INSIDE THE CIA

"I wondered why the diplomat from the American Embassy in Santiago had invited me to such a remote restaurant on the outskirts of the city. As we sipped coffee he explained. 'I'm the local chief for the CIA,' he said. 'We want you to give Uncle Sam a little help in your spare time.' "

'The CIA?' I had heard only vague reference to the organization. [At the time] it was the least known of United States agencies.

'The Central Intelligence Agency,' he said. 'We're in the business of espionage and secret operations.' "

—CIA veteran David Atlee Phillips, on his first contact with the agency, while living in Chile in 1950

SECRETS OF THE CENTURY

INSIDE THE CIA

BY THE EDITORS OF TIME-LIFE BOOKS, ALEXANDRIA, VIRGINIA

CONSULTANTS

Mark M. Lowenthal is a senior principal in the intelligence
directorate at SRA International, a private consulting firm.
He previously served as deputy assistant secretary of state in
the Bureau of Intelligence and Research and, later, as staff
director of the Permanent Select Committee on Intelligence of
the House of Representatives. An authority on the U.S. intelligence community, Dr. Lowenthal is the author of seven books,
including a 1999 textbook on intelligence issues, *Intelligence: From Secrets to Policy.*

J. Kenneth McDonald was chief historian of the Central
Intelligence Agency from 1981 to 1995, where he directed
a classified history program and was general editor of five
volumes of newly declassified documents in the CIA Cold War
Records series. He has taught diplomatic and military history
at George Washington University and the U.S. Naval War College.

H. Keith Melton is an internationally recognized expert on
espionage artifacts and clandestine devices and is a consultant to United States intelligence agencies on historical
espionage equipment. He is the author of *CIA Special Weapons
and Equipment, OSS Special Weapons and Equipment, Clandestine Warfare,* and *The Ultimate Spy Book.*

CONTENTS

PRELUDE:
BEFORE THE CIA   6

CHAPTER 1:
THE COLD WARRIORS   14
ESSAY: TOOLS OF THE TRADE

CHAPTER 2:
COUPS AND OVERTHROWS   56
ESSAY: WAR OF NERVES

CHAPTER 3:
TURBULENT YEARS   102
ESSAY: AIR AMERICA: CIA LINCHPIN IN LAOS
ESSAY: A FLOOD OF REVELATIONS

CHAPTER 4:
ENTERING THE END GAME   152

EPILOGUE:
NEW WORLD, NEW MISSIONS   180

ACKNOWLEDGMENTS AND PICTURE CREDITS   186
BIBLIOGRAPHY   187
INDEX   189

COVER:
Former CIA officer Duane Clarridge evokes the agency's shadowy
mystique in a dramatic 1996 portrait. Clarridge, who played
a key role in organizing Nicaraguan guerrillas in the 1980s,
also served in Nepal, India, Turkey, and Italy.

PRELUDE:
BEFORE
THE CIA

Like most of the 12 million Americans in uniform, Major William Colby was eager to get out of it and get on with his life. Scarcely a month after World War II ended in August 1945, the 25-year-old Colby prepared to resume classes at Columbia University Law School.

But he had one last duty. On September 28, along with nearly 2,000 other members of the Office of Strategic Services (OSS), the wartime intelligence agency, Colby attended a farewell reception. It was held at a roller-skating rink in Washington, D.C., that had served as extra office space for the nearby OSS headquarters in the city's Foggy Bottom section.

The OSS was to be disbanded, and its chief, Major General William J. Donovan, praised the members of America's first centralized intelligence service, calling it "an unusual experiment" for combining intelligence gathering with cloak-and-dagger daring. As the ceremony went on, Colby later wrote, he thought how lucky he was to be alive. In a mission to aid the French resistance, he had been parachuted by mistake into a German-garrisoned town but repeatedly eluded capture. Now, he mused, "Intelligence was over."

But not for long. Within two years, after the start of a bitter Cold War struggle between the United States and the Soviet Union, the OSS would be reborn as the Central Intelligence Agency, or CIA. Soon enough, Colby and many of the other free spirits enjoying their final evening on the polished floor of the rink would be back in the espionage game.

A LEGEND AT THE HELM

The iron-minded man who had founded the OSS was usually called "Wild Bill" Donovan, although rarely to

His face dramatically hidden under a hood, Soviet defector Igor Gouzenko appears on Canadian television in 1954. Nine years earlier, his revelations about Soviet espionage had provided an early glimpse of the decades-long Cold War spy contest to come.

radical scheme and Wild Bill would urge, "Let's give it a try."

By combining intelligence gathering with Donovan's zest for action, the eclectic OSS became, in effect, a prototype for the later CIA. Its secret intelligence branch specialized in espionage—including, for example, the work of spies who found out where German air-craft factories were located. Special operations con-ducted sabotage and supported resistance fighters like the Yugoslav partisans who tied up 15 German divisions. Less colorful but perhaps even more important was research and analysis—the so-called chairborne division—which combined field reports with intelligence ferreted out from journals and other public sources. Among its other branches, the agency also included a gadget shop for weapons, ra-dios, and more esoteric gear and a "black propagan-da" group—morale operations—which often spread false information to demoralize enemy troops.

So many socialites and Ivy Leaguers graced OSS ranks that wags said the initials meant "Oh, So So-cial!" But along with names like Mellon and Vander-bilt, Donovan pulled in professors, doctors, scientists, soldiers, even actors. Hollywood star Sterling Hayden commanded a flotilla of sailing craft that ran a Ger-man blockade of the Adriatic coast. Julia McWilliams, who later married and became famous as French chef Julia Child, correlated secret documents in Ceylon and then China. And, although Donovan was a staunch Republican, his legions also included enough left-wing sympathizers that conservatives cracked OSS meant "Oh, So Socialist!"

his face. The nickname had been applied to Donovan even before World War I, when he was wounded three times leading New York's Fighting Irish 165th Infantry Regiment. By World War II, he did not look wild. Nearing 60, with ruddy cheeks, enormous blue eyes, silvery gray hair and a bland manner, he was an affluent Wall Street lawyer.

In 1941 Donovan had talked President Roosevelt, his old friend and law school classmate, into creating an intelligence service known as the COI, for Coordi-nator of Information. Early in 1942, it became the OSS. As OSS head, Donovan soon bustled around the world. He considered a plot to kidnap Hitler and pushed a plan to snatch Mussolini. Against orders, Donovan landed on Utah Beach under German machine-gun fire a day after D-Day. Suggest the most

Worldwide, the OSS grew to include nearly 12,000 full-time personnel, including many refugees from occupied Europe, engaged in any number of pursuits. Contacts with Vatican emissaries in Japan yielded intelligence on bomb targets there. In Burma, the OSS formed a unit of 10,000 Kachin tribesmen who were said to have killed more than 10 Japanese soldiers for each loss of their own. As the war ended in Europe, OSS men seized Wernher von Braun's team of German rocket builders before Soviet troops could get their hands on them.

Long before the fighting ceased, Donovan lobbied for a postwar future for the OSS. In November 1944 he sent Roosevelt a secret memorandum proposing that the OSS be transformed after the war into an independent "central intelligence service," separate from the military. Like the OSS, it would both collect data and conduct "subversive operations abroad." Operations in the United States, however, were ruled out. The OSS, Donovan added, had "the trained and specialized personnel needed for the task."

At the time, Donovan's notions were savaged. The army and navy jealously safeguarded their own military intelligence. The State Department brooked no rival in foreign affairs. The FBI controlled intelligence in Latin America, and director J. Edgar Hoover wanted to keep it that way. He leaked Donovan's memo to Walter Trohan of the conservative *Chicago Tribune*. Trohan's first blast appeared on February 9, 1945: "Creation of an all powerful intelligence service to spy on the postwar world and to pry into the lives of citizens at home is under consid-

Below, a "Jedburgh" team readies for a jump. Typically composed of three members—an OSS agent, a British agent, and a resistance fighter—the squads aided resistance forces in occupied Europe.

Above, President Truman and a glum-looking Bill Donovan (center) meet in September 1945 with a former French resistance leader. A week later, Truman abolished Donovan's OSS.

eration by the New Deal." Some in Congress likened the proposed agency to the Gestapo.

Roosevelt shelved the idea until the storm calmed. Then in April 1945 he died, and Donovan's hopes withered. He lacked rapport with Roosevelt's successor, President Harry S. Truman. Personal differences aside, the new president also feared a new spy agency might turn into a secret police. Then a government report listed acts of corruption and nepotism by some OSS officers. Donovan, in a last-gasp try for public support, gave the press details of previously confidential OSS exploits. But on September 20, 1945, a week before the farewell at the skating rink, Truman issued Executive Order 9621, terminating the organization.

Even as he broke up the OSS, however, Truman wanted to keep some of its resources. He shifted the secret intelligence and special operation branches to the War Department, and research and analysis to the State Department. Truman certainly saw the need for a coordinated intelligence system. "I had information coming at me from 200 different sources," he said later, "and no one to boil it down for me."

Meanwhile, the State, War, and Navy Departments feuded over the control of intelligence. Clouding matters further was a fight over the makeup of a proposed new Department of Defense. A former OSS deputy even suggested privatizing intelligence by offering contract services to the government through IBM. In January 1946 Truman compromised. He created a Central Intelligence Group, jointly funded and staffed by the three departments. The thinly staffed office soon proved ineffective.

Truman's inclination for a more effective intelligence service grew with the Cold War's dawn. Soon after World War II, Communists, under the watchful eyes of the Red Army, gained control of Poland and Rumania, while a civil war raged in Greece between pro-Communist and pro-Western factions. In February 1946 Soviet leader Joseph Stalin thundered in a speech that war with capitalism was inevitable. The following month, British statesman Winston Churchill, speaking in Truman's home state of Missouri, declared that "an iron curtain has descended" across the continent.

A MASS OF SPIES

As tensions with the Soviets grew, meanwhile, new information about the scope of Soviet espionage in North America emerged. One of the first shocks came with the defection of Igor Gouzenko *(pages 6-7)*, a cipher clerk at the Soviet embassy in the Canadian capital of Ottawa. On the evening of September 5, 1945, Gouzenko had carefully chosen the most sensitive telegrams in the cipher room and stuffed them into his clothes. He did the same with handwritten pages from his supervisor's diary. Then he went off to convince Canadian officials of his and his pregnant wife Svetlana's desire to defect. But the Canadian Department of External Affairs did not believe his tale. The next night, embassy officials broke down Gouzenko's door to arrest him. Gouzenko hid at a neighbor's until the Royal Canadian Mounted Police took him in.

Gouzenko's documents gave details about numerous Soviet spies that had gathered top-secret data on radar, the atom bomb, and the stationing of U.S. troops. He unmasked British atomic scientist Alan Nunn May, who had given

Moscow a sample of U-235, the building block for the bomb. The revelations sent shock waves through top-level officials in Canada and its southern neighbor. Noted Truman, "There must be similar penetrations by the Russians in the United States."

Indeed, that fall Elizabeth Terrill Bentley, a Vassar graduate and American Communist Party member, informed the FBI that many parts of the U.S. government had been infiltrated as well. During World War II, under the code name Smart Girl, Bentley had served as a courier for Soviet agents and contacts in a dozen government agencies, including the War Department. She had shuttled between Washington and her Soviet handlers in New York, her knitting

Testifying before the House Committee on Un-American Activities in 1948, former Soviet agent Elizabeth Bentley lists her contacts in the U.S. government. Her 1945 confession shocked the country.

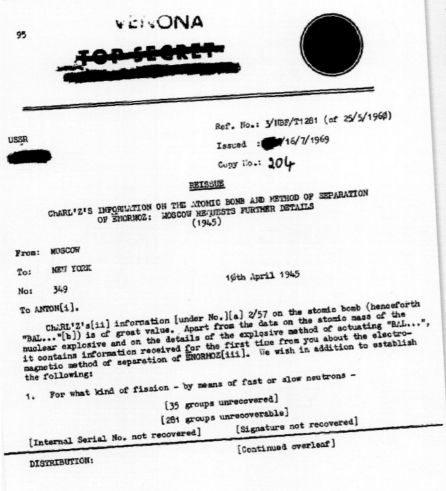

VENONA

95

~~TOP SECRET~~

USSR

Ref. No.: 3/NBF/T1281 (of 25/5/1960)

Issued : 16/7/1969

Copy No.: 204

REISSUE

CHARL'Z'S INFORMATION ON THE ATOMIC BOMB AND METHOD OF SEPARATION
OF ENORMOZ: MOSCOW REQUESTS FURTHER DETAILS
(1945)

From: MOSCOW

To: NEW YORK

No: 349   16th April 1945

To ANTON[i].

ChARL'Z's[ii] information [under No.][a] 2/57 on the atomic bomb (henceforth "BAL..."[b]) is of great value. Apart from the data on the atomic mass of the nuclear explosive and on the details of the explosive method of actuating "BAL...", it contains information received for the first time from you about the electro-magnetic method of separation of ENORMOZ[iii]. We wish in addition to establish the following:

1. For what kind of fission - by means of fast or slow neutrons -

[35 groups unrecovered]

[281 groups unrecoverable]

[Internal Serial No. not recovered]   [Signature not recovered]

[Continued overleaf]

DISTRIBUTION:

At left, the first page of a secret telegram sent from Moscow to New York—and later unscrambled by the army signal corps Venona team—requests data on nuclear fission.

revelations came from an army signals project code-named Venona, which would not be publicly revealed until 1995. Venona had the daunting task of deciphering more than 3,000 Soviet diplomatic telegrams secretly intercepted between 1940 and 1948. Although this work was aided to a degree by cipher clerk Gouzenko's information, the big breakthrough came in the summer of 1946, when linguist Meredith Gardner deciphered the Soviets' "spell table" for coding English letters.

Even so, puzzling out each Soviet message remained a laborious task, and Venona decrypts typically lagged behind events by several years. It was not until years later, for example, that the Venona team would establish that British physicist Klaus Fuchs and American Julius Rosenberg had taken an active part in a wartime spy ring and Rosenberg's wife Ethel had known of it; even then, given the project's secrecy, such evidence would not be produced in court. By early 1947, however, Venona had decrypted enough of the messages to show that scores of Americans were or had been working for the Soviet Union, foreshadowing the decades-long struggle between the intelligence services of East and West that was to follow.

BIRTH OF THE CIA

Meanwhile, amid growing concern over Stalin's intentions in Europe, the U.S. took several decisive steps. In March 1947 the president enunciated his Truman Doctrine, which called for military aid to Greece and Turkey "to support free peoples who are resisting attempted subjugation by armed minorities or by out-

bag stuffed with up to 40 rolls of microfilmed images of sensitive government papers.

Bentley had entered the espionage world partly for personal reasons, having fallen in love with Jacob Golos, a KGB officer and top American Communist Party apparatchik. She found the older, somewhat colorless man "quick, keen, incisive" and "powerfully built"; she later remembered him as "the ideal Communist." Now, however, she had decided to change sides, identifying more than 80 people who she alleged had been spies or simply indiscreet "sources of information," including Assistant Treasury Secretary Harry Dexter White, White House counselor Lauchlin Currie, and Major Duncan C. Lee, an aide to Bill Donovan himself.

Partial confirmation for Gouzenko's and Bentley's

side pressures." In June the Marshall Plan for massive economic aid to Western Europe was proposed.

On the domestic scene, public reservations about the wisdom of creating a centralized intelligence bureau had begun to fade, as some news articles reexamined intelligence failures before World War II and others stressed the growing Soviet threat. "It is generally agreed that a good intelligence service is the first line of defense today," wrote the *Christian Science Monitor*, and legislators agreed. In July 1947 Bill Donovan's vision finally came to pass when Congress approved the National Security Act. The act made the air force a separate branch, unified all three armed services under a secretary of defense, and founded the National Security Council (NSC). It also established the Central Intelligence Agency.

Unlike the Central Intelligence Group, its predecessor, the CIA would be an independent agency, reporting to the president through the NSC. Like the OSS, it could hire its own people and had its own budget. The law also left open the possibility of unspecified "other functions" beyond the coordination of intelligence, which was seen as its primary purpose.

Much of this was what Donovan had proposed two and a half years before. But despite lobbying by influential friends, he was not asked to head the new spy agency. Instead, the nod went to Roscoe Hillenkoetter, a rear admiral who had run wartime naval intelligence in the Pacific and was already serving as head of the Central Intelligence Group. Under Hillenkoetter and his successors, the newborn CIA would soon undertake missions—in the Far East, Western Europe, and central Asia, among other places—as far-flung, secretive, and perilous as those faced by the OSS.

A modest sign on a chain-link fence marks an early CIA headquarters in the Foggy Bottom district of Washington, D.C.

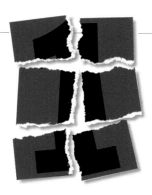

THE COLD WARRIORS

I n the fall of 1950, Communist-inspired guerrillas known as Huks threatened the pro-American government of the Philippines. The Huks—short for the Tagalog name Hukbong Bayan Laban sa Hapon, or People's Anti-Japanese Army—had started out as a resistance force during World War II, but they had never entirely disbanded. Now, angered by the bloodshed and corruption of the 1949 Philippine elections, they had once more taken up arms, this time under the guidance of the Communist Party. To secure the strategic Philippines in the Western camp, the White House called on the Central Intelligence Agency. The CIA, in turn, sent to Manila 42-year-old Edward Lansdale, a lieutenant colonel on loan from the air force.

A former San Francisco advertising man, Lansdale had served during World War II in both army military intelligence and the OSS, the CIA's wartime predecessor. After a previous stint battling the Huks just after the war, he had joined the newly formed U.S. Air Force. His return to the Philippines for the CIA would be seen in its day as one of the agency's early triumphs in the emerging Cold War.

On arrival, Lansdale soon resumed close ties with a dynamic local leader, Defense Secretary Ramón Magsaysay, whom he had gotten to know a few months earlier in Washington. Within weeks, the two had staged a major intelligence coup, rounding up all 105 members of the secret Communist Party politburo in Manila. With Lansdale's active encouragement, Magsaysay then moved to reform the security police and reorganize the Philippine army, making it more mobile and thus better suited to fight the Huks. Along the way, Lansdale's interest in what he rather sinisterly called "the practical-joke aspect of psywar," short for psychological warfare, resulted in some bizarre yet effective tactics.

In one town, for example, officials feared losing their local army garrison; a Huk force had taken up residence on a nearby hill and resisted all efforts to dislodge it. If the troops left, feared the local politicians, the Huks would descend with deadly effect. "Stimulated" by Lansdale's ideas, as his mem-

At left, East German guards in the Soviet sector of Berlin inspect a newly uncovered tunnel built by the CIA and British intelligence. Several hundred feet in length, the tunnel enabled its creators to tap Soviet communication lines for almost a year before it was publicly exposed in April 1956. In the CIA's first decade, such bold experiments were virtually standard practice.

oirs related, a local "psywar squad" responded with a brutal, and effective, trick. First they spread word that an *asuang,* or vampire, was in the area. Then, late one night, they fell on the last man in a column of Huks following a forest trail. After taking him into the bush, the soldiers punctured his neck twice, vampire-style, and hung him upside down until the flow of blood became a trickle. They then placed the blood-drained body—by now a corpse—beside the trail, where his comrades soon found it. Thoroughly spooked, the Huks abandoned the hill the next morning.

Incidents like that became part of the Lansdale legend that he himself helped to fashion in the years ahead, as he became one of several larger-than-life figures from the agency's first years. While vigorously combating the Huks, Lansdale also became a backstage political mentor and public relations adviser to Magsaysay, encouraging him to adopt agrarian reforms and other policies that Lansdale believed would make democracy pay off for the average Filipino. After Magsaysay swept to power as the new president in 1953, Lansdale, by now a full colonel, returned to Washington and a glowing reputation among many top policymakers.

Lansdale's next stop on behalf of the CIA, in 1954, would be Vietnam, which had been divided into North and South after the defeat of the French. There he concocted a successful propaganda campaign to persuade many of North Vietnam's one million anti-Communist Catholics to move to the

CIA officer and air force colonel Edward Lansdale (below, left) and Philippine defense secretary Ramón Magsaysay relax in the bungalow they shared in the early 1950s. Originally sent to the Philippines to suppress Communist rebels, Lansdale became a key Magsaysay adviser, helping him win the 1953 presidential election.

At top, a choir of children performing in a Radio Free Europe program sings songs banned behind the Iron Curtain; the poster below displays the radio network's credo. Secretly funded by the CIA from its inception until 1973, Radio Free Europe had a potential audience of 78 million in Eastern Europe, whose exiled leaders were often showcased in its programs. It also operated a peerless information-gathering service on events in the Communist zone that proved useful to many analysts—including those at the CIA.

South. Among the physicians the CIA enlisted to help the hard-pressed refugees was Dr. Tom Dooley, who gained fame for his humanitarian work. As in the Philippines, Lansdale also threw his support behind a local leader, Ngo Dinh Diem, who became president in 1956. The supposedly clandestine officer became so well known that he appeared in fictional form, thinly disguised as the likable Colonel "Hillandale," in the 1958 bestseller *The Ugly American*.

Barely three years old when it sent Lansdale to the Philippines, the CIA would over time undertake many covert actions. But the new agency had many other duties as well: among others, producing intelligence and analyses, thwarting enemy spies, disseminating anti-Communist propaganda, and experimenting with new technology, ranging from spy planes to truth serums.

Within these broad parameters, the agency would take on an extraordinary array of projects in its first decade, sometimes succeeding, sometimes falling short. Among other efforts, the CIA silently bankrolled Radio Free Europe and Radio Liberty, networks that were set up in 1950 and 1951 to beam news and pro-American information behind the Iron Curtain. It trained guerrillas for raids against the new Communist rulers of China and tried to slip agents into Eastern Europe and the Soviet Union. Some of the agency's espionage specialists struck intelligence gold in a key Soviet agent named Pyotr Popov, while others, in tandem with the British, built a tunnel to tap communications lines in the Soviet sector of Berlin.

BATTLING FOR BALLOTS

All this was still to come, however, in the fall of 1947, when the White House tapped the CIA for its first major covert-action mission, a scheme to block local Communists from winning control of a key Western European country. In August the CIA's short-lived predecessor, the Central Intelligence Group, had informed President Truman of a high-level Soviet document secretly taken from a safe in Eastern Europe and microfilmed. The memorandum outlined the Communist strategy in Western Europe, including a general strike in Italy to weaken that country's prime minister and the incitement of labor unrest in France and Belgium. Aside from the specifics in the document, the Soviet playbook for subverting vulnerable countries was already known to include propaganda; bribery; infiltration of unions, the military, and the police; and encouragement of civil unrest.

Late in 1947 Italy looked especially at risk. World War II had destroyed four-fifths of its industry, rendered the lira nearly worthless, and left millions out of work. A coalition government of Christian Democrats, Socialists, and Communists had taken office in 1946 to deal with the disarray but had unraveled the following year. The Communists were well positioned to win control of the government in elections slated for April 1948.

Since the war, Communist governments had already assumed power in Poland, Rumania, Bulgaria, and in May 1947, Hungary. Now the fear that Italy could be next in line galvanized Washington. "Our whole position in the Mediterranean, and possibly in western Europe as well, would probably be undermined," wrote George Kennan, the State Department's leading Soviet expert.

The National Security Council ordered the CIA to keep the Communists from gaining Italy. This the new agency was eager to do, but there was a potential obstacle. In establishing the CIA as an intelligence-gathering body just a few months before, the National Security Act had said nothing about manipulating the internal affairs of nations. Yet leading policymakers such as Defense Secretary James Forrestal felt they must not handicap the U.S.—and, in particular, the CIA—in the gloves-off contest with the Soviets. With Truman's blessing, Forrestal pushed through a secret National Security Council directive that approved covert political action, euphemistically referred to as "psychological operations," in order to counter Communist propaganda and influence abroad. The way was cleared for action in Italy and, over time, around the world.

At agency headquarters in Washington, OSS veteran James Jesus Angleton played a

James Jesus Angleton, shown here in 1944 while serving in the London OSS office, became head of an OSS counterintelligence unit in Rome later that year. His local knowledge helped the CIA as it planned to keep Communist candidates out of the Italian government in 1948.

"He liked to sit up talking until four or five in the morning and often spoke in riddles that you had to interpret or feel, rather than analyze with cold logic."

—Teddy Kollek, future mayor of Jerusalem, on Angleton in the late 1940s

As part of a propaganda campaign preceding the 1948 elections, CIA officers and their agents blitzed Italy with anonymous pamphlets and other printed matter. Much of the material was patterned after items distributed by the Christian Democrats, who devised the poster above, which combines a skeleton in a Red Army uniform with the slogan "Vote or he'll be your boss."

key supporting role in the work to come. During the war, Angleton had served as the OSS counterintelligence chief in Rome. After the collapse of the Fascist government there, he had secured the former government's archives and located the lost royal treasures of Ethiopia—a nation that had been among Mussolini's first victims. Angleton then remained in Rome, working for army military intelligence, well into 1947. Now newly returned to Washington, he was able to tap a network of sources through agents remaining in Rome to give the agency up-to-date estimates on the changing political winds there; he is also thought to have offered those still on the scene some concrete tactical advice as they worked frantically to affect the fast-approaching election.

From Rome, meanwhile, agency officers cabled headquarters that $10 million would be needed to thwart the Italian Communists at the polls. CIA director Admiral Roscoe Hillenkoetter arranged for the cash to be siphoned from the Economic Stabilization Fund, created after the war to check wild swings in foreign currencies. The money was laundered through the bank accounts of individuals, who then "donated" the funds to charities that were actually CIA fronts. To ward off IRS investigation of these fraudulent tax deductions, participants marked the contributions on their tax returns with a special three-character code.

By all accounts, the agency spent its money cannily. Lifting a page from Tammany Hall, CIA officers quietly paid for anti-Communist leaflets and posters and plied centrist politicians with "walking-around" money to canvass voters. "Passing black bags to affect a political election is not really a terribly attractive thing," Mark Wyatt, an officer then stationed in Italy, later commented. "But we only had a few months to do this, and that was the principal thing that we did."

Wyatt, like Angleton, was a member of the agency's Office of Special Operations, or OSO, which specialized in intelligence collection. Although the Italian operation hardly came under that heading, he and other OSO officers were among those assigned to the task simply because the CIA then had no covert-action experts. As the election approached, agency officers helped circulate unsavory rumors in Italy about the sexual adventures of Communist leaders, forging letters that gave substance to the lies. Anonymously published pamphlets luridly described rape and pillage by Moscow's soldiers in the Soviet sector of Germany, implying the same could happen in Italy. Funds also went to Italy's anti-Marxist press, where "Communist apparatchiks in cartoons had three nostrils in their noses," as well as bushy, Stalinesque mustaches, Wyatt recalled. The Soviet dictator quickly became known in Italy as *il Buffone*—the Clown.

To complement the CIA's secret propaganda role, the U.S. government orchestrated an overt effort as well. While the State Department brandished the stick—an aid cutoff if the Communists won the election—the White House dangled the carrot, asking Congress for millions in assistance to Italy and donating 29 ships to the Italian merchant marine. At the same time, other factors helped turn the tide. The American Marshall Plan to revitalize Europe's economies began to breathe new life into Italy. A February 1948 Communist coup in Czechoslovakia put the Soviets in a bad light just two months before election day. And Italy's influential Catholic Church constantly inveighed against the godless Communists.

As the election approached, strikes and other Communist-led disrup-

At left, Frank Wisner, the tireless head of the CIA's first covert-action wing, the OPC, chats with sons Hugh and Frank Jr. in the family's well-appointed Georgetown home. Like many of those associated with the agency at the time, Wisner was a man of some social standing; according to one of his colleagues, joining the agency in the early days was "rather glamorous and fashionable and certainly a most patriotic thing to do."

tions shook Italy. But the final result deeply gratified Western leaders. Of more than 200 parliamentary seats the CIA had targeted, anti-Communist parties won all but two. The Christian Democrats' margin was large enough to deny their opponents a significant place in the government.

Despite that outcome, however, CIA director Hillenkoetter was among many concerned by the idea of intelligence gatherers plunging into such direct action. If similar missions lay ahead, it seemed vital to outfit the CIA with an organization geared expressly for covert operations. That was certainly the view of one upbeat man on the move, Frank Gardiner Wisner, another OSS veteran.

Forty years old and brimming with energy, Wisner was, like many CIA officers of the day, a child of privilege. Born into a prominent family in Laurel, Mississippi, he had attended a Virginia prep school, then the patrician University of Virginia. Stocky and fiercely competitive, he had been a star hurdler, good enough to compete in the 1936 Olympic trials. After attending the university's law school, Wisner had worked as a Wall Street attorney. Six months before Pearl Harbor, he had joined the navy, and in 1943 was assigned to the OSS, which sent him to Egypt, Turkey, and near the war's end, Germany and Rumania. In the Rumanian capital of Bucharest, Wisner had watched helplessly as Soviet troops herded thousands of citizens, some of whom he knew personally, onto boxcars for transportation to Stalin's labor camps. The experience was seared into his memory.

After a brief stint back in the law, the restless Wisner had headed to Washington in 1947, taking a high-level job with the State Department's Office of Occupied Territories. His assignment: to figure out how to counter Moscow's empire building. That question became ever more urgent as the Soviets solidified their hold on Eastern Europe. In 1948 Moscow tried to squeeze the U.S., Britain, and France out of their sectors of occupied Berlin by blockading the city—a ploy thwarted by an 11-month airlift of vital supplies. That same year, a Soviet invasion of Western Europe seemed possible to many. General Lucius Clay, American high commissioner in Germany, warned Washington in the spring of 1948 that war "may come with dramatic suddenness."

It was at this juncture that Wisner argued fervently for an instrument of covert action beyond that offered by ad hoc arrangements like the one in Italy. He found powerful supporters in Kennan and Forrestal. In June 1948 the advocates of action got what they wanted when President Truman signed a Kennan-crafted National Security Council directive. Blandly titled NSC-10/2, it created a new bureaucratic entity, later called the Office of Policy Coordination. Technically "within the structure of the CIA" in time of peace, and paid for with agency funds, this innocuous-sounding corner of American bureaucracy was also to coordinate its actions closely with representatives of the State Department and Pentagon.

Behind the blandness lay a declaration of secret war. Among the duties listed in the directive were "any covert activities related to: propaganda; economic warfare; preventive direct action, including sabotage, anti-sabotage, demolition and evacuation measures; subversion against hostile states, including assistance to underground resistance movements, guerrillas and refugee liberation groups, and support of indigenous anti-Communist elements in threatened countries of the free world." Moreover, all such operations were to be clandestine, so that the U.S. government could "plausibly disclaim any responsibility." This was the first, but hardly the last, reference to the key CIA notion of plausible deniability.

To head the new organization, Hillenkoetter tapped Frank Wisner, the human whirlwind. Wisner recruited staff at a headlong pace and brainstormed endlessly about OPC tactics. He did so with a large degree of autonomy. The generals at the Pentagon were kindred spirits, his liaison at the State Department an old OSS friend. The relationship with CIA management was strictly at arm's length. Wisner, the former track star, could run hard, fast, and unfettered.

OPERATION BG FIEND

In March 1949 Wisner undertook what proved to be OPC's biggest project when he embraced a British proposal aimed at Communist Albania. A small, mountainous nation in the Balkans, Albania was estranged not only from the West but also from its neighbor, Marshal Tito's Yugoslavia—unique in the Communist bloc for its independence from Moscow. Albania's ruler, Enver Hoxha, was the brutal and paranoid dictator of a poverty-stricken land divided by class and clan hatreds. A fervent believer in Stalinist ideas, Hoxha had deeply unsettled the populace by suppressing religion, eliminating private property, and clamping down on any vestige of individual liberty. A Westerner who visited briefly in January 1949 later said, "I have never been so glad to leave a country in my life. I think we have had a glimpse of hell." To the British and Wisner, Albania seemed the perfect place to start raising the Iron Curtain.

The British Secret Intelligence Service, or SIS—also known as MI-6, its original title—was well acquainted with Albania through wartime links with its resistance forces. SIS had considered unseating Hoxha in late 1948. But the British, still economically devastated by the war, lacked the cash to ignite a popular revolt. Instead, they suggested a joint venture with the United States. An enthusiastic Wisner, with backing from the National Security Council, felt a successful uprising in Albania might spark counterrevolutions throughout the Soviet empire. Albania was to be "a clinical experiment to see whether larger rollback operations would be feasible elsewhere," the OPC chief explained.

With Wisner in the lead, OPC optimists discounted a downbeat CIA intelligence report by the agency's Office of Research and Estimates that saw dim prospects for revolt. "A purely internal Albanian uprising at this time," the analysts forecast, "would have little chance of success."

That gloomy assessment aside, the outcome of the Albanian gambit would in large measure lie in the hands of an up-and-coming British intelligence officer, Harold "Kim" Philby. The 37-year-old son of a famous explorer and Arabist, Philby had attended Cambridge University and subsequent-

Enver Hoxha

Shown here four years after he took control of Albania in 1944, Enver Hoxha transformed the country from a semifeudal vestige of the Ottoman Empire into a Stalinist state, brutally achieving his goals through executions and other forms of summary justice. Under his iron rule, which lasted into the 1980s, the government collectivized farms and abolished religious institutions.

Harold "Kim" Philby

Born in India to a British intelligence officer and nicknamed for Rudyard Kipling's fictional spy hero, Harold "Kim" Philby (above, in 1955) excelled as a secret agent for the Soviets while rising to a high rank in British intelligence. When investigators finally verified Philby's true allegiance in 1962, the KGB spirited him to safety aboard a Soviet-bound freighter.

ly worked as a foreign correspondent, earning a reputation for staunch right-wing views. His aristocratic stutter and rumpled insouciance charmed most people, including the largely upper-class leadership of SIS, and he was recruited into the intelligence elite. As SIS's official liaison officer in Washington to both the CIA and the FBI, Philby was fully briefed on the Albanian enterprise.

Unknown to all—and despite his upper-class patina—Philby had been one of several Cambridge students recruited by Soviet intelligence in the early 1930s. He had already passed on a wealth of SIS secrets. Now, with his windfall posting to Washington, he could monitor American moves as well.

As required by the directive that created the OPC, the Albanian adventure was to be arranged so that the U.S. government could plausibly deny it had played any role in the affair. The ready solution was to employ Albanian volunteers as proxies. Driven from their homeland as the Communists took over, thousands of Albanians were living in refugee camps. Many were eager to help subvert Hoxha's regime.

Initially, the British handled recruitment for the joint effort, now code-named BG Fiend. (Most CIA projects begin with a two-letter prefix, or digraph, indicating the region involved or type of mission.) The numbers were kept small to maintain secrecy and to allow the forces to operate in a swift-moving, guerrilla style. Through their contacts among the Albanian émigrés, the British signed up about 30 young men from camps around Naples, Italy, and whisked them away for training. Wisner offered to conduct their education at an American base in Libya, but his partners had a better idea—Malta, a British island possession since 1799, which was closer to Albania. In his memoirs, Kim Philby would one day quote Wisner as saying cheerfully, "Whenever we want to subvert any place, we find that the British own an island within easy reach."

In Malta, BG Fiend recruits were schooled in the arts of subversion at Fort Bin Jema, an old castle. Over 10 weeks, trainees learned map reading and radio communications, and practiced landing small boats on the rocky shores of Adriatic coves. To contain ricochets, the fort's empty moat was set up for small-arms and grenade practice.

Discipline was less than taut, the British having learned from training refugee fighters in World War II that a collegial atmosphere worked better. Rules forbade neither liquor nor nocturnal jaunts to nearby towns, with predictable results. On an Albanian national holiday, for example, a few of the recruits, drunk on ouzo, tossed celebratory grenades into the moat for the simple pleasure of hearing them explode. In general, the Albanians inspired little confidence in their instructors, who derided the would-be insurgents behind their backs as "pixies." An Albanian leader in exile wrote of them as "men with narrow chests and necks like chickens," too insubstantial for the task at hand.

On the evening of October 3, 1949, a ship named the *Stormie Seas* approached Albania's shores. Piloted by two former British naval officers, the

Stormie Seas appeared to be a charter on a Mediterranean luxury cruise. Concealed belowdecks, however, were nine Albanians with a mission of insurrection—the first contingent from BG Fiend. Secret compartments in the big schooner held radios, propaganda leaflets, weapons, and photographs of prominent Albanian exiles who had been chosen as prospective leaders of a new, non-Communist government.

Once ashore, the nine agents split into two groups and started toward their designated regions, only to find that traps had been laid for them by Albania's security service and its 80,000-strong army. Government forces ambushed one group of four, reportedly killing three, according to locals; the other man escaped. The men in the second group learned from a young girl that security police had been lurking near the coast for days. "Brothers, you're all going to be killed," she warned them.

Despite the peril, the second group pressed on. Moving constantly to elude pursuers, they handed out the leaflets and the photos, explained how to form opposition cells, and promised listeners that Britain and the United States would aid their resistance. The agents found some sympathizers, but many doubters. "Why are there only five of you?" they asked.

Meanwhile, the *Stormie Seas* landed two more bands, totaling 11 Albanians, farther along the coast. These, too, met with immediate trouble. One group, forced on the run, trekked along mountain paths by night, hid in dank caves by day, and drank rainwater and dew drained from groundsheets. A relative whom one agent managed to recruit was swiftly arrested and executed. "It was impossible," a survivor later recalled. "The Communists had too tight a grip." Having failed to incite the slightest hint of a revolt, those who were not killed escaped overland to Greece.

Below, four British-trained Albanian guerrillas—called pixies by their instructors—pose with their weapons. Part of the first landing party in a joint CIA-British scheme to liberate Albania, the four were ambushed by government troops after going ashore on October 3, 1949; the man at far left escaped, but the other three died.

Pondering the eerily efficient performance of Hoxha's security apparatus, OPC and SIS decided that either the Albanian recruits had been indiscreet during their training or spies had observed the movements of the *Stormie Seas*. One high-ranking CIA officer concluded that Albanian émigrés in Rome who knew of the project must have leaked word. No one imagined that high-level betrayal contributed to the losses. An undaunted Frank Wisner told Philby, "We'll get it right next time."

Two members of a group of CIA-trained Albanian guerrillas proudly pose in their uniforms, complete with the Albanian national symbol, a double-headed eagle. Hysen Salku, at left, airdropped into Albania on October 15, 1951, but broke both legs on landing; government forces killed him the next day. The fate of Jusuf Dema (above, right) is unknown.

"People talked of nothing else. It was a tragedy, a searing defeat, a perfectly terrible thing."

—OPC officer Tom Braden, on the Albanian operation

But they did not. As the operation continued and expanded, men continued to die futilely, apparently confirming the earlier CIA analysts' estimate that Albania was not ripe for insurrection. The British withdrew from the operation in 1952, but Wisner's OPC pressed on gamely for another year before giving up. The Americans chose to parachute in the Albanians, using small aircraft piloted by former members of the Polish air force, who were given cyanide pills in the event of capture. The Poles trained at a U.S. air base in Wiesbaden, West Germany; upward of 40 Albanians drilled at an OPC camp near Heidelberg. Because time was short, recruits performed no practice jumps before undertaking perilous nighttime drops. Albania's very poverty confounded the operation. The country had almost no electricity, and therefore few lights; pilots could not locate drop zones in the dark. Two disastrous airdrops led to nothing but the show trial of captured agents, who were tortured into denouncing American or British imperialism, then convicted and executed.

Kim Philby could not have directly betrayed the later missions. He had returned to England in May 1951 under deepest suspicion after two other members of his Cambridge ring fled to Moscow. But by then he had done enough damage, having filed the reports that warned Hoxha at the outset. A Soviet agent who penetrated the Albanian exile community later verified his story and secured details about agent drops. The net result of Philby's treachery, combined with other adverse conditions on the ground, was appalling. As many as 200 agents fell into the brutal hands of Albanian security, and several thousand other Albanians may have been executed simply because they had family or other ties to the intruders. The OPC knew none of the details at the time. It could only recognize that its "clinical experiment" had unequivocally failed to overthrow Hoxha.

At home, meanwhile, some U.S. leaders worried about OPC's swashbuckling ways. George Kennan later told a congressional committee that setting up a covert action unit "did not work out at all the way I had conceived it." He explained that "we had thought that this would be a facility which could be used when and if an occasion arose when it might be needed. There might be years when we wouldn't have to do anything like this."

But nonstop action was in Frank Wisner's blood. By September 1949, just months after BG Fiend started, he had begun sending agents into the western periphery of the Soviet Union itself. This small first infiltration consisted only of two couriers sent to contact resistance forces in the Ukraine. But the larger, ultimate goal of such insertions—to incite rebellion—was not entirely unrealistic, for at the time Stalin did not have all the Soviet republics completely under his yoke. In Lithuania alone, anti-Communist partisans at one point numbered about 30,000, and in almost a decade of battling to regain independence, would kill tens of thousands of Soviet soldiers. In the Ukraine, an even larger resistance army struggled against Stalin's forces.

Far more agents, of course, would be needed to provide real help in the fight. Just as Wisner had sought his Albanian provocateurs among refugees, now he looked to Europe's many displaced-persons camps, home to thousands of refugees from the Soviets, as a source of highly motivated manpower. For both American and British intelligence, displaced persons were the perfect candidates to contact existing insurgent groups behind the Iron Curtain. Who better to make such overtures than those who spoke the language of the resistance fighters, knew the terrain, and hated Communism?

In a reprise of the Albanian project, OPC and SIS inserted such recruits into the Baltic Soviet republics, the Ukraine, and several Eastern European nations. Although the effort began with high hopes and continued for several years, it too yielded little but tragedy. In 1951 SIS airdropped a total of 18 men into southern Poland and the Ukraine; all disappeared. At about the same time, OPC sent teams into the Baltic republics as well as the Ukraine and Moldavia, all to no avail. In 1952 and 1953, 16 more CIA-trained agents vanished. "It was a horrible mistake," recalled an OPC officer managing some of the missions. "None of them survived." From agents spirited into the Baltic republics came only radio messages that the Soviets were about to arrest them. The following year, OPC finally halted the program.

THE CAT BECOMES THE MOUSE

Even as their security forces wrapped up virtually every agent sent eastward by Britain and the United States, the Communists added insult to the injuries with a massive trick that netted them both considerable treasure and a major propaganda victory. In the summer of 1950, a Pole who had fought both German and Soviet occupation forces in his country arrived in London and looked up an exiled Polish general, Wladyslaw Anders. The visitor brought thrilling news: Although the West believed the Soviets had extinguished all military opposition, a small but tough resistance army still survived in Poland. Named Wolnosc i Niepodlegtosc (Freedom and Independence), or WIN, the force had 500 active fighters and 20,000 part-timers, the visitor announced. He added that 100,000 sympathizers stood ready to join an anti-Soviet uprising.

General Anders shared these glad tidings with the CIA and asked for aid to build up WIN. He found a receptive audience, this being the sort of opportunity that set Frank Wisner's pulse racing. However, the Americans wanted to know more about WIN's leaders. Anders, as the link to the newly discovered resistance force, was in a position to reveal the names of his contacts, but he feared that any leak could imperil the entire enterprise. In violation of basic intelligence craft, OPC did not press the matter. OPC settled instead for evidence of WIN's accomplishments—photographs of burned-out Soviet tanks and blasted barracks and police stations.

Over the next two years, the agency airdropped weapons, explosives,

"The thought of an American general, hanging from a parachute, descending into a Communist country, gave us some pause."

—John Bross, deputy manager for WIN project

timers, and radios to WIN locations throughout Poland. The Americans also contributed more than one million dollars in gold coins to be handed out as bribes. This lavish support seemed to pay off handsomely. Reports from Poland now indicated that WIN controlled whole regions of the countryside, posing a genuine challenge to the Communist regime. Wisner felt that antitank guns were all the resistance forces needed to "drive the Red Army out of Warsaw." At last the West seemed poised to liberate a Soviet-controlled nation.

The awful truth began to dawn after WIN contacts requested that senior American military officers be sent to help guide the underground army. As OPC officer John Bross later remarked, "the thought of an American general, hanging from a parachute, descending into a Communist country, gave us some pause." More sobering yet, aerial reconnaissance and electronic surveillance of Poland contradicted WIN's claims that it had caused widespread havoc.

On December 27, 1952, a two-hour broadcast by Radio Warsaw confirmed the calamity. In tones alternating between contempt and outrage, Polish authorities revealed that WIN was an elaborate hoax, designed to showcase the West's supposedly aggressive instincts. The Polish resistance had indeed been wiped out years earlier, but some of its leaders had agreed to become double agents, with Polish intelligence officers posing as other WIN officials. Phony battles had been staged to conjure up the wrecked tanks. All the money and military gear the Americans had dropped into the country had been a handsome, unintended gift to Poland's security forces.

Radio Warsaw also asserted that Poland, through the WIN ruse, had discovered a U.S. "volcano plan" for World War III in Europe. The Americans, it was claimed, intended to defend Western Europe through a scorched-earth strategy. Italy, Germany, France, and Great Britain would be a vast wasteland. The story, while pure disinformation, made riveting propaganda. An American intelligence official termed the WIN debacle "one of the worst operations ever run by the CIA." Inspired by the Polish scam, the Soviets set up phony resistance groups in Estonia and other parts of their empire.

Michael Burke, a former OSS officer whose wartime experiences had inspired the 1946 film *Cloak and Dagger,* starring Gary Cooper, managed many of the OPC airdrops into Soviet territory. Summing up the whole array of Iron Curtain operations in this period, he later wrote, "World War II-type paramilitary resistance movements simply were not on for Eastern Europe. There were very realistic limits to what could be accomplished by the CIA."

Wisner's OPC did enjoy some true successes. It was the OPC that sent Lansdale to the Philippines, securing that nation in the Western camp. It was also the OPC that poured some $30 million a year into Radio Free Europe and Radio Free Liberty. And the organization slipped shiploads of weapons to Tito, strengthening his stance as Yugoslavia's anti-Soviet Communist strongman.

In October 1950, while Wisner was still steadfastly putting agents into Albania, the CIA leadership changed. Frustrated by the agency's failure to predict the outbreak of the Korean War that summer, President Truman re-

TAKING ON COMMUNIST CHINA
IN A "BIG BOYS' GAME"

During a 1956 stop in Thailand, CIA director Allen Dulles (holding hat) reviews local mercenaries hired for operations against the Communist Chinese. Thailand was one of several Asian countries where the CIA trained men for military missions.

Enthralled by a CIA recruiter's tales of parachuting behind enemy lines and organizing resistance networks against the Communists in Asia, newly minted Yale graduate John Downey joined the agency in 1951. The recruiter, however, had not mentioned, and probably did not know, that enemy infiltrators frequently compromised the secrecy of the missions. Downey learned that the hard way when the plane in which he and another young CIA colleague, Richard Fecteau, were traveling was shot down over Manchuria. Their whereabouts betrayed by a turncoat radio operator, the pair spent the next two decades in a Chinese prison.

Downey and Fecteau were just two small parts of a CIA effort designed to roll back Communism in the Far East. Motivated by the Communist takeover of China in 1949 and the Korean War that followed on its heels, the

agency mounted an aggressive campaign against the people they called the ChiComs. CIA officers fanned out throughout Asia recruiting and training agents, then inserted them into hostile territory and bolstered their missions with airdrops of weapons and supplies.

Except for Edward Lansdale's work in the Philippines and Vietnam *(pages 15-17),* most of the agency's early efforts against Communism in Asia were relatively small affairs that reminded one CIA veteran of "a flea biting an elephant." Often poorly conceived, many of them also ended tragically. Of 212 Chinese agents recruited by the CIA who parachuted into the mainland between 1951 and 1953, 101 were killed and 111 were captured. Almost as complete was the failure of other CIA-recruited agents operating inside North Korea during the war. Most were caught and "doubled" by the Communists—made to radio

Richard Fecteau

John Downey

Richard Fecteau and John Downey face the future with confidence in these youthful photos. A CIA officer for just five months prior to the pair's capture in 1952, Fecteau served 19 years of a 20-year jail term. Downey, sentenced to life, was freed in 1973, after President Richard Nixon visited China.

Below, Cessna 195s of the Civil Air Transport's fleet idle on a Chinese field in the late 1940s. Founded in China by two Americans, CAT became the first of several CIA-owned air transport companies.

back misinformation to their CIA handlers. "We were led into lies, deceit, deception and traps," said one rueful CIA veteran. "We were children in a big boys' game."

In Tibet, occupied by the Chinese in 1950, the CIA had more mixed results *(overleaf)*. It scored one stellar success in 1959 in aiding the escape of the ruling Dalai Lama. CIA agents supplied a carefully crafted script to a monk who routinely passed on oracular messages to the Dalai Lama. In an evening session, the monk repeated the words, recommending that the ruler leave immediately and even providing a detailed escape route. The Dalai Lama followed the directions and fled to India and safety.

Beginning in the late 1950s, the CIA also supported a Tibetan guerrilla movement, even training some of the fighters in Colorado. Of the Tibetans sponsored by the CIA, 90 percent died or committed suicide to evade capture.

In the early 1960s, however, Tibetan guerrillas scored a notable coup when they captured papers that exposed details of the Chinese-Soviet rift as well as the early efforts of Chinese Communists to develop an atomic bomb.

Its successes against China were few, but the CIA kept trying. By the end of the 1950s, the agency had spent hundreds of millions of dollars on arms and ammunition and developed a network of Asian allies for logistical support and training sites. It even acquired an airline, Civil Air Transport *(above)*, a precursor to Air America, which provided reliable, secure service for agency personnel and their recruits. The establishment of the airline and other facilities may have been the most lasting achievement of the CIA's anti-China adventures, creating a paramilitary infrastructure that would help sustain its Far Eastern operations for the next 15 years.

Above, Tibetan guerrillas pause during their exercises at Camp Hale, Colorado, in 1961. CIA trainer Roger E. McCarthy (right) was one of a select group of agency personnel that put the men through paramilitary training at the camp, whose high mountainous setting closely resembled the Tibetans' homeland.

The Dalai Lama, third rider from the front, escapes from Tibet to India along a route, planned with CIA help, that took him over the Himalayas. The agency stayed in close touch during the three-week trip until his safe arrival was assured.

placed Hillenkoetter with General Walter Bedell Smith. Smith soon took control of the OPC from the State Department, bluntly announcing to Wisner, "You work for me." He objected to the constant sparring between the OPC and the OSO, the "special operations" office that served as the agency's intelligence-gathering force. In their respective specialties of covert action and espionage, the OSO and OPC often operated independently—or at cross-purposes—in the same countries.

Bit by bit, General Smith forced a merger. In December 1950 he established a new CIA position euphemistically called deputy director for plans, charged with overseeing all clandestine operations, including both the OPC and the OSO. Jolted by this loss of autonomy, Wisner was much relieved when he learned the job would go to Allen Dulles, an old comrade from Wall Street and the OSS. Indeed, as Wisner hoped, little would change under the new regime.

The avuncular Dulles was an intelligence legend, author of a recent book on his secret role in negotiating the German army's surrender in northern Italy toward the end of World War II. A large, cheerful, pipe-smoking man with a bristling mustache, he looked like an amiable professor, but he was iron willed and shrewd. Dulles had first tried his hand at intelligence as far back as 1916, as a foreign service officer in Bern, Switzerland. In that World War I posting, he had adroitly built up a network of refugees who shed useful light on events in the kaiser's Germany. But he had also missed a golden opportunity: On a Friday afternoon in the spring of 1917, in order to make a tennis date with a sweetheart, young Dulles brushed off a meeting with a Russian émigré named Vladimir Lenin. He did not know that Lenin would depart by train the next day to make a Russian revolution. Dulles would later tell this story to countless CIA trainees, stressing the moral: Never turn down a chance to gather intelligence.

After World War I, Dulles practiced international law in the powerhouse New York firm of Sullivan and Cromwell, run by his older brother, John Foster Dulles. World War II brought him back to intelligence work. Joining the OSS, he returned to Bern in 1942, and from that location produced one intelligence triumph after another. Dulles learned that the Nazis were working on long-range missiles and the atomic bomb. He steered help to the Italian dissidents who overthrew Mussolini in 1943. He also collected 1,600 top-secret German documents from master spy Fritz Kolbe, a highly placed official in the German Foreign Office who handed over the Japanese fleet's order of battle.

With mocking affection, Dulles's CIA colleagues twisted a catch phrase of the day—"the great white hunter"—to call him the "Great White Case Officer." A case officer is the basic job title of a CIA operations officer who recruits and manages foreign agents to do the actual spying, and the nickname reflected Dulles's lasting affection for the excitement of work in the field.

Dulles and Wisner saw the need for covert action, as did the National Security Council, and OPC continued on its aggressive way. Even now, Wisner sometimes went a bit far. On learning that Stalin might visit Paris for a 1952 summit conference, he proposed planting a bomb in his car—an idea that was quickly quashed within the agency. The agency's forceful approach became more vigorous than ever after Dwight D. Eisenhower became president in 1953. Within a few weeks of his inauguration, he made Dulles the first civilian director of central intelligence. Dulles's brother John Foster was named secretary of state, becoming the third member of the family to hold that position.

Assisted by Frank Wisner, who now replaced him as deputy director for plans, Allen Dulles would lead the agency in a relentlessly venturesome style for eight years, with the full support of an eager White House. During that time, the CIA stage-managed coups in Iran and Guatemala and attempted one in Cuba *(pages 56-91),* among other places; it also conducted high-altitude overflights of the Soviet Union by U-2 spy planes and supervised construction of the world's first spy satellite. Yet, as befitted an agency with a renowned case officer at the helm, some of its most successful projects took place in quieter quarters of the CIA's charge, in classic feats of espionage and intelligence collection.

A VITAL VOLUNTEER

On New Year's Day 1953, a young American vice-consul in Vienna, Austria, found an envelope in his car addressed in misspelled German to the American high commissioner, seat of U.S. authority in that tense city. Divided into four sectors of occupation and situated at the fault line between Western and Eastern Europe, Vienna was a prime location for cloak-and-dagger intrigue during the Cold War.

Inside the outer envelope was another, and within that, a note in faultless Russian. "I am a Soviet officer," it said. "I wish to meet with an American officer with the object of offering certain services. Time: 1800 hours. Date: January 1, 1953. Place: Plankengasse, Vienna 1."

Thus began the CIA's dealings with Pyotr Semyonovich Popov of the GRU, the Soviet military-intelligence service. At a time when the West was in desperate need of firsthand information about Soviet military assets and intents, Popov would be a jewel beyond compare.

Popov, not yet 30, had his share of flaws. He drank heavily and cheated on his wife. As a spy, he would display a terrible memory for important detail and an alarming casualness about security. Wounded during Red Army service in World War II, he had later been inducted into the GRU, evidently less by merit than by virtue of his rural background—peasants were then thought to epitomize the cherished Soviet working class. His assignment in Vienna was to recruit agents, which he did poorly; although his wife taught German, he spoke little of it himself and found the city's cosmopolitan culture baffling. Nonetheless he made the rank of lieutenant colonel, which let him roam freely through the local GRU headquarters, picking up sensitive documents as he wished.

In return for the secrets he offered, Popov wanted money. He first re-

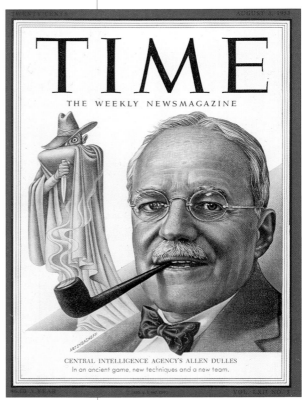

CENTRAL INTELLIGENCE AGENCY'S ALLEN DULLES
In an ancient game, new techniques and a new team.

In 1953, 60-year-old Allen Dulles made the cover of Time after succeeding Walter Bedell Smith as director of central intelligence. In his eight-year tenure, Dulles, whom the magazine described as having "the cheery, manly manner of a New England prep-school headmaster," shaped the CIA's organization and outlook for years to come.

"Allen was shrewd—but cold as ice."

—Louis Auchincloss,
former law firm colleague

quired 3,000 Austrian schillings to pay for an abortion for his Serb mistress, Milica Kohane. "She is a sensible girl," he told George Kisevalter, his astute, Russian-born CIA handler. "She knows I have a wife and children."

Yet Popov's motives were not purely mercenary. The GRU colonel despised the Soviets for the collectivization measures that abolished individual farms and brought terrible suffering to his own family of farmers. Popov was weary of being considered a chattel of the state. "The only thing is," he pleaded to Kisevalter in an early meeting, "treat me like a human being!"

Popov quickly built a trusting relationship with Kisevalter. At their first meeting, he divulged the names and assignments of 24 GRU case officers—the first of 650 he would pass on. He later unveiled a coveted manual on the Red Army's organization and tactics. At another meeting, he turned over a handwritten copy of the entire GRU payroll in Vienna, down to the last clerk and driver. Popov returned from a trip back home to the Soviet Union in mid-1954 with data on nuclear submarines and missiles, and he would subsequently supply details on missile-guidance systems. In grateful acknowledgment of the intelligence lode, Allen Dulles himself sent his ace spy a pair of gold cuff links, emblazoned with the helmet of Athena for wisdom and a sword for bravery.

When the Allied occupation of Austria finally ended in April 1955, Popov returned to the Soviet Union and dropped out of touch. The case seemed closed. But in January 1956, the GRU assigned him to a town in East Germany, and the Russian brashly reestablished contact. When a British military mission toured the area, Popov seized the opportunity to slip one of the officials a note, indicating he should forward it to the CIA. On its way, the missive passed through the SIS station in Berlin. Among those who may or may not have seen it there was George Blake, the man who headed SIS operations against the Soviets. SIS did not know that Blake was also a Soviet agent, appearing in KGB files under the code name Diomid.

An intelligence officer in Seoul at the outbreak of the Korean War, Blake had been captured early on when Communists overran the city. During his war-long internment in North Korea, a Soviet case officer had persuaded him to switch sides. Many years later, Blake would write that he subsequently passed to the KGB anything of interest that crossed his desk. He insisted, however, that he did not see Popov's letter and so could not have betrayed him at that time.

Unaware of any damage the letter may have caused, the CIA promptly dispatched Kisevalter to Berlin to work again with Popov, who traveled to the city on a variety of pretexts. Nearly a decade after the war's end, many structures in Berlin remained burned-out shells. Still divided, as Vienna had been, into four parts, the city was in effect split between the Soviet sector to the east and the American, British, and French sectors in the west. Passage between the two sections was relatively uncontrolled, however, and East Berliners fled by the thousands to the western sector. Ease of travel made the city a hotbed of intrigue as Soviet and Allied intelligence officers lived, worked, and rode the U-Bahn, or subway, in uneasy proximity. As documented in the groundbreaking 1997 book *Battleground Berlin,* written by a senior CIA officer who had served in Berlin and his KGB counterpart, Berlin became one of the world's spy capitals. Over a single two-year period, 40 politically motivated kidnappings by East German security occurred there.

In this place of tension and peril, Popov resumed his flow of secrets to Kisevalter and other CIA contacts. In March 1957 he handed over a blockbuster, a transcript of a speech by Soviet Defense Minister Georgy Zhukov to senior commanders. It dealt with ultrasensitive matters such as the Red Army's combat readiness, an estimate of the U.S. Army's nuclear strength, and Soviet strategies in the event of a European war—including plans for a two-day blitzkrieg in which Soviet forces would drive to the English Channel. Although closely held by the CIA, a copy of the document found its way to the SIS office in Berlin. In all likelihood, George Blake read the transcript and passed word to the KGB that Zhukov's speech had fallen into Western hands. Popov, who had been present in the audience, was now certainly among those under suspicion.

At that time, Popov was in charge of shepherding GRU agents as they passed through Germany to assignments abroad under false cover. As the agents came through, Popov identified them to the CIA so that they could be closely watched. One he named was Margarita Tairova, who had been dispatched to New York City. Once there, heavy-handed surveillance—including an FBI break-in of her hotel—put her on alert. Tairova reported to her Soviet superiors that she was being tailed. They in turn realized Popov was one of but three people who could have blown the operation. The GRU dispatched a colonel from Moscow to grill Popov. "The colonel spoke to me yesterday and I didn't sleep all night," Popov told Kisevalter. "So you see, perhaps, we shall never meet again!"

It was a wonder that Popov had not been caught long before, given his chronic absentmindedness. He once forgot the address of a safe house for a meeting with the CIA. Another time he left a notebook with emergency phone numbers at home. Compounding his error, he asked his wife for them from a telephone at the GRU's East Berlin headquarters, hardly a secure location. On a third occasion, he mistakenly took a subway express from East Berlin through West Berlin—off-limits to most Soviet officers. When he exited the U-Bahn, Soviet military police briefly took him into custody, and the GRU reprimanded Popov for his unauthorized transit. As Popov once remarked, "He who does not make mistakes is not working."

From Vienna, Milica Kohane, his now estranged lover, unwittingly caused him new difficulties. After Austrian police stopped another drunken GRU officer from entering her apartment, a GRU investigation uncovered her relationship with Popov, as well as the fact that she had helped expose election fraud by the Austrian Communist Party. To atone for the security lapse of keeping a foreign mistress, particularly a politically unreliable woman like Kohane, Popov was ordered to undergo the Soviet ritual of contrition known as self-criticism. He wept openly about the incident in front of his CIA contact. The pressure and peril of his work no doubt contributed to his headaches and high blood pressure.

Not long after the Kohane incident, Popov was recalled to Moscow.

A HIDDEN WORLD OF FACTS, FIGURES— AND DANGER

The Central Intelligence Agency began in 1947 with a small staff and a large mission: to keep the president, and his National Security Council, informed about international events affecting the nation's security. Originally, this meant coordinating reports from other departments, but the CIA was soon gathering and analyzing intelligence itself. Ever since, that task has remained at the core of its work.

Seemingly every kind of information is useful for this work. At CIA headquarters in Langley, intelligence officers watch foreign television news broadcasts and glean other facts from a sea of "open sources" that includes journals, newspapers, speeches, and the ever-growing Internet. Added to the mix is a wealth of secretly gathered information such as spy-satellite images, intercepted phone and radio signals, and some quirkier data as well. Among its other duties, for example, the CIA monitors the health of key foreign leaders and has on occasion arranged to collect and analyze their hair and other specimens, which can reveal hidden physical problems. The riskiest, yet in some ways most vital, intelligence gathering of all is "HUMINT," the vital human intelligence that provides key missing facts and personal insights.

Managing the tricky HUMINT process is the task of the CIA's operations officers. Although operations staff have tackled everything from training guerrilla fighters to planning escapes or "exfiltrations," most spend their days as case officers, responsible for recruiting and supervising foreign agents—chauffeurs, cleaning staff, military officers—who do the actual work of spying.

The delicate process of persuading someone to become a spy—frequently an act punishable by death— is an art that requires an intuitive grasp of what makes different kinds of people tick. Motives can range from money to friendship, from a desire for world peace to a deep hatred of an existing regime. Gaining the trust of a new agent can require months or years of contacts, as well as secret training sessions with cameras, bugging gear, and the like.

Putting together the resulting reports, along with the other vast array of intelligence, is the work of the agency's analysts, who create numerous reports, including a daily "brief" for the president. The brief, which has been called the world's most exclusive daily paper, is tailored as much as possible to each chief executive's preferences. For example, because Lyndon Johnson often reviewed important documents in bed, for some time the brief was completed and delivered in the late afternoon; Johnson later decided to read it before the morning papers, and the entire preparation cycle was rescheduled for a 6:30 a.m. delivery.

Although its exact size is a secret, by the late 1990s, the CIA had an estimated 16,000 to 17,000 employees, of whom only about 1,000 were overseas operations officers. The rest include a wide range of specialists, from economists and historians to computer scientists, disguise artists, cabinetmakers, and leatherworkers. All new employees must pass a background check that reaches back seven years, as well as a polygraph exam, which may be repeated at intervals throughout their careers.

Among its many unusual features, a job at the CIA can carry high risks, especially for those in the field. Proudly displayed on a marble wall in the CIA's entrance hall are 78 stars commemorating officers who have died in the line of duty. Below them, an open book supplies names for fewer than half the stars. The other dead officers remain anonymous, having lost their lives under circumstances still considered too sensitive to be acknowledged.

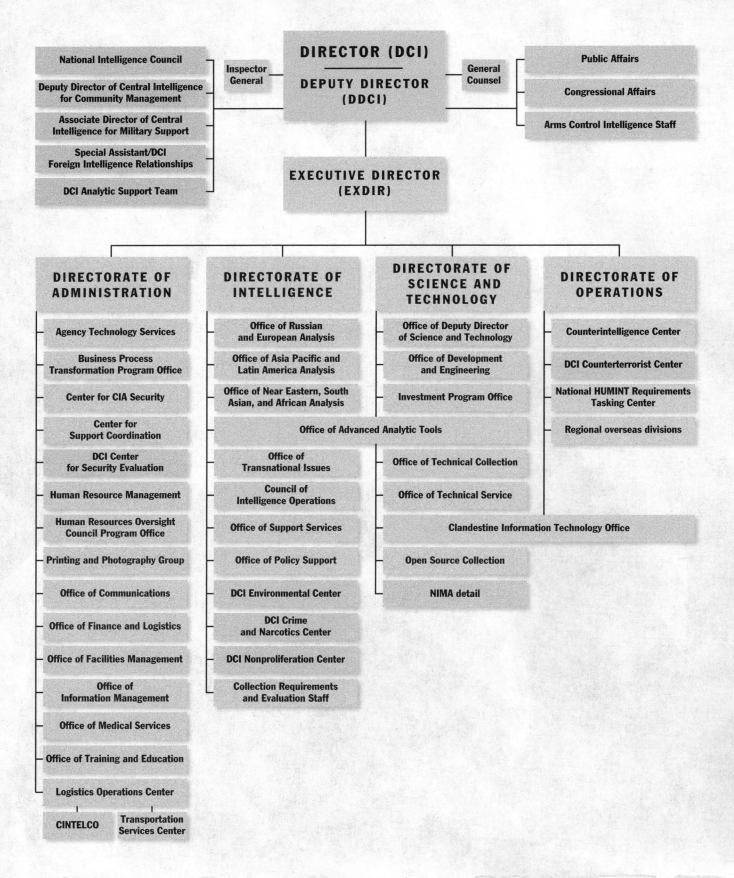

DIRECTOR (DCI)
—
DEPUTY DIRECTOR (DDCI)

Inspector General

General Counsel

National Intelligence Council

Deputy Director of Central Intelligence for Community Management

Associate Director of Central Intelligence for Military Support

Special Assistant/DCI Foreign Intelligence Relationships

DCI Analytic Support Team

Public Affairs

Congressional Affairs

Arms Control Intelligence Staff

EXECUTIVE DIRECTOR (EXDIR)

DIRECTORATE OF ADMINISTRATION

Agency Technology Services

Business Process Transformation Program Office

Center for CIA Security

Center for Support Coordination

DCI Center for Security Evaluation

Human Resource Management

Human Resources Oversight Council Program Office

Printing and Photography Group

Office of Communications

Office of Finance and Logistics

Office of Facilities Management

Office of Information Management

Office of Medical Services

Office of Training and Education

Logistics Operations Center

CINTELCO

Transportation Services Center

DIRECTORATE OF INTELLIGENCE

Office of Russian and European Analysis

Office of Asia Pacific and Latin America Analysis

Office of Near Eastern, South Asian, and African Analysis

Office of Advanced Analytic Tools

Office of Transnational Issues

Council of Intelligence Operations

Office of Support Services

Office of Policy Support

DCI Environmental Center

DCI Crime and Narcotics Center

DCI Nonproliferation Center

Collection Requirements and Evaluation Staff

DIRECTORATE OF SCIENCE AND TECHNOLOGY

Office of Deputy Director of Science and Technology

Office of Development and Engineering

Investment Program Office

Office of Technical Collection

Office of Technical Service

Clandestine Information Technology Office

Open Source Collection

NIMA detail

DIRECTORATE OF OPERATIONS

Counterintelligence Center

DCI Counterterrorist Center

National HUMINT Requirements Tasking Center

Regional overseas divisions

A Structure of Secrecy

As illustrated in the color-coded chart at left, the director of central intelligence, or DCI, actually has two jobs. The DCI is the head of the CIA, which includes the units indicated here in gray. But the director also leads the intelligence community, a group of agencies that includes the CIA; the National Security Agency; several military-intelligence branches; and sections of the FBI, and the State, Energy, and Treasury Departments. As part of that second job, the DCI manages the offices shown here in pink, which are staffed by top members of the larger intelligence community, including generals and admirals. Still other units, depicted in tan, link the CIA, the community, and other government offices. For example, the National Imagery and Mapping Agency

(NIMA), which interprets satellite images, is a Defense Department unit, yet a large group of CIA employees, as shown here, work closely with it.

Since 1963, the CIA itself has been divided into four broad divisions, or directorates, each headed by a deputy director. Administration *(far left)* handles the routine of running a government agency—but with a twist. Employees' telephones, for example, do not come from a commercial supplier but from a more secure internal company, CINTELCO. And the medical services office maintains lists of psychiatrists with security clearances, enabling employees to receive care without a security breach.

Intelligence, the next directorate, is staffed largely by analysts, often with Ph.D.s and other advanced degrees. Based mainly at agency head-

quarters in Virginia *(below)*, specialists not only sift through facts but also reach conclusions that help shape U.S. policy. For technical data related to satellites, computers, and communications, they rely heavily on the science and technology directorate.

Science and technology also supplies the very stuff of spy craft: concealed cameras, bugs, disguises, false identity cards, invisible inks, hidden weapons. These and other items are put to use by the shadowy operations directorate (formerly called plans), which almost certainly includes some hidden divisions not listed here. Operations officers once guarded their identities so carefully that they ate in a separate cafeteria at headquarters. They remain a group apart, living under assumed identities for much of their agency careers.

In a view from the 1990s, CIA headquarters takes on a rosy glow at sunset. Located near Washington, D.C., the complex is ringed with security measures, including trained dogs; remote audio surveillance is discouraged by special glass walls.

Early the next year, 1958, a CIA miscue accidentally removed any doubt about the Soviet officer's double life. The agency sent to Popov's home a coded letter with mailing addresses for communicating with his handlers. The KGB, which had Popov under surveillance, intercepted the letter, photographed it, then returned it to the envelope as if unopened.

In Moscow, Popov continued to work for the CIA, not realizing the KGB now was tracking him around the clock. When the watchers finally pounced and accused him of treachery, Popov confessed immediately but showed such remorse that the KGB tried for a time to use him as a double agent—still appearing to spy for the CIA, but in reality working for the Soviets again. In that role, Popov followed through with prearranged "brush contacts" with a CIA officer based at the American embassy, slipping him small notebooks as they passed each other at agreed-upon locations. The reports contained military data—and clues that something was amiss. Popov had previously numbered his reports; these were unnumbered. Moreover, he wrote front to back in the notebooks, not back to front as before. The reports also contained little of value.

The CIA began to smell a rat. Then, at a meeting in the men's room of a Moscow restaurant, Popov confirmed the agency's suspicions with his boldest action to date. He slipped his CIA contact a small cylinder covered by cloth; he had hidden the cylinder by hanging it from a string within his pants. The cylinder held eight tiny handwritten messages revealing he had been under KGB control for seven months.

Although Popov continued to play the role of double agent, in the end the Kremlin decided he could not be trusted. On October 16, 1959, both he and his CIA contact were arrested as they passed notes on a Moscow bus. Five KGB agents hustled the CIA man to an interrogation room, where he sat mute through two hours of threats before being released. Popov was tried and sentenced to death as a traitor. According to one story, GRU officers hurled him, alive, into a furnace. Reports in the 1990s, however, made it apparent that Popov had been executed by firing squad the year after his arrest, just as the Soviet press had reported at the time. "A bullet at the end of a contemptible life," commented the Soviet newspaper *Izvestia*, "is not only a punishment but an act of mercy." Although the CIA had more than once offered Popov the chance to retire in safety in the West, its daring if reckless agent had always declined.

UNDERCOVER UNDERGROUND

During the Dulles years, Berlin would also be the scene of a less deadly intelligence feat, one seemingly more appropriate to a Hollywood script than real-life spy work. This time, the intelligence would come from a giant, but secret, construction project in the heart of Cold War Berlin.

In the early 1950s, the CIA and SIS had become preoccupied with the difficult task of eavesdropping on Soviet communications, especially in the key German and Austrian occupation zones. Increasingly, the Soviets sent

George Blake

During World War II, George Blake served briefly with the Dutch resistance before joining British intelligence. After being captured by the North Koreans in 1950, he began a double life in service to the KGB; among the secrets he betrayed were clues to the identity of a key CIA source, Pyotr Popov.

sensitive messages by landlines—overhead wires and buried cables—rather than by radio transmissions, which could be intercepted. Soviet patrols also regularly checked overhead wires for tampering, sharply limiting opportunities for tapping them. The first breakthrough in solving this problem came in 1951, in Vienna, when SIS secretly dug a 70-foot tunnel from the British part of the city into the Soviet sector and then plugged into an important underground Soviet cable. They called the project Operation Silver.

In 1952, SIS and the CIA formed a partnership for a similar, but far more ambitious, project in Berlin. On the city's southern edge, in a mostly empty area of shacks and farmland, three important cables passed within several hundred feet of the boundary between the U.S. and Soviet zones. Buried in soft soil alongside a major highway, the cables carried phone traffic within East Berlin and between it and Soviet military bases elsewhere.

Instead of a 70-foot tunnel, as in Vienna, getting at the cables in Berlin would require a tunnel nearly 1,500 feet long. Not all of it would be in Soviet territory; to avert suspicion, the secret entrance on the Allied side would be hundreds of feet from the border. If the Vienna tunnel had been Operation Silver, a project of this magnitude had to be code-named Gold.

At the time, the CIA's local chief in Berlin was Bill Harvey, a former FBI counterintelligence agent who, before joining the CIA, had suspected Philby was a mole and had had him investigated. Nicknamed "the Pear" for his hefty bulk, Harvey had a well-earned reputation as a womanizer, a drinker—and a gung-ho cold warrior. He went armed at all times, often carrying pearl-handled pistols in holsters under each armpit. Yet for all his bravado, Harvey was also highly competent.

A Treasure Trove from the Third Reich

As the CIA set up shop in Western Europe, it inherited a highly useful intelligence asset—the so-called Gehlen Organization. One of Hitler's top spymasters, Reinhard Gehlen, shown here in his lieutenant colonel's uniform in 1944, had developed a comprehensive network of sources on the Soviet "eastern front" during World War II. In the spring of 1945, his accurate, but ominous, reports on the strength of advancing Soviet troops led Hitler to fire him. Gehlen then buried his files and went into hiding with his staff. A month later, he surrendered to American forces, who soon saw the value of what Gehlen had to offer.

In 1946, under U.S. Army sponsorship, Gehlen's organization—made up largely of his former officers and foreign agents, some now in Communist-controlled Europe—was back in business. By the time it formally passed over to CIA control in 1949, the enterprise employed some 4,000 Germans. Shortly after West Germany resumed its independence in 1955, Gehlen's organization became the official West German intelligence service, the BND, with Reinhard Gehlen still firmly in command.

"He was disciplined and superb at making ops," remarked another CIA officer. "He thought out every detail."

The voluble Harvey enthused about the Berlin wiretapping gambit and headed for Washington to brief Dulles and Wisner at CIA headquarters. Said a senior officer who heard Harvey's pitch, "I don't think the Director or Frank Wisner would have gone ahead with it if they hadn't had a guy like Harvey in West Berlin." Harvey's zeal carried the day, and Dulles approved Gold in January 1954. He considered the potential intelligence bonanza worth the operation's $20 million-plus price tag.

Given the barren local landscape and the operation's sheer scale, a cover story was clearly required—a false construction project that would mask the laborers and heavy equipment of a tunneling operation. The intelligence services settled on an ingenious ruse—the construction of a warehouselike building, fitted with antennas, that was meant to suggest a radar-intercept station to curious Soviet observers. In fact, the warehouse would be the tunnel's starting point. It was designed with an extra-deep foundation to hold the huge volume of dirt that would pile up as diggers worked their way toward the target.

To determine the precise distance and direction to the cables, CIA officers crossed into the Soviet sector, drove over the highway that ran above the targeted site, and staged the changing of a flat tire. During the brief stop, one officer stuck a small reflector by the road. From a peephole in the warehouse, a surveyor then directed a beam that bounced off the reflector, yielding an exact measurement.

Before work began on the tunnel, American army engineers built a 450-foot test tunnel in New Mexico, in soil similar to the German site. Then, in Berlin, U.S. Army teams worked continuous eight-hour shifts with pick and shovel over six months to remove 3,100 tons of dirt. The resulting passage was six and a half feet in diameter and almost five football fields long. It burrowed toward the target cables with its floor at a depth of just over 16 feet, deep enough to deaden the sounds of digging. To prevent a cave-in, the tunnel was lined with hundreds of circular steel collars, each precoated with rubber to muffle the clanking noise of engineers bolting them together. Air conditioners in the warehouse pumped fresh, cool air to the diggers below. In their Vienna excavation, British engineers had learned how to dig upward without collapsing the ceiling. It was SIS that built the vertical shafts at each end of the tunnel.

As the work progressed, Harvey visited the construction site, but only at night, and only after changing cars to elude KGB tails. By the spring of 1955, the job was done. At the top of the vertical shaft, the circuits were tapped in the aptly named tap room; microphones in the room were ready to pick up the sounds of intruders. Fifty feet inside the tunnel, a massive steel door was placed to discourage Sovi-

"If you ever know as many secrets as I do, then you'll know why I carry a gun."
—William Harvey

A former FBI spy catcher who moved to the CIA soon after its founding in 1947, Bill Harvey later became CIA base chief in the American sector of Berlin. Harvey led the effort to build the Berlin tunnel, which his colleagues nicknamed "Harvey's Hole."

William King Harvey

Smooth Operator

In 1998, research into East German archives offered a rare look at one of the many foreign agents recruited by the CIA during the Cold War. Originally a believer in Communism, telephone installation engineer Gertrud Liebing (above) changed her mind after a run-in with Soviet authorities and began spying for the CIA in 1955. Assigned to the Central Committee of the Socialist Unity Party in 1959, Liebing tapped the phone lines of key officials. She offered her apartment for meetings between East German intelligence officers and informants—and tapped the telephone there as well. Using coded radio transmissions and letters, Liebing reported to the CIA until 1966. Then East German postal inspectors discovered that her correspondence with a West Berlin friend included numbers written in invisible ink. Already in ill health, the 55-year-old informant died after serving two months of a 12-year prison term.

ets or East Germans who might discover the project. Harvey also posted a forceful, although mysterious, sign that blared a warning in German and Russian, "Entry is forbidden by order of the Commanding General."

Once the tunnel was in place, the British handled the tapping, delicately withdrawing the 273 separate wires within the three cables, then applying clips that stole the smallest possible increment of signal voltage to avoid alerting the Soviets that someone was listening in. The resultant faint signals went first to amplifiers within the tunnel and then to a battery of tape recorders in the warehouse. Each day, 800 reels of tape recordings were flown under armed guard to London and Washington for analysis; SIS analyzed the telephone signals and the CIA took the teletype traffic. At Building T-32 near the Lincoln Memorial, some 50 CIA officers sat in a cramped, windowless room wearily translating from Russian and German. The building was cased in steel sheathing to stop electronic impulses from leaking out to the Soviets' own eavesdroppers.

For 11 months and 11 days, Gold worked handsomely, with hundreds of thousands of messages caught on the electronic fly. Then, in the early morning hours of April 22, 1956, Soviet troops were spotted above the far end of the tunnel. As they began to dig, Harvey rushed to the American end of the tunnel. Within an hour, one of the microphones at the Soviet end picked up amazed Russian and German voices as they discovered the elaborate tap chamber. Working carefully, East German technicians entered the tunnel itself around midday. When they found their progress blocked by the steel door, they dug around it. "It goes all the way under the highway!" the interlopers exclaimed. "How did they do it? It's fantastic!"

Although disappointed at the discovery, the CIA team stood ready to fend off too close an encounter. Harvey had positioned a .50-caliber machine gun on the American side of the tunnel, just past a dip in the structure that blocked the view ahead. The gun was not loaded, but the intruders could not know that. As they approached, Harvey himself, just out of sight, pulled back the bolt of the gun, then released it, making the unmistakable sound of a round being chambered. The Soviets and East Germans quickly withdrew. But at 3:35 p.m., the taps went dead.

An internal CIA history of the operation concluded that the Soviets were drawn to the site when one of the cables malfunctioned after heavy rains. "Analysis of all available evidence—traffic passing on the target cables, conversations recorded from a microphone installed in the tap chamber, and visual observations from the site—indicates that the Soviet discovery was purely fortuitous," the report read.

Not quite. In reality, the end of Gold had nothing to do with bad luck or a troublesome cable. It was later learned that the KGB had known about the tunnel from the start, having been alerted by George Blake, the same mole within British intelligence who had helped bring down Pyotr Popov. Even before the first shovel hit the dirt, Blake had passed along information on the covert excavation.

For a year before the staged "discovery" of the tunnel, the Soviets had let the West listen in on their communications, never making the slightest

effort to intercede. The KGB's apparent reason: thwarting the operation might have led to the exposure of Blake, whom the Russians valued more than the information the West might glean from the taps. Some in the West later wondered if the KGB had also salted the cable traffic with disinformation, but in the 1990s, a study of KGB records indicated this was not so. Evidently the intelligence service believed the intercepts could do no great harm. The highest-level communications of the military, the Communist Party, the Soviet foreign ministry, and the KGB traveled across carefully guarded overhead lines instead.

In the immediate aftermath of the tunnel's closure, opinions differed within the CIA and SIS as to the worth of what they had heard, a harvest so huge that transcription and analysis would continue for two years after the tunnel's closing. Some intelligence officers thought the take was of little use—mostly routine, low-level chatter. Others noted the cable taps supplied a solid picture of Soviet military assets in the region. They revealed an East German transportation system so decrepit that a surprise Soviet attack on Berlin would have been very difficult.

Allen Dulles himself was in no doubt. Calling Gold "one of the most valuable and daring projects ever undertaken," he awarded Harvey the Distinguished Intelligence Medal. Years later, he proudly recounted the story of the Berlin tunnel in his 1963 book, *The Craft of Intelligence.* Built on a vast scale and wrapped in its layers of clever deception, the tunnel project epitomized the CIA's confidence and zest for direct action in the Allen Dulles era, as Dulles surely knew.

The Soviets, as the planned dupes of the enterprise, saw matters rather differently. They had intended the staged discovery of the tunnel to be a propaganda coup, proof of U.S. underhandedness in what was depicted as a purely American project. Soviet and East German authorities even set up a beer and sausage stand at what they expected to be Berlin's newest tourist attraction. But, in a final irony, their attempts to indict the United States and its intelligence agency backfired. In comments typical of many, the *New York Herald Tribune* praised the operation as a "striking example of the Americans' capacity for daring undertakings." And the *Washington Post,* in an editorial headlined "The Tunnel of Love," noted that West Germans reacted with "astonishment and delight," viewing the project as "evidence that the tradition of Yankee resourcefulness and ingenuity is not a myth after all."

Soon after German technicians uncovered the eastern end of the Berlin tunnel on April 22, 1956, Communist officials led journalists on guided tours, resulting in some of the photographs shown here. Clockwise from top: East German guards near a makeshift tunnel opening stare across at the American "warehouse" covering the other end of the tunnel; a photographer crosses the underground border between the Soviet and American sectors; and a Soviet technician examines specialized tapping equipment underground.

PORTABLE DIALER
The dialer below could attach to a telephone line, then ring a phone inside to check if a site was unoccupied before an agent secretly entered.

TOOLS OF THE TRADE

By the time the CIA started work in 1947, specialized espionage equipment was a staple of the intelligence game. The new agency benefited greatly from the past efforts of the wartime OSS; in fact, many experts from the OSS research and development branch came back to form the nucleus of the CIA's technical services staff. In the years to come, the TSS would continue to grow, recruiting engineers, locksmiths, disguise artists, and other specialists who pitted their skill against the Soviets and their allies.

Shown here and in the pages that follow are classic intelligence-gathering tools used by the CIA in the first decades of the Cold War. Although some were created in TSS workshops, in its early years the CIA also depended heavily on equipment developed elsewhere, either by civilian manufacturers, American military intelligence, or the FBI. Not only did this off-the-shelf approach allow the CIA to take advantage of the latest gadgetry, it also made the items harder to trace. No matter the source, however, the label "CIA" never appeared on any agency equipment.

Although possessed of a certain period charm today, many of the devices illustrated here were technical marvels in their time—cutting-edge innovations that pushed the limits of miniaturization, concealment, and portability. Together, they gave the CIA's officers and agents the means to acquire photographic, audio, and other intelligence—and to deliver or transmit it safely home.

WRISTWATCH CAMERA
Produced in the late 1940s, the Steineck ABC Camera (left) let its wearer take photographs while pretending to check the time. Below, illustrations from a U.S. government manual demonstrate its use; an arrow indicates the right-angle viewfinder.

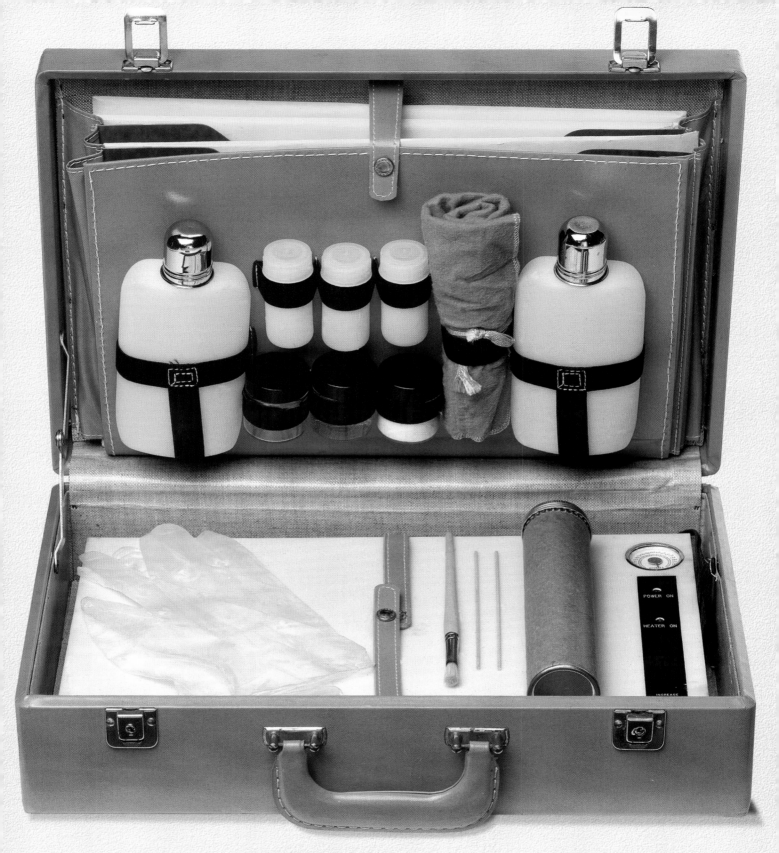

A LETTER-INTERCEPTION KIT

The "flaps and seals" case above was designed for surreptitiously opening envelopes. Steam produced by the white-heat table at the bottom, combined with mechanical and chemical manipulation, could open and reseal almost any piece with no sign of tampering.

CLANDESTINE PHOTOGRAPHY

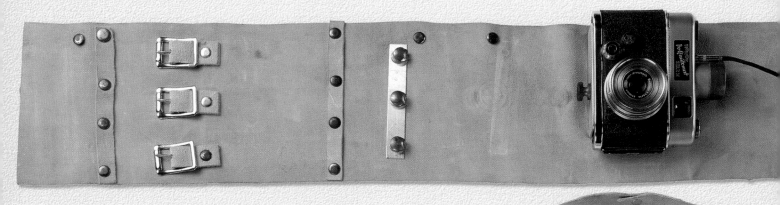

CIGARETTE-PACK SURVEILLANCE

The world's smallest motor-driven 35 mm camera, the Swiss Tessina fit snugly into a cigarette pack modified by CIA technicians. A metal frame built into the box supported the camera and kept the lens aligned with tiny perforations through which the camera could shoot. The shutter release was pressed through the box, just above the holes.

PERFORATIONS —

CRUSH·PROOF BOX

Warning The Surgeon General Has Determined That Cigarette Smoking Is Dangerous to Your Health

Winston

20 FILTER CIGARETTES

FULL·RICH
TOBACCO FLAVOR

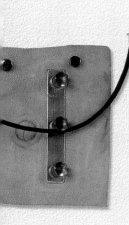

WAIST-BELT CAMERA

With a spring-motor film advance and remote shutter-release cable, the German-made Robot Star II camera could be mounted between the two layers of an agency-supplied waist belt, as shown here and in the diagram at right. The belt came with a set of several matching coat buttons (far right) that included one see-through piece meant to be placed over the camera lens.

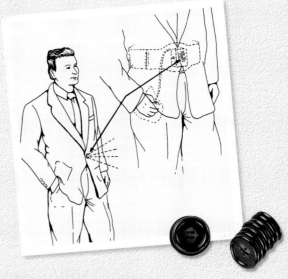

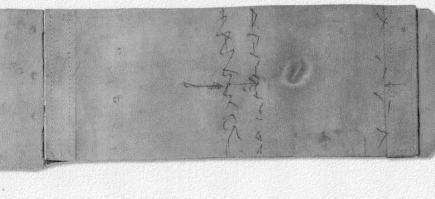

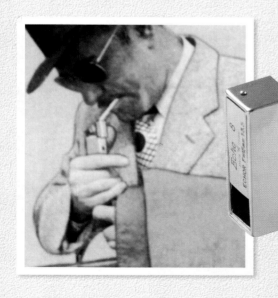

PHOTOS FROM A LIGHTER

Even smaller than the Tessina on page 46, the Japanese Echo 8 fit into a lighter case side by side with a fully functional lighter. As shown at far left, the user opened the device to light a cigarette, then aimed the camera with a right-angle viewfinder. The lens aperture is visible as a small square on the side of the case.

MICRODOT MESSAGES

A staple of the spy trade, microdots—tiny pieces of photographic film like the one shown at upper left on a glass slide—can contain a full page of text in a space less than a millimeter across. During the late 1960s and early 1970s, the CIA's microdot gear for the field included a readily concealable reader (far left) and the astonishingly compact microdot camera at left.

DOCUMENT PHOTOGRAPHY

A favorite with intelligence services since its introduction in 1938, the Minox camera is ideal for secret document copying; the Model III, shown here with a film cartridge, was used extensively by the CIA throughout the 1950s. Attached to the left side of the camera is a measuring chain that, when fully extended, sets the proper focal length for photographing flat objects (diagram, right).

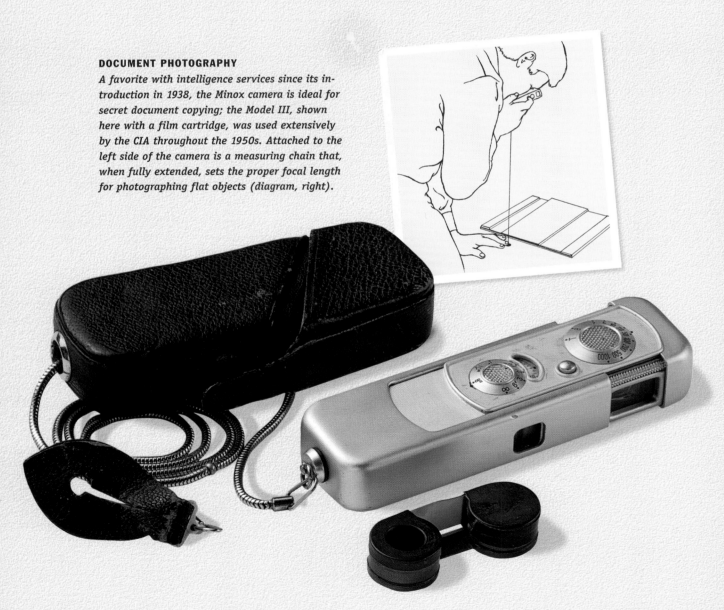

HIDDEN FILM

Transporting film and other items could require concealment inside such innocent-looking items as this modified battery and shaving cream can. Both are hollow with screw-on closures; to deceive searchers, the can also contained a small amount of dispensable cream.

DEAD-DROP SPIKE

Another way of relaying photographs or other small items was by means of prearranged locations, known as dead drops, where items could be left for retrieval. The spike above, designed to hold film, would have been driven into the ground at such a site and left for later pickup.

COVERT COMMUNICATIONS

CODES ON A STAMP

Nothing more than lists of number groups used to generate codes, "one-time pads" come in pairs, one for the sender and one for the receiver; if each sequence is used once and then discarded, the coded transmission is almost unbreakable. The pad below, hidden on the back of a Polish stamp, was used by CIA operatives in the late 1940s.

RADIOS FOR THE FIELD

For work in hostile areas, the CIA used rugged, compact military radios like the Delco 5300, made in "agency black" instead of army green. The example below was used in Cuba during the 1960s.

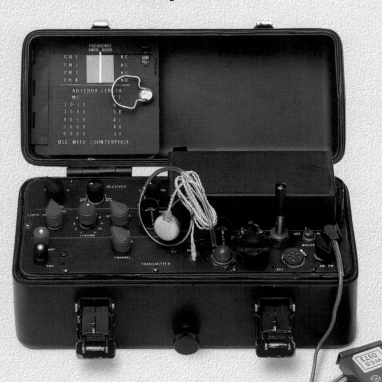

HOTEL-LAMP TRANSCEIVER

Meant for operations that required short-range communications between agents—for example, between hotel rooms—the compact transceiver above, left, could be hidden in a lamp base. If necessary, it could be set up as a listening device.

TO CALIBRATE RECEIVER
1. REMOVE ANTENNA
2. REDUCE VOLUME
3. TURN BFO TO ZERO
4. PRESS "CAL" BUTTON
5. SET DIAL TO .5MC POINT CLOSEST TO OPERATING FREQUENCY & TUNE FOR ZERO (0) BEAT
6. TURN "ADJ. CAL." CONTROL TO MATCH DIAL READING
7. AFTER CALIBRATING REPLACE ANTENNA & READJUST VOLUME
VOLUME
TUNING
KEYER
MANUAL
CRYSTAL
SEND
GND
2 AMP
PRESS TO CAL.
CAL ADJ.
BFO
BAND-SWITCH
4.5-10MC
10-22MC
"0" IS OFF
AC LINE SWITCH
90-250 VAC
50-400 CYCLES
RECEIVER
TRANSMITTER
POWER SUPPLY

ATTACHÉ-CASE RADIO

During the Cold War, the CIA made extensive use of radios fitted into reinforced attaché cases like the one shown here. Designed to use only Morse code, which is more secure than voice transmissions and can be employed over a greater range, the radio could reach about 3,000 miles when an outdoor antenna was deployed.

EXT
ACL

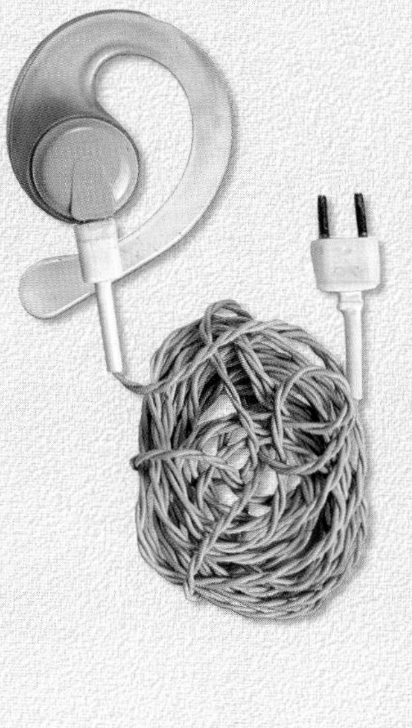

MORSE-CODE TRAINING KEY

All CIA covert-operations officers learn many forms of radio communication. This practice key was used to hone trainees' Morse code skills during the 1950s.

AUDIO SURVEILLANCE

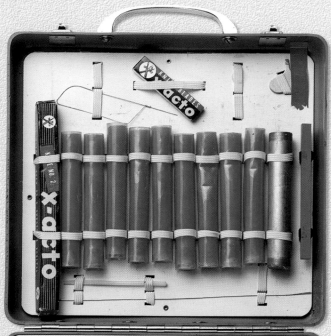

FINE-WIRE KIT

Used by U.S. intelligence and law enforcement personnel, this case holds gear to lay undetectable wiring for hidden microphones and transmitters. With it, fine wires—stored here in paper-wrapped spools—could be inset into cracks or soft building materials and covered where necessary with wax from the enclosed red tubes.

A CLASSIC BUG

Concealed in a 110-volt electric plug, this microphone/transmitter used by the CIA in the 1950s could pick up conversations within 15 feet and relay them to a listening post. It was powered by current passing through the electric line.

HIDING IN A SPINE

In the 1960s, transistorized electronics made it possible for U.S. intelligence experts to create a thin listening device (left) that could be concealed in the spine of a book, as shown above.

A CLANDESTINE BASE STATION

Produced for law enforcement but also used by the CIA, the Bell & Howell SK-8A Intelligence Case (below) contained a receiver and tape recorder that enabled it to serve as a "base station" for transmissions from nearby bugs. Concealed in a hard plastic briefcase, the SK-8A drew power from batteries or an automobile cigarette lighter adapter and could record for up to six hours.

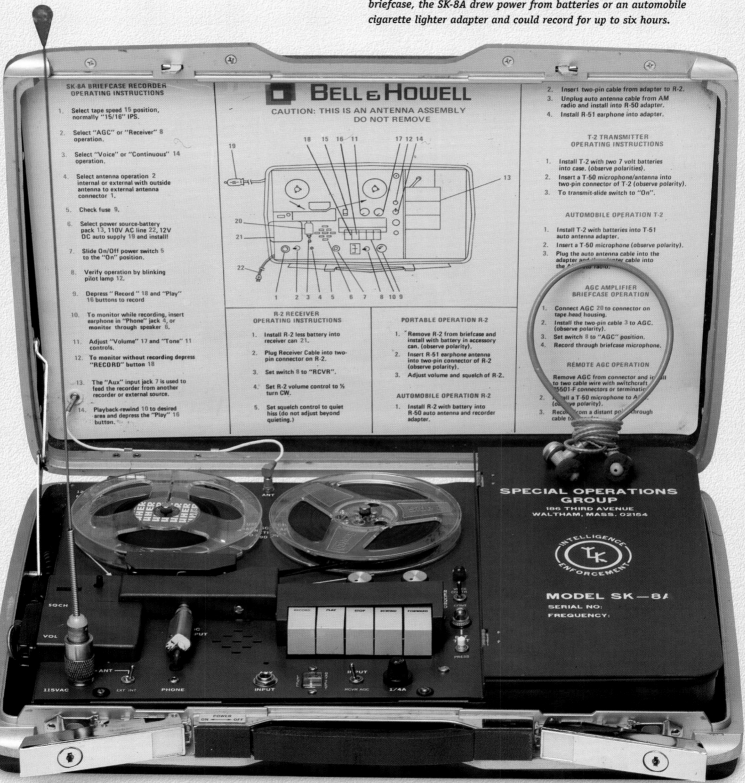

SURREPTITIOUS ENTRY

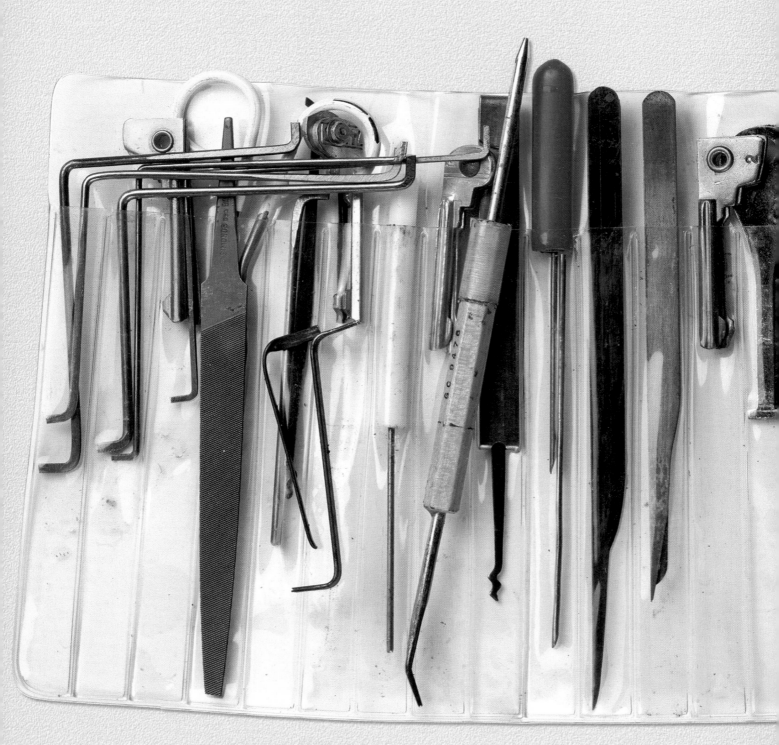

A LOCKSMITH'S SPECIAL GEAR

*One of a kind, the lock-pick collection above was assembled by
a locksmith employed by the CIA in the 1960s. Each agency lock expert had a set, based partly on the locks that might be encountered;
besides devices to open tumbler- and lever-type locks, this one holds
special keys (far right) to fit more old-fashioned locks as well.*

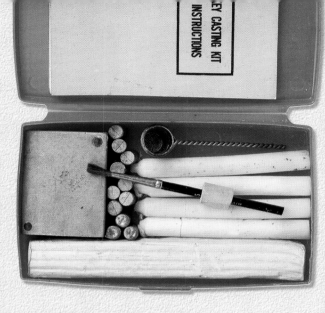

A POCKET KIT TO COPY KEYS

Tools needed to reproduce a key from a clay impression fit snugly into the case above, which includes clay, candles, a ladle, slugs of an easily melted alloy, and a two-piece aluminum mold (shown open in the enlarged view at left). Once a clay impression was obtained, the mold was used to make an alloy copy; a key-cutting machine could then create a hard key for use.

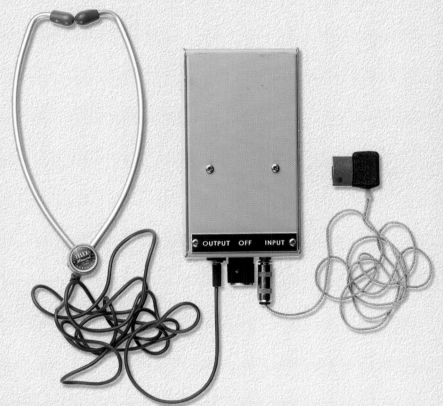

OUTPUT   OFF   INPUT

A SAFECRACKER'S ELECTRONIC EARS

The electronic stethoscope above allowed a CIA locksmith to detect the sounds made by the combination tumbler mechanisms used in most safe locks before 1965. With the red-tabbed contact microphone attached next to the safe's dial, the high-gain amplifier (center) magnified the sound more than 10,000 times through the operator's headset.

COUPS AND
OVERTHROWS

ust after midnight on August 1, 1953, the CIA's top man in the Iranian capital of Tehran lay down in the back seat of an unmarked black sedan and pulled a blanket over his head. After a brief drive, an armed guard waved the car, seemingly empty except for its driver, inside the gates of the royal palace. The CIA officer pulled aside the cover and sat up expectantly. Through the gloom a thin figure approached the sedan and climbed into the rear seat. Muhammad Reza Pahlavi—the 34-year-old shah of Iran—greeted Kermit Roosevelt.

In his horn-rimmed glasses, the witty, professorial Roosevelt hardly looked the part of a man of action. A grandson of President Theodore Roosevelt, Kermit Roosevelt had been a leading OSS expert on the Middle East during World War II. He went on to write the book *Arabs, Oil, and History*, then joined the CIA in 1950. Now, he was at work on his most ambitious assignment to date: plotting the ouster of the shah's 72-year-old archrival, Prime Minister Muhammad Mosaddeq.

A fervent nationalist and a spellbinding speaker, Mosaddeq had nationalized Britain's Anglo-Iranian Oil Company two years earlier, prompting a British boycott of Iranian oil. U.S. policymakers were equally troubled by Mosaddeq's on-again, off-again ties to the Tudeh—Iran's Communist Party—and his openness to warmer relations with the Soviet Union. In the summer of 1953, the United States was just concluding a brutal war against Communism in Korea, and Senator Joseph McCarthy, near the peak of his influence, was still making unnerving claims of Communist subversion within the United States. The newly arrived Eisenhower administration, elected in part on a platform of "rolling back Communism," saw Iran as a test case.

In their nighttime meeting—one of several held by the two men that summer—Roosevelt and the shah agreed that the latter would issue two firmans, or royal decrees. One would dismiss Mosaddeq as prime minister; the other would appoint a mutually agreeable successor, General Fazlollah Zahedi.

Castro's Cuban troops hit the ground near a burning bus—typical of the civil-ian vehicles used to convey their forces—as they take fire from attacking Cuban exiles during the CIA-directed Bay of Pigs invasion in 1961. The planned overthrow of the Cuban government was the most ambitious of several similar efforts mounted by the agency in the 1950s and early 1960s.

The shah, a realist, knew those legal documents alone would carry no weight with Mosaddeq; they would have to be enforced by the people, and elements of the Iranian army, in the streets of Tehran. That support could be readily marshaled, Roosevelt assured him, noting that the CIA's network of Iranian agents could "distribute pamphlets, organize mobs," and "keep track of the opposition." As for Iran's armed forces, he told the shah, all "except for a very few at the top" were devoted to him. But the shah remained cautious. He decided to fly north to the Caspian Sea and remain outside the capital until the outcome of the power play was known.

The effort to oust Mosaddeq enjoyed high-level support back home, having been approved two months earlier by a group that included not only CIA director Allen Dulles but also his brother, Secretary of State John Foster Dulles; Undersecretary of State— and former CIA director—Walter Bedell Smith; and Secretary of Defense Charles Wilson. As Roosevelt later recalled in his 1979 memoir, *Countercoup,* the response to his 22-page plan, code-named Ajax, received a thumbs-up. "So this is how we get rid of that madman Mosaddeq!" John Foster Dulles exclaimed. British intelligence would also be involved, working jointly with the CIA.

In essence, Roosevelt aimed at exploiting two existing factors: Iran's economic distress from the oil boycott and Mosaddeq's growing political weaknesses. By assuming the post of defense minister, Mosaddeq had already angered the army; by dissolving the national assembly, he had infuriated its members; by dallying with the Communist Tudeh Party, he had put off the ayatollahs, Iran's religious leaders. Even the Tudeh was distrustful. Mosaddeq had crushed a Communist-inspired demonstration two years before, at the cost of a hundred lives. As the CIA saw it, Mosaddeq was ripe for a fall. All that was needed was a final push.

That push began in July when Roosevelt drove into Iran, entering at a remote border post to avoid attracting attention. He set up shop in Tehran, was briefed by local CIA officers, and finalized plans with the shah. Still, the plot had not yet been set in motion. Then, on August 8, 1953, a week after Roosevelt's last meeting with the shah, Mosaddeq began talks on trade with the Soviet Union. President Eisenhower immediately granted final approval for Ajax. The next day, Roosevelt sent an Iranian colonel up to the Caspian Sea to obtain the shah's signature on the firmans. Bad weather delayed the officer's return, so Roosevelt waited at the home of Bill Herman, the CIA station chief in Tehran. "We sat, in daytime around the pool, after dark in the living room," Roosevelt remembered. "Smoking, drinking mild vodkas with lime juice, playing hearts with the children or backgammon with each other."

The signed royal decrees finally came back on Wednesday, August 12—just in time for another delay, the start of the two-day Iranian weekend that Thursday. As the CIA team continued to wait, Roosevelt recalled, "the pool was no solace," and "cigarettes and vodka-limes tasted awful."

After another anxious period Saturday, the clatter of tanks were heard on the city streets that night. Before dawn on Sunday, Herman learned that

Kermit Roosevelt

Described by a former British intelligence officer as "the last person you would expect to be up to his neck in dirty tricks," scholarly looking Kermit Roosevelt headed the CIA's 1953 effort to oust the shah of Iran's rival, Prime Minister Muhammad Mosaddeq.

"So this is how we get rid of that madman Mosaddeq!"

—John Foster Dulles, as quoted by Kermit Roosevelt

Held aloft by his supporters, Mosaddeq is carried through the streets of Tehran in 1951. A still-active 72 by the time he left office in 1953, Mosaddeq had been involved in Iranian politics for some four decades.

the street outside Mosaddeq's house was filled with armored vehicles. It soon became obvious, however, that word of the secret plan had leaked out: The troops were there not to remove the prime minister but to protect him. When an officer arrived to deliver the shah's firmans to Mosaddeq, he was arrested. At 7 a.m., Mosaddeq announced on the radio that the shah, encouraged by "foreign elements," had attempted an illegal seizure of power. He was therefore "obliged" to assume total control of the country. Roosevelt quickly arranged to conceal Zahedi, the nominal prime minister, in a friendly cellar. The shah, no longer finding the Caspian Sea sufficiently remote, fled without luggage to Rome. There he stayed at the Excelsior Hotel. Also at the Excelsior was Allen Dulles, who happened to be in Rome at the time and anxiously scanned the cable traffic at the U.S. embassy for news of Iran.

The next morning, things went from bad to worse for the planned coup as several thousand nationalists and Tudeh members rioted, looting shops and toppling statues of the shah. As the crowd got out of hand, rioters even hurled stones at mosques; according to one scholar, the CIA may have hired some in the crowd to blacken the Tudeh's name. Roosevelt, undaunted, persuaded Ambassador Loy Henderson to warn Mosaddeq he would order all Americans to leave the country if the riots persisted. The threat to Iran's tottering economy worked: Mosaddeq directed the police to quash the demonstrations with tear gas and night sticks.

With the pro-Mosaddeq crowds silenced, it was time for the CIA to unleash its own mob. The next day, the agency's Iranian contacts hired circus strongmen and tumblers to lead a protest march from the sweltering city bazaar to Mosaddeq's residence. A huge crowd, swelled by police and soldiers—and by the cash handed out by agency operatives—shouted "Long live the shah!" and ransacked government and Tudeh offices. It was at this

Jubilant supporters wave the shah of Iran's portrait from atop an army tank during the 1953 coup. What Time magazine called a "spontaneous popular uprising" ended with an impromptu street auction of former prime minister Mosaddeq's furniture.

crucial moment that a day-old message from Walter Bedell Smith arrived. Convinced the coup had flopped, Washington wanted to cut its losses; Roosevelt was ordered to stop work. Instead, he radioed back an optimistic falsehood: "Happy to report Zahedi safely installed."

Roosevelt then set off to fetch Zahedi from the cellar. As a boisterous throng lifted up Zahedi and rushed into the street, word spread that pro-shah troops were streaming to Tehran. Later that day, tank units led by Zahedi assaulted the troops and armor defending Mosaddeq's home. In the ensuing gun battles, 300 died. The Tudeh, meanwhile, stayed on the sidelines. Mosaddeq fled for his life, and the shah made a triumphant return. After a congratulatory visit to the palace—uncloaked and sitting upright, for once, in an official embassy car—Roosevelt was quietly whisked out of the country on a U.S. military transport. Mosaddeq was later sentenced to three years' imprisonment, followed by house arrest.

With the shah in charge, control of Iran's petroleum production passed to a consortium of Western oil companies. Roosevelt himself, after leaving the CIA, became a vice president for Gulf Oil and a consultant for Iran. The CIA's role in the coup became something of an open secret. Years later, asked if the CIA had spent millions to incite a riot, Allen Dulles replied, "I can say that the statement that we spent many dollars doing that is utterly false."

Whatever its cost—estimates by participants ranged from $100,000 to almost $20 million—Ajax was not only a bargain but a triumph in the eyes of U.S. policymakers. To President Eisenhower, a commander who knew the cost of military intervention, such coups d'état seemed a cheap and ready means of replacing unfriendly governments. At a modest cost and no loss of American life, strategically important Iran was returned to the Western camp. For more than 25 years, Iran's close ties to the United States would make it a cornerstone of U.S. Middle East policy, as well as a key base for collecting electronic intelligence on the Soviet Union. The relationship abruptly terminated with the shah's January 1979 overthrow, followed 11 months later by the seizure of hostages at the U.S. embassy in Tehran.

At a White House debriefing for Eisenhower and cabinet leaders, Roosevelt recalled years later, he noticed a disturbing enthusiasm among his audience. According to Roosevelt, the view of such listeners as Secretary of State John Foster Dulles was that the agency "could solve any problem anywhere in the world." Amid the excitement, Roosevelt remembered sounding a cautionary note: "If we, the CIA, are ever going to try something like this again, we must be absolutely sure that the people and the army want what we want. If not, you had better give the job to the Marines."

That advice, however, was rarely followed during the 1950s and early 1960s, as the Cold War contest between the United States and its allies and the Soviet bloc intensified. In 1956 and 1957, for example, the CIA enlisted Syrian officers in a failed coup attempt to keep the left-wing Baath Party from power. In 1958 the agency provided World War II-vintage bombers to back a failed revolt by Indonesian colonels against President Sukarno, who

Following a six-day exile in Rome, Shah Muhammad Reza Pahlavi— flanked by his new prime minister, General Fazlollah Zahedi (left)— makes a triumphant return to Tehran. At the airport, some exuberant well-wishers embraced the shah's legs and kissed his boots.

had wanted to put Communists in his cabinet. One of the CIA pilots was shot down after mistakenly bombing a church. Other examples abounded.

As this secret history began to emerge years later, critics argued that such missions—and several failed CIA plans for the assassination of foreign leaders—interfered with other countries' efforts at self-determination (*pages 144-147*). Supporters and many agency veterans saw these efforts equally clearly as part of a justifiable effort to contain Communism around the world. Whatever history's verdict, it was the attempted, and sometimes successful, coups of the 1950s that led the agency straight into its first great public disaster—the ill-fated effort to topple Cuban leader Fidel Castro at the Bay of Pigs. That debacle was inspired most directly by the CIA's previous success elsewhere in the region, in the Central American nation of Guatemala.

LAND OF THE OCTOPUS

Even as the agency hatched its Iranian intrigue, the Eisenhower administration was already keeping an eye on disturbing events in Guatemala, where newly elected president Jacobo Arbenz Guzmán seemed to be playing a pro-Communist, antibusiness role similar to that of Mosaddeq in Iran. Although he had been chosen democratically, Arbenz was guilty of a

Eager to end a dictatorship in Guatemala, Jacobo Arbenz Guzmán, shown above with his wife, Maria, helped stage a 1944 coup that led to his election as president in 1950— and to policies that angered the U.S.

Samuel Zemurray

Traditional thatched houses re-created by United Fruit (foreground) contrast with the firm's modern worker dormitories on 65,000-acre Tiquisate Plantation, part of its vast holdings in Guatemala. Through a close relationship with a previous regime, company president Sam "the Banana Man" Zemurray (inset) had won large land concessions for the Boston-based firm.

number of sins in Washington's eyes, from legalizing the Communist Party to including prominent leftists among his circle of friends. The Guatemalan Congress even observed a minute of silence after the death of Stalin.

From that perspective, a particularly galling act—and one that would prove his undoing—was Arbenz's approval in June 1952 of a Communist-drafted reform bill that redistributed 234,000 acres of banana plantation to landless peasants. The bill was meant to benefit Guatemala's rural poor, mostly Indian farmers whose literacy rate was barely five percent and daily wage less than a quarter, and it provided compensation to the land's previous owners. Much of the land in question, however, was owned by the powerful, Boston-based United Fruit Company. Practically a shadow government within Guatemala, the firm would not be trifled with. Along with its vast acreage, el Pulpo (the Octopus), as it was called, owned the nation's rail and telephone lines and ran its principal port. By Guatemalan standards, United Fruit paid its workers generously, although it opposed unionization.

United Fruit also benefited from powerful U.S. connections. John Moors Cabot, the assistant secretary of state for Latin America, was a major stockholder; his brother Thomas had been company president. President Eisenhower's personal secretary was married to its public relations director. John Foster Dulles had done legal work for a bank that had helped the corporation take over Guatemala's railroads. Sam "the Banana Man" Zemurray, the owner of United Fruit, pressed his anti-Arbenz campaign before the public by hiring the influential public relations firm of Edward Bernays; he also retained Washington insider Thomas "Tommy the Cork" Corcoran as a lobbyist.

In early August 1953, within days of the successful Iran coup, Eisenhower's National Security Council authorized the CIA to devise a means of removing Arbenz. Arranging the matter was a job for deputy director for plans Frank Wisner, who had previously managed several covert actions in Eastern Europe, and his deputy, Tracy Barnes. A smooth, unflappable product of Groton, Yale, and Harvard Law, Barnes had served, like Wisner, in the OSS. During the war, Barnes and one of his comrades had captured a French town by fooling its German garrison into believing they were part of a much larger attack force. His men would employ similar tactics of deception and psychological warfare in Guatemala.

Barnes and Wisner needed an operational commander. Kermit Roosevelt was the obvious choice, but he declined the job. They settled instead on Albert Haney, a rugged former army counterintelligence colonel who had corralled German agents in the Panama Canal Zone during World War II. Haney's deputy, the husky William "Rip" Robertson, had just returned from the Korean War, where he had taken pleasure in accompanying

Central America and the Caribbean saw heavy CIA involvement in the 1950s and early 1960s. Following its successful coup in Guatemala in 1954, the agency returned there in 1960 to set up training camps for the Bay of Pigs invasion. Honduras and Nicaragua also provided important staging areas during the decade, while tiny Great Swan Island was home to the CIA's Cuban radio transmitter.

Key to the CIA's plan to overthrow Arbenz were Tracy Barnes, who managed logistics, and Rip Robertson, who helped train the rebel army. Seven years later, both men worked on the Bay of Pigs invasion.

C. Tracy Barnes

William "Rip" Robertson

covert commando squads into North Korea—in defiance of his CIA orders.

Once chosen, Haney reported directly to Wisner, bypassing the CIA's chief of Western Hemisphere operations, Joseph Caldwell "J. C." King, who did not take the affront lightly. He met with Haney, urging him to make direct use of United Fruit's considerable assets and influence; when Haney disagreed, King exclaimed, "If you think you can run this operation without United Fruit, you're crazy!" Crazy or not, Haney focused instead on influencing the poorly trained 6,200-man Guatemalan army. Arbenz's popularity with the Guatemalan people would not matter if the military turned against him. This could be accomplished in several ways: discrediting Arbenz by playing up his Communist ties, launching a destabilizing propaganda campaign, and lastly, providing an external threat—an "invasion" of anti-Arbenz dissidents.

The first order of business was to recruit a replacement for Arbenz, someone who could head the token invasion force and then proceed into office—ideally, a relatively prominent Guatemalan, yet one who would be easily controlled. Haney and King recruited a former army colonel named Carlos Castillo Armas, a graduate of the Guatemalan military academy who had also attended classes at Fort Leavenworth, Kansas. Castillo Armas enjoyed a certain cachet among some Guatemalan exiles, having escaped from prison in Guatemala following his own failed coup attempt in 1950, in which he had been wounded. At the same time, "he was a small, humble, thin guy," one CIA operative observed. "He didn't know what he was doing. He was in way over his head."

In the early fall of 1953, Castillo Armas was flown to Florida for a secret meeting with King, who spoke on behalf of the CIA. The agency promised Castillo Armas to create a political party for him, the National Liberation Movement; build a small paramilitary force; and provide three million dollars in funds. The United Fruit Company would furnish arms to his soldiers in return for getting back the lands Arbenz had appropriated. Castillo Armas accepted the deal.

Although he cooperated with Haney on that front, King was soon voicing his strong objections on Haney's strategy to Wisner. "He'll be starting a civil war in the middle of Central America," he protested. "Do we want another Korean War right at our doorstep?" Wisner stuck by Haney, but the debate continued for months. It was not until early 1954 that Allen Dulles, after assembling the key players over cocktails at his Highlands estate in Georgetown, gave final approval to the plan, optimistically codenamed PB Success. By then, most of the groundwork for the invasion was already firmly in place.

With a staff of 100 and a budget that may have reached $20 million (as is often the case with covert operations, exact financial figures are difficult to determine), Haney had set up headquarters at the little-used Opa-locka Marine Corps air base in Florida. He sent Rip Robertson to Nicaragua, whose dictator, Anastasio Somoza, felt threatened by Arbenz's land reforms. There, across the border from Guatemala, Robertson and others set up two camps where 300 Guatemalan rebels and mercenaries were trained in guns, sabotage, and maneuvering. The agency's role and the names of the trainers were carefully concealed. "Our instructors," one exile wryly recalled, "were taciturn, friendly Americans whom we knew only by first name. They were all called Pepe or José."

At the same time, the agency prepared for a propaganda campaign by establishing clandestine radio transmitters in Nicaragua, Honduras, the Dominican Republic, and even the U.S. embassy in Guatemala. Some were set at a frequency that would jam the official government broadcasts. In charge of the propaganda for the operation were David Atlee Phillips, a handsome former actor, and E. Howard Hunt, a sometime mystery writer. Phillips trained several Guatemalan exiles in psychological warfare; the team wrote scores of anti-Arbenz tracts and prerecorded radio broadcasts for their "Voice of Liberation."

A CIA officer (below, far left) reviews rebel forces prior to the Guatemalan coup in this photo from an internal agency history declassified in the 1990s. The CIA supplied money, arms, and training to the troops, most of whom dressed in ordinary civilian clothes.

John E. Peurifoy, U.S. ambassador to Guatemala, displays copies of progovernment Guatemalan newspapers for reporters. Peurifoy regarded any support for Arbenz as evidence of Communist leanings in the Guatemalan press.

"I am definitely convinced that if the President [Arbenz] is not a Communist, he will certainly do until one comes along."

—Ambassador Peurifoy, after meeting Arbenz

Meanwhile, Tracy Barnes assembled a motley air force of surplus World War II fighters and transports: three C-47 cargo planes, six P-47 fighter-bombers, one P-38 fighter, and two civilian Cessnas. To fly the planes, Barnes recruited a squadron of freelance American pilots, most with military or CIA experience. Pilots pocketed $500 a month for training, twice that for combat.

With the Dulles brothers in charge, cooperation between the State Department and CIA was extraordinary; U.S. ambassadors assigned to the region were carefully selected with the coup in mind. The newly installed ambassador to Honduras, Whiting Willauer, was one of the founders of Civil Air Transport (CAT), the CIA's air arm that later became Air America. The experienced Willauer organized rebel air bases in Honduras and Nicaragua. In Guatemala itself, the new ambassador was Jack Peurifoy, an activist diplomat fresh from a stint as ambassador to Greece; while there, he had helped put together the country's ruling right-wing coalition. After a brutal, six-hour "get-acquainted" meeting with Arbenz, Peurifoy reported, "I am definitely convinced that if the President is not a Communist, he will certainly do until one comes along." Perfectly suited for his role of intimidating Arbenz, the thickset, swaggering Peurifoy packed a pistol and often sported a feathered green Borsalino hat.

Just as the pieces were falling into place, however, a serious security breach emerged. In January 1954 a Castillo Armas courier betrayed the details of the project to President Arbenz, including staging areas and invasion routes as well as the complicity of both Nicaragua and the "government of the North." Arbenz made the documents public, but the American press readily accepted the State Department's indignant denials. Arbenz grew desperate; knowing Castillo Armas's invasion was imminent, he decided on drastic measures.

On May 15 a nondescript Swedish freighter, the *Alfhem,* docked at Puerto Barrios, a port located on Guatemala's Atlantic coast. Armed guards surrounded the ship as crates labeled Optical and Laboratory Equipment were unloaded onto waiting boxcars. The crates, in fact, contained 2,000 tons of rifles, artillery, mines, and ammunition from Communist Czechoslovakia—and the U.S. government knew it. A CIA agent pretending to be a birdwatcher had observed the *Alfhem*'s loading and departure from a port in Poland.

Arbenz's plan had been to secretly hand out the weapons to worker militias. But the gamble to save his regime became a public relations disaster when the State Department publicly announced what the *Alfhem* was carrying. U.S. newspapers, the public, and Congress exploded in rage. One legislator likened the shipment hyperbolically to "an atom bomb planted in the rear of our backyard." President Eisenhower ordered the navy to search ships bound for Guatemala. The fact that most of the ordnance was

too obsolete for combat hardly mattered. Two days after the *Alfhem* docked, Allen Dulles scheduled Castillo Armas's invasion for the following month. In addition, he ordered a commando team to secretly enter Guatemala and blow up the munition-laden boxcars.

It was an assignment tailor-made for Rip Robertson, with his love for action behind the lines. On May 20 he led a band of raiders through the jungle from the Honduran border to a secluded position along the rail line outside Puerto Barrios. Unobserved, they planted dynamite along the track. But as they lay in wait, a sudden tropical rainstorm saturated the ground. When the train arrived and Robertson pushed the detonator, only one charge exploded, barely cracking a rail. His team then opened fire on the freight train. They killed a soldier and lost one of their own before the railroad cars chugged out of sight, still packed with Czech arms.

An increasingly unnerved Arbenz, meanwhile, lurched into more extreme acts, rounding up hundreds of dissidents, many on the CIA payroll.

With a revolver thrust into his belt and a flashlight in his hand, Carlos Castillo Armas, the CIA-chosen successor to Arbenz, leaves his headquarters on the night before the invasion. Below, some of his troops, armed with Soviet-bloc weapons supplied by the CIA to avoid revealing the U.S. role, engage Arbenz's forces.

His government executed 75 people and buried them in mass graves. Events on both sides were building to a climax.

On the CIA's propaganda front, Phillips and Hunt broadcast messages aimed at the Guatemalan officer corps claiming Arbenz planned to disband the army. On June 4 a retired air force colonel defected to Nicaragua. Phillips's team asked him to tape a message urging Guatemalan pilots to follow his lead. The colonel demurred, since his family was still in Guatemala City. His handlers expressed understanding and offered him one drink, then another. "The pilot was a good aviator and a poor drinker," Phillips recalled. The CIA operatives casually asked him what he would say if he were to make such a broadcast. "The pilot was eloquent and fiery in the best Latin tradition as he delivered a hypothetical speech to his friends persuading them to defect with their planes and to join Castillo Armas and his rebels."

A truckload of armed CIA-backed rebels heads to the front. In all, Castillo Armas's exile army numbered no more than 400 members at its peak.

The colonel dozed off, unaware his exhortation had been secretly taped. It was broadcast the next morning.

On June 18 the long-awaited, albeit small-scale, invasion began. Riding in his staff car, a dilapidated station wagon, Castillo Armas led a convoy of trucks carrying a hundred men across the Honduran border. Meanwhile, a C-47 transport plane blanketed the capital with leaflets threatening to bomb the presidential palace and demanding the resignation of Arbenz.

The next day the aerial assault started with little fanfare. One of the small, single-engine Cessnas appeared over Puerto Barrios. The copilot opened his window and dropped a hand grenade and stick of dynamite onto fuel tanks, causing modest damage. A few days afterward, another pilot ran out of fuel and crash-landed in Mexico. Ground fire put two other aircraft out of action.

A mishap of another type occurred when Robertson got word that a British freighter, the *Springfjord,* was about to unload supplies for Arbenz's forces. Frantically he contacted Barnes and Haney at Opa-locka for permission to bomb the ship. Fearing an international uproar over the matter, they refused, but they suggested covert alternatives, such as having frogmen blow up the target. Robertson plunged ahead with an aerial assault anyway. One of his pilots scattered leaflets over the vessel, warning the crew to abandon ship. Then, on his second pass, he dropped a 500-pound bomb squarely down the smokestack.

Unfortunately for Robertson, the ruined ship had been carrying only coffee and cotton; luckily, no one was killed. When Dulles heard the news, he fired Robertson. Wisner rushed to the British embassy in Washington with profuse apologies. The agency ultimately paid at least a million dollars to Lloyd's of London, the ship's insurer.

As a government soldier looks on, gasoline spurts from storage tanks strafed by a single rebel plane. Although limited, the damage was enough to force gasoline rationing in Guatemala City.

On the ground, meanwhile, Castillo Armas was proving to be no Napoleon. His small liberation army pulled up six miles inside the border at the town of Esquipulas and called for air support. It failed to seize two other towns, defeated by 30 soldiers in one skirmish and by police and armed dockworkers in a second. But reality mattered less than the impression created by the CIA's propaganda machine, now working overtime. A model of disinformation, Voice of Liberation broadcasts claimed that two powerful columns of Castillo Armas's army—which in fact never grew to more than 400 men—were sweeping aside all resistance. Arbenz's minister of communications, swayed by false stories, informed friends that rebel forces "were being swelled by thousands of volunteers."

A different kind of deception occurred during bombing raids on Guatemala City, when loudspeakers on the roof of the U.S. embassy blared sounds of explosions to make the actual, and puny, aerial assault seem substantial. The air attacks, although wreaking little harm, were nicknamed *sulfados*, laxatives, for their powerful effect on the government and residents of the capital. President Arbenz, already suffering from depression, began drinking heavily. Guatemalans fled the capital to escape what many believed to be an impending siege.

Most important to the CIA's effort, the leaders of Guatemala's armed

Coup Climate

Long before the Guatemalan coup began, the American public was concerned about the state of affairs in that country. Much of the worry was fueled indirectly by United Fruit, which waged an aggressive public relations campaign targeted to journalists. Masterminded in part by Edward Bernays—considered the father of modern public relations—United Fruit's effort included press junkets, special briefings, and a confidential newsletter.

Among those who took Bernays's bait was Daniel James, managing editor of the *New Leader*, who wrote a series of articles on Guatemala and a book titled *Red Design for Central America*, published by a company with CIA ties. The cartoon above, which appeared in the *New York Times*, offers an apt synopsis of Guatemala's emerging image. As a hat-wearing Guatemalan dances to the Communists' tune, a smiling Joseph Stalin remarks, "Just call me José."

forces surmised the United States would not permit Castillo Armas to lose and would, if need be, launch a full-scale invasion with American troops—a plausible-enough scenario given the long history of U.S. military intervention in Central America. Resistance, therefore, became fragmented. At the town of Zacapa, a government army refused to fight a rebel force. On June 25 a panicky Arbenz ordered arms distributed to the people, angering the conservative officer corps. The military decided Arbenz had to go. In a June 27 palace session with his army chief of staff, Colonel Carlos Díaz, Arbenz, exhausted, agreed to turn over power.

That evening, Arbenz broadcast his farewell address. Ironically, many Guatemalans never heard it because of the CIA radio jamming. "A cruel war against Guatemala has been under way," Arbenz declared. "The United Fruit Company, in collaboration with the governing circles of the United States, is responsible."

The fallen leader walked across the street to request asylum in the Mexican embassy. His sudden resignation stunned propaganda chief David Phillips. "We thought we'd lost," he later wrote. "We were so surprised by his departure." Another interested observer of the relatively quiet coup was Ernesto "Che" Guevara, an Argentinian medical student and pro-Arbenz activist. He later gave Fidel Castro advice the Cuban took to heart: "We cannot guarantee the Revolution before cleansing the armed forces."

In Arbenz's wake, five provisional governments swiftly formed and as quickly fell. Finally, on July 3, the leader of the National Liberation Movement entered Guatemala City. Downtown, a boisterous crowd of 150,000 welcomed Castillo Armas, with many in attendance setting off CIA-supplied firecrackers. On July 13 he addressed a vast throng before the National Palace. "The battle has begun," he intoned, "the hard battle that requires us to demand each citizen to be a soldier of anti-Communism. Workers and peasants have in me their best friend."

Within a month, Castillo Armas returned United Fruit's appropriated acreage, outlawed the banana workers' union, and placed suspected Communists on a watch list. He also disenfranchised most of the voting population by establishing a literacy test for would-be voters. A few weeks later, he outlawed all labor unions and political parties.

Back in Washington, the CIA basked in the glow of another successful coup. Eisenhower hosted the major players at a celebratory debriefing. "You've averted a Soviet beachhead in our hemisphere," the president declared. United Fruit, the corporation that had seemed to benefit so dramatically from the coup, was less ecstatic. The week after Arbenz left office, the firm was sued by the Justice Department for violating antitrust laws with its banana monopoly.

Few foresaw the events that the coup helped to set in motion. In 1957 Castillo Armas was assassinated by one of his guards. In the years that followed, Guatemala sank into a savage, decades-long civil war as government security forces—trained in part by the CIA—tortured and murdered civilians in a hunt for suspected Communists. By the time the war ended in 1996, an estimated 200,000 Guatemalans, mostly poor indigenous Indians,

HIGH-FLYING SPIES:
ADVENT OF THE U-2

Above, Lockheed test pilot Tony LeVier guides the U-2 during its maiden flight on August 4, 1955.

Richard M. Bissell Jr.

The secrecy required of U-2 project manager Richard Bissell (left) extended to his home, where safes and color-coded phones were installed.

When CIA director Allen Dulles handed his special assistant a top-secret assignment on Thanksgiving weekend in 1954, he had every confidence Richard Bissell would get the job done. Bissell had proved himself earlier that year with his first CIA assignment—assisting Frank Wisner with the Guatemala operation. Now he would be in charge of a still more vital mission: developing a state-of-the-art spy plane.

Newly endorsed by a presidential task force set up to find ways of studying the Soviet military, the plane would be a technical marvel, capable of flying long missions without refueling and of soaring to more than 70,000 feet (about 13 miles), just beyond the reach of Soviet antiaircraft missiles. Even from that height, its special cameras would be able to photograph details less

than 10 feet across. It sounded good on paper. But the aircraft—later named the U-2—had yet to be built.

Bissell quickly assembled a crack team, including Lockheed's chief designer, Kelly Johnson, who had previously drafted plans for such a plane. Johnson's tireless staff performed miracles of high-speed engineering. Less than eight months after Lockheed came on board in December 1954, the first U-2 prototype took flight *(above)*.

After the test, Bissell kept the momentum up. Over the next several months, 20 planes were commissioned, air force pilots were trained and secretly assigned to the CIA, and covert U-2 bases were established. On July 4, 1956, a U-2 flew over the USSR for the first time; Bissell later recalled "standing around a long table with Dulles next to me, both of us chuckling with amazement at the

Almaza Air Base, Cairo, at 10:20 GMT, 11/1/56

During a pause in Soviet over-flights in the fall of 1956, a U-2 took the reconnaissance image at left of Egypt's Almaza airfield during the Suez crisis, in which British, French, and Israeli forces attacked Egypt. Minutes later, the U-2 passed the same field, only to find it in flames from a bomb drop (below). The closely timed pair of images helped demonstrate the plane's effectiveness, impressing President Eisenhower.

"Ten-minute recon-naissance, now that's a goal to shoot for!"

—President Eisenhower,
on Egyptian airfield images

Almaza Air Base, Cairo, at 10:40 GMT, 11/1/56

clarity of those incredible black-and-white photos." Over the next four years, U-2s gathered intelligence on Soviet bombers, airfields, and missile and nuclear development.

Although the Soviets could not yet challenge the U-2 with surface-to-air missiles, they often tracked its flights by radar. Partly because of this, President Eisenhower personally authorized each U-2 flight plan, sometimes canceling flights entirely. His fear was that the Soviets would mistake a U-2 flyover for a prelude to a nuclear attack and launch a preemptive strike. The president was especially reluctant to authorize a nine-hour mission that would be the longest ever undertaken by a U-2. Ultimately scheduled for May 1, 1960, the planned 3,800-mile flight extended from a base in Pakistan, over several locations in the Soviet Union, and then on to a landing in

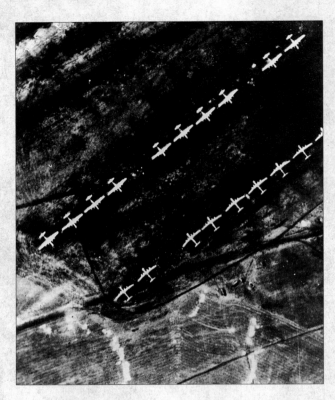

Soviet authorities claimed this picture was taken during Powers's flight. It was actually a photo of outdated aircraft.

Other items used to fuel Soviet propaganda on the downed U-2 include a photograph of Powers after he was taken prisoner (right) and his poison suicide needle, still unused in its sheath.

Norway. Hesitating in part because it would occur close to his May 16 summit with Soviet leader Nikita Khrushchev, Eisenhower finally gave the mission the go-ahead.

And then the U-2's luck ran out: The Soviets managed to loft a missile high enough to bring down the spy plane, piloted by Francis Gary Powers. Bissell had predicted "one chance in a million" that the pilot of a downed U-2 could survive. But the damage in this case was not caused by a direct hit; instead, the culprit was shock waves from a nearby missile detonation—enough to stop the plane but not enough to kill its occupant. In his struggle to escape the craft, Powers was unable to destroy the camera, proof of the plane's mission. After parachuting down, he was captured and imprisoned.

Following U.S. denials of the nature of the mission,

the Soviets exhibited items from the wreckage in Moscow as crowds of onlookers filed past. Eisenhower then admitted the U-2's purpose, stating that such missions were "distasteful but necessary" because of the Soviet "fetish of secrecy." Tensions ran so high, however, that the summit was canceled. (Powers was later exchanged for a Soviet spy and returned to the United States.)

The incident marked the end of the U-2's flights over the Soviet Union, but its missions continued elsewhere. Although the aircraft remained in use through the 1990s, responsibility for the U-2 shifted to the air force in August 1974. By then, aerial reconnaissance had long since been supplemented by images from orbiting spy satellites. Development of the first of these, tested in the late 1950s, had been managed by none other than Richard Bissell.

"We caught the American spy—like a thief, red-handed!"

—Nikita S. Khrushchev, May 18, 1960

Standing on a wicker chair, Khrushchev addresses reporters at the May 11 exhibition in Moscow of debris from the downed U-2 plane. "Only countries which are at war with each other can act this way," he shouted. "Impudence, sheer impudence!"

had perished. In 1999 the United States formally apologized to the Guatemalan people for its part in the tragedy.

Criticism of the U.S. role in the coup long predated that apology, however, and so did CIA veterans' defense against such critiques. "Our job was simply to get rid of Arbenz. We did that successfully," Richard Bissell, Dulles's special assistant in the Guatemalan affair, once wrote. "But this does not assure a happy ultimate outcome." As the director's "eyes and ears," Bissell had a privileged insider's perspective on the Guatemalan project. He would go on, years later, to play a key role in another coup undertaken at the request of the White House, an effort expected to repeat the agency's success in Guatemala. But Castro's Cuba would prove a more elusive prey.

DESTINATION: CUBA

By 1960, six years after the CIA ousted Arbenz, the agency had changed considerably. Allen Dulles was still director, but hobbled by gout and shaken by the 1959 death of his brother John Foster, he kept a lower profile. The Eisenhower administration itself, noted for its close ties between ranking officials and the CIA, was winding down; in 1961 John F. Kennedy, a president less familiar with the ways of the secret agency, would take over the Oval Office. Bissell, now Dulles's heir apparent, had taken over as deputy director for plans from Frank Wisner in 1959. Tragically, the dynamic Wisner had been gripped by severe manic depression several years before. The illness led to his departure from the agency and eventual suicide.

In his new position, Bissell inherited Wisner's shadowy empire of more than 50 overseas CIA stations and a "black" budget of $100 million in unvouchered monies. The lanky, six-foot three-inch Bissell reminded one assistant of a great stork. A bundle of nervous energy, he constantly paced his office or fidgeted with objects on his desk. Bissell was an avid sailor, known for staying the course in the midst of tempests. He was also a superb planner. As a civilian during World War II he had masterminded the complex convoy schedules for merchant shipping. Afterward, he wrote many of the documents on which the Marshall Plan for rebuilding Europe was based. Before taking over for Wisner, Bissell had also managed the complex project of developing the U-2 spy plane *(pages 72-75)* and begun work on one of the world's earliest spy satellites, the Corona.

In 1960, at the same time that Richard Bissell was grappling with the fallout over the Soviet Union's shootdown of a U-2, his division was running assassination plots against certain foreign leaders, including Cuba's Fidel Castro. Although those efforts failed, Cuba and its newly installed prime minister were becoming a matter of serious concern for the agency and for the administration.

Just 90 miles away, Cuba had long been of special interest to the United States, which had helped free it from Spain in 1898, and then in 1903 extracted as one reward a permanent deep-water naval base at the island's Guantanamo Bay. When Castro and his dusty guerrilla band overthrew the island's brutal dictator, Fulgencio Batista, on January 1, 1959, the Eisenhower administration was quick to recognize the new government, but it

At a May Day rally in 1960, Cuban prime minister Fidel Castro warns of plans for a U.S.-sponsored "aggression against Cuba through Guatemala"—the nation, now friendly to the United States, where the CIA would soon be training hundreds of Cuban exiles for combat.

was not long before Castro's administration raised alarm bells. Castro proved a full-blown Communist who nationalized U.S.-owned businesses, publicly supported Soviet premier Nikita Khrushchev, sent guerrillas to stir up revolution in Panama and Haiti, and executed hundreds of dissidents.

Although CIA documents as early as 1959 mention the possibility of assassination, the administration's main impulse was to arrange an armed overthrow of Castro. Toward that end, in March 1960 President Eisenhower secretly approved a CIA-drafted "Program of Covert Action against the Castro Regime." The president cautioned Dulles that the plan should above all avoid revealing the U.S. role. Instead, it would be governed by a doctrine known as "plausible deniability," so that the CIA, and certainly the White House itself, could credibly disavow any direct role in Castro's overthrow.

Bissell devised a scheme for Cuba that in some respects mimicked the agency's successful Guatemalan coup, combining a "powerful propaganda offensive" with a paramilitary force trained by the CIA. This time, in place of a local strongman such as Guatemala's Colonel Castillo Armas, the CIA would ready a "responsible and unified" government in exile—a true democratic alternative to Castro. The agency also planned to foster local resistance to Castro before the invasion.

Like Wisner six years earlier, Bissell bypassed the CIA's Latin American chief, J. C. King, in choosing a project head. Instead, he gave operational control to one of the leaders of the Guatemalan coup, Tracy Barnes. As his deputy and project director, Barnes then recruited Jake Esterline, an opera-loving former guerrilla fighter who had managed the Washington operation center during the coup against Arbenz. David Phillips, another familiar face from Guatemala days, was once again put in charge of radio propaganda; Phillips's old comrade Howard Hunt was sent to Miami, where he negotiated with the often-fractious Cuban exile community to form the desired replacement government, known as the Frente.

Up in Washington, the headquarters team set up shop in a dilapidated former Waves (Women's Reserve of the U.S. Naval Reserve) barracks, called Quarters Eye, near the Lincoln Memorial. When Quarters Eye received word from agents in Cuba that Castro was receiving a significant volume of Soviet weapons—soon to include front-line MiG fighters—the tempo and scale of the undertaking increased. Both the $4.4 million originally earmarked for the project, and the original cadre of 40 CIA operatives, increased by a factor of 10. The invasion plan itself, meanwhile, escalated from the introduction of a small paramilitary group and a tiny force of 20 to 150 guerrillas into a full-blown invasion of some 1,500 troops.

As the planned operation mushroomed in size and importance, some in the CIA were unenthusiastic, including such influential figures as Bissell's rival Richard Helms, director of operations within the plans directorate, and Asia specialist Edward Lansdale, who considered the invasion force far too small. For the moment, their views were disregarded. A more annoying problem was that Barnes found he was getting castoffs from other agency offices as his project expanded. As he later reflected, "You'll get a certain number of people that their supervisors let you have with crocodile tears." According to the CIA's own highly critical inspector general's report on the Cuban endeavor, which would not be declassified until 1998, "the project was not staffed throughout with top-quality people."

One somewhat erratic agent was Gerry Droller, a short, balding German-born agent pulled from the Swiss desk to work beside Hunt with the exile government. He spoke no Spanish and lorded over his Cuban charges, reminding them haughtily that "I carry the counterrevolution in my checkbook." According to Peter Wyden, author of a well-regarded 1979 account of the attempted coup, Droller once held a meeting with a Cuban émigré—without Hunt's knowledge—in a Miami motel room. They grew so loud that a woman in an adjoining room could plainly hear the two heavily accented voices discussing revolution. She took notes and called her brother, an FBI agent.

Fortunately for the operation, damage was limited to a severe reprimand for Droller, but as the project grew, the supposedly secret enterprise became an open book. Hunt himself entertained contacts at Miami's finest

Manuel Artime

E. Howard Hunt

Psychiatrist Manuel Artime, left, and CIA liaison E. Howard Hunt relax outside a Florida safe house early in 1961. Hunt alienated other Cuban groups and their leaders by consistently backing Artime as leader of the Cuban exiles.

"Our hand should not show in anything that is done."

—President Eisenhower to Allen Dulles on the planned Cuban operation nightspots. He had so many men from the Frente visiting his home after dark that some neighbors took him for a bookie.

Meanwhile, David Phillips was laying the groundwork for the planned propaganda effort by establishing a secret radio transmitter on Great Swan Island, a tiny, guano-covered speck off the Honduran coast. To create programming, Phillips recruited polished announcers from the Cuban exile community and built them a first-class studio in Miami. Always a stickler for detail, Bissell decided that the result was "too professional, too American" and directed Phillips to "go back and put some rough edges on it." In response, Phillips told his broadcasters to speak colloquial Spanish and had the rugs removed from the studio so their chairs and shoes could be heard scuffing. Hunt and Droller also gave Frente leaders CIA funds to buy radio time on the station. But the various political factions spent as much air time attacking each other as they did Castro. In the end Hunt's liaison work was so ineffective he was returned to Washington.

For the invasion force, anti-Castro refugees were mustered from around Miami, in a recruitment drive that proved difficult to conceal. One assembly camp was in a residential area, where neighbors could hear orders in Spanish and see formations drilling. When some American youths threw firecrackers through the fence, the Cubans, thinking Castro's agents were attacking, burst out of the barracks with guns blazing. One youngster was wounded. The *Miami Herald* investigated. Under pressure from Allen Dulles, however, they canceled an exposé of the training.

Each recruit was given an enlistment number—starting with 2500 to mislead Cuban intelligence on the size of the force—and sent to Camp Trax, a CIA-staffed training ground in Guatemala. The force was soon renamed Brigade 2506, after the number of the first man killed in training. But the new name suggested a unity that wasn't entirely real. Chafing under over-

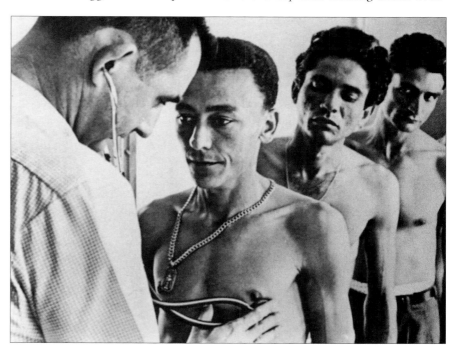

At right, a CIA doctor examines potential recruits for the exile brigade. In addition to physical examinations, the men underwent psychological workups and polygraph tests to determine if they were Communists or homosexuals.

Members of Brigade 2506, who adopted the insignia at upper left before the invasion, go over a map during a jungle training exercise.

An airplane and a stack of bombs await a call to action on a Guatemalan airstrip set up by the CIA for the brigade's planes.

BRIGADE 2506

When Robert Davis, CIA station chief in Guatemala, was assigned to set up training facilities for a small group of Cuban exiles, he called a friend. Soon 20 or so radio operator trainees were moving onto a 5,000-acre coffee plantation, setting up camp in the guesthouse and working in a barn. As plans shifted from guerrilla support to an outright invasion, the group swelled into the hundreds. Barracks and an airstrip were built. The site became known as Camp Trax.

Camp graduates later recalled skirmishing in the mountains and running tactical field exercises. "Sometimes they would make us walk a long way through the jungle to get the feel of it—to be wet, without food and to experience danger," recalled one recruit. Early on, a trainee fell 2,000 feet from a cliff to his death; in his honor, the brigade was named after his service number, 2506. Instructors also set up a mock cargo net on a wooden fence. Carrying weapons, the men crawled up and down the net to simulate disembarking from a troop ship.

Despite difficult conditions and sometimes strained relations between Brigade 2506 members and their instructors, the Cubans remained confident. Boarding the trucks that would start them on the journey toward the invasion, the exiles sang the Cuban national anthem. As Erneido Oliva, armored battalion commander, recalled, "It was a great spectacle."

weening American commanders, the brigade was split by infighting among rival groups struggling for political control. Key ringleaders were detained after two battalions briefly mutinied.

To provide air cover for the brigade's arrival in Cuba, Tracy Barnes rounded up 16 surplus B-26 bombers as well as eight C-46 and six C-54 transports. None of the American-trained Cuban exile pilots had combat experience, and most had fewer than 100 hours of flight time. They also faced a daunting challenge. For the sake of plausible deniability, bases in Florida within easy range of Cuba had been vetoed. Instead, the pilots flew out of bases in Nicaragua and Guatemala, making a grueling six-hour round trip for a brief window of 30 minutes over Cuba.

The exile pilots performed well, however, when they went into action—in Guatemala. When the Guatemalan army tried to stage a coup in November 1960, Brigade 2506 planes helped put it down. The CIA feared a new government might close down its training sites.

Meanwhile, CIA efforts to airdrop supplies to the anti-Castro resistance in Cuba proved ineffective. Of 30 attempted supply drops to guerrilla forces, only four succeeded. In the first drop, the supplies missed their target by seven miles, landing on a dam where they could easily be seized by Castro's men. The agent for whom the drop was intended was killed, and after the mission the pilot got lost and landed in Mexico. Increasingly, the emphasis turned to Brigade 2506 as the linchpin of the plan.

To plan the brigade's landing on the beach, Barnes and Esterline brought in marine colonel Jack Hawkins. A tough veteran of Iwo Jima, Hawkins plotted an invasion on Cuba's south coast near a supposed hotbed of anti-Castro sentiment. As with any amphibious invasion, victory would depend on complete air superiority. Barnes's squadron of B-26s would have to destroy Cuba's limited number of aircraft on the ground during two planned preinvasion strikes.

Even with full air support, however, Hawkins knew no brigade of 1,500 men could defeat the 200,000-strong Cuban army and militia. Instead, he expected the troops to seize and hold a beachhead—it was hoped their numbers would be swelled by local volunteers—while a small force of paratroopers and local guerrillas broke up Cuban troop movements. With the invasion force in place, Frente leaders would then be flown in to proclaim a "provisional government." At that point the Cuban people, it was assumed, would rebel. In case things didn't go as planned, Hawkins also included an escape scheme. If the beachhead broke, the invaders might retreat into the nearby Escambray Mountains and join guerrillas operating there.

To conceal any American involvement, the invasion fleet would consist primarily of five small, rusty freighters the agency chartered from a Cuban firm. Although the U.S. Navy aircraft carrier *Essex* and five destroyers were to escort the small armada to Cuba, they were expressly forbidden to support the landings. The sole authorized American support would come from two CIA officers, each positioned on an infantry landing ship converted into a command vessel and expected to act as a troubleshooter for the ground troops; the troops, in turn, would be ferried ashore by seven assault

Jack Hawkins

Grayston L. Lynch

Two veteran military men—marine colonel Jack Hawkins and army captain and amphibious-operations expert Grayston Lynch—played key roles in the invasion of Cuba. Hawkins planned the landing, whereas Lynch was one of two CIA liaisons at the scene.

landing craft. One of the two designated officers was Grayston "Gray" Lynch, a former army captain who had earned Purple Hearts at the Battle of the Bulge and Korea's Heartbreak Ridge. The other was Rip Robertson, who had quietly returned to the agency's payroll after being fired during the Guatemala affair.

The chess pieces were at last in place, but the players were changing. President Eisenhower, who had enjoyed agency triumphs in Iran and Guatemala, left office in January 1961. His successor, John F. Kennedy, had been briefly informed of the planned invasion before taking office. Soon after becoming president, he asked for the Joint Chiefs of Staff to assess the scheme. Their study gave it just a 30 percent chance of success, assuming everything went as planned. It criticized the plan's lack of adequate shipping, training, and engineering support. In briefing the president on the study, however, Richard Bissell optimistically termed the project's chances as "fair," and his evaluation went unchallenged.

Meanwhile, the scheme's cloak of secrecy grew ever more frayed. The *New York Times* bluntly reported on January 10, 1961, that a U.S.-trained army of Cuban exiles was being readied in Guatemala. "Castro doesn't need agents over here," President Kennedy exploded. "All he has to do is read our papers." Keenly aware of the looming assault, Castro stationed militia in every landing zone and jailed tens of thousands of potential opponents.

On March 11 Bissell gave Kennedy a full-dress briefing. The new president, worried about political fallout in Latin America and with Moscow, wanted the project scaled down. "Too spectacular," he commented to Bissell. "It sounds like D-Day. You have to reduce the noise level."

A few days after the briefing, David Phillips visited the operations room at Quarters Eye to find paramilitary officers wearily poring over charts. "There's been a change in the plan," a colonel informed him. "Now we are going to land here," indicating a point 100 miles to the west. "Bahía de Cochinos?" Phillips scoffed. "How can propagandists persuade Cubans to join the Brigade at the 'Bay of Pigs'?"

The locale, which happened to be Castro's favorite fishing spot, had been chosen because of its proximity to an airstrip that could handle the exiles' B-26s. The drawback was the new site lay 60 miles from the Escambray Mountains and was ringed by a vast swamp. If the landings failed, there was nowhere to retreat to.

Lynch and Robertson, the agency's troubleshooters on the scene, did not learn about the switch in landing sites until April 1. By then other things were going wrong as well. A Pentagon observer was not reassured by watching the loading of the fleet in Nicaragua. Gasoline drums were stacked next to ammunition crates. Many of the small landing crafts' outboard motors would not start. A Pentagon representative who observed the preparations remarked that "logistically, the operation would likely fall apart." Lynch examined reconnaissance photos of the Bay of Pigs and noticed a dark area just offshore that looked like coral. "I want to know about this stuff under here," he demanded. "Oh yeah," a CIA photo interpreter replied, as Lynch later recalled. "That's seaweed all along here. You won't have any problem." In fact, as the invasion force would discover to their dismay, it was coral.

As he mulled over the planned undertaking, Kennedy ordered more changes to maintain "plausible deniability." Each made the project a bit more risky. The marginally trained troops were ordered to stage a chancy night landing. There were also several postponements, until at last the date was set for April 17.

With all the alterations and delays, an air of fatalism overtook Quarters Eye. Esterline and Hawkins wanted out. On April 8 they went to Bissell's home and told their chief they were resigning. Bissell remained calm in the face of mutiny. The project was too far along to abort, he explained; their departure would only lessen chances for success. Dejectedly, they agreed to stay on.

The invasion had taken on an irresistible momentum. Even though the president reserved the right to call the whole thing off on a day's notice, he, too, leaned against cancellation. During his election campaign, Kennedy had supported aid to Cuban rebels, and he did not want to open himself to charges of being soft on Communism. Any thought of canceling the assault was also complicated by the question of what to do with the rebels. As Allen Dulles once put it to Kennedy, "Don't forget that we have a disposal problem." If the brigade's soldiers were disbanded, he noted, "We can't have them wandering around the country telling everyone what they have been doing." In a sense, it seemed too late to turn back.

For their part, meanwhile, Bissell and others assumed that the administration, once the operation was under way, would guarantee victory. "It never occurred to Bissell that if push came to shove, Kennedy wouldn't 'put in his stack,' " recalled Kennedy's national security adviser, McGeorge Bundy, using a poker metaphor. An optimistic April 13 cable from Hawkins, on an inspection tour of the brigade, also gave reason for optimism. Praising the "remarkable smoothness" of the embarkation, Hawkins wrote that the exiles "have supreme confidence they will win all engagements against the best Castro has to offer." April 13 was also the day that the CIA put one

"We felt that when the chips were down, any action required for success would be authorized rather than permit the enterprise to fail."

—Allen Dulles, on the decision to proceed

more precaution into place: Manuel Zuñiga, one of the exile pilots, was directed to pose as a defecting Cuban pilot in a shot-up bomber. Shortly before the invasion forces landed, he would land in Miami with the goal of showing the world the action against Castro was homegrown.

CARIBBEAN CATASTROPHE

With months of planning, preparations, and second thoughts finally behind them, the pilots of Brigade 2506 swung into action on Saturday, April 15, flying out of Nicaragua to execute the first of two planned strikes against Cuba's three airfields. They were a smaller force than originally planned: The day before, when Bissell explained that 16 of the brigade's planes would execute the strike, President Kennedy had balked again at the "noise level" and demanded a change. Bissell reluctantly reduced the number by half.

Following the strikes, as planned, Zuñiga and his B-26 landed in Miami. Zuñiga quickly claimed to be a defector. The plane had bullet holes that a CIA officer had blasted into it with a .45. At the United Nations, Ambassador Adlai Stevenson—unaware of the hoax—displayed a photo of the craft. "It has the markings of Castro's air force on the tail," he asserted. Briefed by Bissell just a week before on the covert operation, Stevenson had been assured there would be no overt U.S. role.

The deception soon turned out to be as full of holes as the plane, however. Reporters noticed the plane's gunports were still covered with tape. They had obviously never been fired. Stevenson, furious, fired off an angry telex to Secretary of State Dean Rusk.

"The whole world knows the attack was made with Yankee planes piloted by mercenaries paid by the United States CIA," shouted Castro at a funeral for those who had died in the bombings. "Even Hollywood would not try to film such a story."

Although the raids that day destroyed much of Cuba's small air force, seven combat aircraft remained undamaged. The second strike, scheduled for the next day, Sunday, April 16, was sorely needed to establish air superiority, but a chance conversation torpedoed it. On Sunday afternoon, the team at Quarters Eye went ahead with preparations. To maintain a low profile for the invasion, Dulles was out of the country. His deputy director, General Cabell, stopped by Quarters Eye after a golf outing. Curious about whether the strike had high-level approval, Cabell casually contacted Secretary of State Rusk. Rusk, never an enthusiastic supporter of the invasion, and doubly cool after the telex from Stevenson, phoned the president and argued against the second strike. Kennedy agreed, replying "I'm not signed off on this." Bissell uncharacteristically declined to make his case. "We had to go ahead and make the best of it," he recalled.

That night, the five dilapidated freighters, seven small landing craft,

Brigade frogmen pose aboard the command ship Balgar, bound for Cuba. Their orders were to scout the beaches, mark them with landing lights, then expedite the unloading of men and matériel.

A Cuban commercial airliner erupts in flames at the Santiago de Cuba airport, the result of a bombing raid by the exile force two days before the Bay of Pigs invasion. The photo appeared in Castro's daily paper, Revolucion, as part of a larger effort to encourage Cubans to resist the rebel troops.

and two command ships of the invasion force moved slowly into the still waters of the Bay of Pigs. Lynch and Robertson, disobeying orders, accompanied their teams of frogmen to the beach on rubber rafts. In a twist of fortune typical of combat situations, Lynch's team met with a surprise as it approached the landing site on the southeast of the bay. As he later recalled, the secret-invasion beachfront was "lit up like Coney Island" by a construction site's vapor lights.

Losing precious time, Lynch turned his raft toward a darker spot a few hundred yards away. Almost immediately it bottomed out on the sharp coral that photo analysts had told him was seaweed. The men climbed out and started dragging the raft and supplies 80 yards to shore. Then, Lynch heard a Jeep approaching down the beach; they had been spotted. The Jeep swung around its headlights, clearly illuminating the raft. Lynch emptied his Browning automatic rifle into the vehicle. His men joined in, killing a Cuban militiaman inside.

About one in the morning, Lynch was called back to the ship for an urgent communication from the command post in Washington. "I had that now familiar sinking sensation," he recalled. The message read: "Castro still has operational aircraft. Expect you will be under air attack at first light. Unload all men and supplies and take the ships to sea."

This proved impossible. Landing craft carrying heavy equipment could not clear the coral reef until high tide at 7 a.m. While they waited out the intervening hours, the first planes appeared—not the brigade's own B-26 bombers, but the fighter aircraft from Castro's air force that had survived the brigade's first, and only, advance airstrike. The antiquated British-built Sea Furies and a T-33 jet—a trainer retrofitted with 20 mm cannons—were hardly formidable. Once the lumbering B-26s arrived, however, the Cuban planes proved more than a match for them, downing two. The Cuban air forces also took a terrible toll on the brigade's ships. Off the bay's northern landing zone, a Sea Fury rocket tore a gaping hole in the freighter *Houston* at 6:30 a.m. After the captain beached his vessel, a company of frightened troops refused to disembark. Rip Robertson rafted by, screaming at the hesitant invaders, "Get off, you bastards, it's your damn war!"

Meanwhile, during the early morning hours, the operation's propaganda team had swung into action as well. Around midnight, Howard Hunt had called up the public relations consultant working with the Frente and shortly after 2 a.m. had "Bulletin No. 1" issued on behalf of the exile government. At 3:44 a.m., radio broadcasts from Great Swan Island chimed in, urging Cuban soldiers to join the revolt, "Take up strategic positions that control roads and railroads! Make prisoners or shoot those who refuse to obey your orders! See that no Fidelist plane takes off." As far as can be determined, the pleas were roundly ignored.

About 9:30 that morning, off Lynch's southeast end of the bay, Castro's planes fired rockets into the *Rio Escondido,* which carried many of the brigade's supplies. The ship disappeared in a gigantic mushroom cloud. From his landing site Robertson radioed Lynch, "God Almighty, what was that? Fidel got the A-bomb?"

The truth was less dramatic, but devastating for the attackers. Just hours into the invasion, the exile forces had lost their supply of aviation gasoline, meaning that B-26s would be unable to land and refuel on the beachhead. The loss of a communications van broke contact between air and ground forces. Worst of all, the ship had carried 10 days' worth of ammunition. The invading forces now faced a numerically overwhelming foe with only the ammunition in their packs. With most of the brigade now ashore, Quarters Eye ordered the remaining supply ships to withdraw from the invasion zone. One ship, the *Caribe*, fled 200 miles from the bay and only returned when a U.S. destroyer fired across its bow.

On shore, the arriving forces fanned out from the two beaches and dug defensive positions as Castro's troops—backed by artillery and heavy tanks—closed in. On the first day, Brigade 2506 troops dealt out heavy losses, particularly to a unit that became known as the Lost Battalion of Castro's militia. But the men were in trouble, desperately short of food and ordnance. They also required air support against the remaining Cuban planes.

> "Castro still has operational aircraft. Expect you will be under air attack at first light."
>
> —CIA operational headquarters to Bay of Pigs landing force

The freighter Houston spews fire and smoke after taking a hit from one of Castro's planes. Because the ship lacked an adequate number of lifeboats, exile troops were forced to jump overboard; many drowned.

In Washington, President Kennedy reluctantly approved further air strikes. Many of the exile Cuban crews, exhausted by around-the-clock flying and demoralized by the air team's heavy losses, refused to go. Without informing the president, Bissell then allowed American bomber crews drawn from the Alabama National Guard to go in their place. Two planes were shot down, and four Americans were killed.

On Tuesday Castro's reinforcements poured in, forcing the brigade to abandon the northern beachhead for the other landing. The bone-weary troops were near collapse. At a 7 a.m. meeting, Richard Bissell requested that Kennedy authorize the carrier *Essex* to launch air raids. The president was torn; to his brother, Attorney General Robert Kennedy, he said, "I'd rather be an aggressor than a bum." In the end, however, he told Bissell to maintain "minimum visibility." Throughout the day at Quarters Eye "the cables kept coming in. It got worse and worse," recalled a Kennedy adviser.

Around midnight Bissell rushed again to the White House. The presi-

dent and ranking cabinet members, back from the annual Congressional Reception, were in white tie and tails. Hastily assembled White House staffers were in sweatshirts and corduroys. Before this oddly assorted gathering, Bissell insisted the project could be saved, but only if the president approved carrier air strikes immediately. This Kennedy refused to do, determined to avoid an open U.S. role in the invasion.

Instead, he authorized six navy fighters—with their markings hurriedly painted out—to escort the brigade's B-26s for one hour the next morning, with strict orders for the navy fighters not to fire. But even that modest help was not to come. Back at Quarters Eye, the worn-out staff failed to allow for the one-hour time difference between Cuba and the bombers' Nicaraguan base. The navy pilots were still on the *Essex* when the B-26s passed overhead. Two more were lost.

On Wednesday the brigade broke up into small groups and tried to hide out in the swamps. Pepe San Román, its commander, sent a final radio message: "Am destroying all equipment and communications. I have nothing left to fight with." To his CIA handler, he added, "And you sir, are a son of a bitch." Castro's militia rounded up the survivors. Of the 1,543 brigade fighters, 114 died and 1,189 were captured; others escaped or were never landed.

The mood at Quarters Eye was funereal. Jake Esterline was ashen, while his assistant was bent over and vomiting into a wastebasket. "Everyone was crying," Barnes's secretary recalled, except her boss, "who was stoic." Colonel Hawkins, wrote David Phillips, held one hand over his face, "as if hiding," not listening as Tracy Barnes tried to cheer up the group. Phillips remembered that he went home, got drunk, then "wept for two hours."

By then, the role of the United States in the invasion, a poorly concealed secret all along, was plain for all to see. "Plausible deniability," concluded the CIA's top-secret report on the Bay of Pigs, had turned into a "pathetic illusion." The report also concluded the project had probably been doomed to fail, and the CIA should have acknowledged as much. At a press conference that week, President Kennedy took the blame for the fiasco. "There's an old saying that victory has a hundred fathers and defeat is an

At top left, Castro's troops fight off Brigade 2506 members in the Laguna del Tesoro; at bottom left, antiaircraft personnel fire at rebel planes overhead. Below, Cuban army reinforcements head for the front. Contrary to the CIA planners' optimistic predictions, popular support for the invasion never materialized, and the brigade encountered stiff resistance.

Guarded by Castro's troops, Cuban exiles sit dejectedly on the soil they had hoped to regain. After a trial and lengthy negotiations, the survivors were released 20 months later in exchange for $53 million in food and medicine.

"Now, many heads are going to roll as a result of this."

—Richard Bissell

At right, President John F. Kennedy accepts a Brigade 2506 flag from two of the unit's members during an emotional rally in Miami after their 1962 release from prison in Cuba. The president promised that the flag (above) would be "returned to this Brigade in a free Havana." Instead, it remained in storage for almost 15 years and was then given back to the exiles.

orphan," he said. "I am the responsible officer." In private, however, he raged against the CIA and its smoothly persuasive briefers. "All my life I've known better than to depend on the experts. How could I have been so stupid?"

For Allen Dulles, the disaster meant the end of his long, golden career as CIA director. During the late 1950s, Dulles had planned a new, architecturally innovative headquarters for the agency that would shift it from scattered government offices downtown, like Quarters Eye, to a beautiful campus in northern Virginia. Although the headquarters was completed, he was not able to preside over the new home he had helped design. On November 28, 1961, Dulles's last day in office, President Kennedy dedicated the new building in Langley, Virginia, awarding Dulles the prestigious National Security Medal as a last gesture before retirement.

The next day John McCone was sworn in as CIA director. After the chaotic Cuban project, Kennedy wanted a no-nonsense administrator with experience in the business world. Although McCone had government experience as undersecretary of the air force and chairman of the Atomic Energy Commission, he had also established the influential Bechtel engineering firm, and he seemed a perfect choice. Given Kennedy's estrangement from the agency, his lack of any previous CIA experience was a plus.

Richard Bissell, the man whom many had expected to succeed Allen Dulles as CIA director, left soon after Dulles, having been advised by the president months earlier that he would "have to go." During McCone's tenure, the rift between the administration and the agency soon healed, aided by the agency's key role during the crises over the status of Berlin and over nuclear missiles in Cuba *(pages 92-101)*. The CIA's next major paramilitary role would be of a different nature and far broader scope, as the agency plunged into large-scale undertakings in Laos and Vietnam.

WAR OF NERVES

Except for the ticking of the clock on the mantel, the meeting room in the Soviet embassy in Vienna was deathly quiet as Nikita Khrushchev and John F. Kennedy concluded their June 1961 summit talks. What had begun as a tense but amicable discussion had escalated into a heated exchange about Berlin, the former capital of Germany, which had been partitioned since World War II into a Communist eastern sector and a democratic western sector.

West Berlin, an isolated pocket of freedom deep within Soviet-controlled East Germany, had been a source of friction between the superpowers for years. Now, Khrushchev insisted, it was time to unify the city under Communist rule, and he would begin preparing to do so within six months—with or without Kennedy's consent. "If that is true," Kennedy replied, "it's going to be a cold winter." As the two men exited the building (left), photographers noted that the president was no longer smiling.

On the night of August 13, East German work crews hastily erected a barbed-wire barrier around West Berlin. Within weeks they had replaced most of the fence with a fortified wall. Kennedy ordered U.S. troops to the city and for the first time publicly acknowledged the possibility of nuclear war. In the months ahead, the CIA would play a central, behind-the-scenes role in supplying Kennedy with the information he needed to chart a course through one of the most dangerous periods of the atomic age, beginning with the Berlin crisis and extending into the Cuban missile crisis.

A VITAL SOURCE

In its reports to Kennedy, the agency relied on many sources, including aerial reconnaissance. Perhaps the most remarkable was a colonel in the GRU, Soviet military intelligence. Oleg Penkovsky had established a covert connection with the CIA less than four months before the Berlin Wall went up.

Penkovsky's efforts to make contact had begun on a rain-soaked night in 1960, when he stopped two

The September 15, 1961, issue of Life magazine emphasized the deepening crisis between the two superpowers. Its cover story featured a letter from President Kennedy (bottom) that made the possibility of a nuclear attack on America sound all too real.

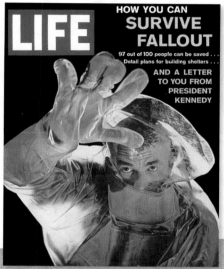

US ARMY CHECKPOINT

young American tourists out for a stroll in Moscow's Red Square. After chatting for a few minutes, he revealed his true purpose. "I have some information which I wish to give directly to the American embassy," he said. Pressing a letter into their hands, he implored them to go there immediately. "Your government will be very grateful," he added. Despite misgivings, one of them did as he asked.

Months would pass, however, before Penkovsky gained a stable link with the West, connecting first with SIS, the British secret service, and later with the CIA as well. "What concerns me," he cautioned both agencies, "is the West's failure to understand the true motives of the Soviet Union as a dangerous foe who wants to be the first to attack and smash us."

While working with the CIA and SIS, Penkovsky had supplied numerous photographs he had taken of secret technical documents, many related to the Soviet nuclear program. Now, in face-to-face debriefings during the crisis, he argued that, in his words, "they are not ready" for a nuclear exchange—meaning the West could stand its ground with relative safety. He added emphatically, however, "Khrushchev's statements about this are all bluff, but he is preparing as fast as possible."

FLASHPOINT BERLIN

With East and West Berlin now physically divided, the city became a point of daily contention between the superpowers. The heavily guarded wall effectively halted the flood of East German refugees, while police at border checkpoints restricted movement from West to East. The tension came to a head in late October when sentries denied passage to two American military police who refused to show their passports; armed U.S. soldiers then escorted the MPs across the border. For two days tempers flared as Americans continued to defy East German border police, until finally Soviet and U.S. tanks faced each other at Checkpoint Charlie *(opposite)*. True to Penkovsky's prediction, however, Khrushchev then backed down.

The Americans "can't turn their tanks around and pull them back as long as our guns are pointing at them," the Soviet leader told his commander in Berlin. "They're

Oleg Penkovsky, whose credentials as a member of the GRU intelligence service appear below, met with CIA and SIS handlers during his assignments abroad. In a 1961 London meeting, he posed in the uniform of a U.S. army colonel brought by the Americans to honor his contributions; his SIS handlers loaned him a British uniform for a similar portrait.

**TIMELINE:
APRIL 20-NOVEMBER 1961**

APRIL 20-MAY 6, 1961
Soviet GRU colonel Oleg Penkovsky and a CIA/SIS team hold their first series of meetings in London.

JUNE 4, 1961
Kennedy-Khrushchev summit in Vienna breaks down when Khrushchev threatens to cut off access to West Berlin.

JULY 18-AUGUST 7, 1961
Second series of London meetings with Penkovsky (above, with a CIA officer).

JULY 25, 1961
President Kennedy addresses the nation on the crisis in Berlin and announces a further defense buildup; the next day, Khrushchev calls this a declaration of "preliminary war."

AUGUST 13, 1961
Construction of the Berlin Wall begins.

**SEPTEMBER 20-
OCTOBER 14, 1961**
In Paris, Penkovsky and CIA/SIS team meet for the last time.

OCTOBER 27-28, 1961
The Berlin crisis reaches a climax when U.S. and Soviet tanks confront each other for 16 hours.

NOVEMBER 1961
John McCone succeeds Allen Dulles as CIA director (above, from left, Kennedy, Dulles, and McCone).

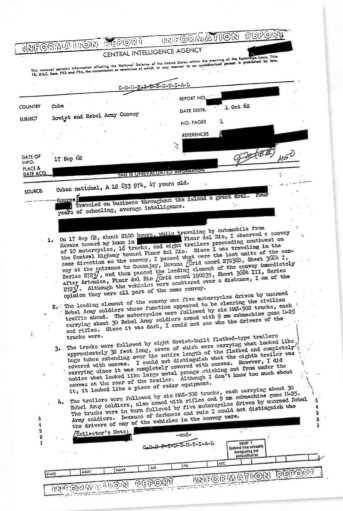

An October 1962 CIA report details a Cuban citizen's sighting of Soviet trucks hauling suspicious-looking cargo. Sensitive information in the document—including the informant's identity—was blacked out prior to declassification.

Analysts (below) from the National Photographic Interpretation Center examined thousands of feet of film to verify there were Soviet missile sites in Cuba. Kennedy later called NPIC "instrumental in identifying the nature and magnitude of the threat to world peace."

ERECTOR/LAUNCHER EQUIPMENT

TENT A

8 MISSILE TRAILERS

EQUIPMENT

looking for a way out, I'm sure, so let's give them one." The Soviet tanks departed, and soon the American armor did as well. The peaceful resolution that day did not signal a thaw in superpower relations, however. The coming year would produce yet another crisis that would bring the world to the brink of nuclear war.

SOVIET MISSILES IN CUBA

In August 1962, CIA director John McCone had in his possession reams of intelligence reports that revealed ominous-looking developments in Soviet-allied Cuba. The files included photographs taken by U-2 spy planes, accounts from agents and ordinary citizens living on the island, and thick files of Soviet documents provided by Penkovsky. In the aerial photos McCone saw what looked like several surface-to-air missile (SAM) batteries, far removed from existing airfields or government installations. What could the SAMs be protecting, he wondered. The field reports noted Soviet ships unloading thousands of men and ordnance, as well as convoys of tarpaulin-covered trucks traveling after dark. McCone reached a troubling conclusion: "There was nothing else to ship to Cuba but missiles."

The other members of Kennedy's inner circle of advisers, however, dismissed McCone's argument. The Soviets had never placed offensive missiles outside their own territory, and Khrushchev had repeatedly denied—both publicly and privately—that such weapons would be stationed in Cuba. Still, the president ordered that a contingency plan be prepared. "I was quite disillusioned," recalled McCone, "because usually a contingency plan goes in the bottom drawer." The CIA also sent a message to Oleg Penkovsky, requesting any information on "measures being undertaken by the USSR to convert Cuba into an offensive military base. In particular we would like to know if Cuba is to be provided with surface to surface missiles." But the usually prompt and reliable agent did not respond. What the CIA could not know was that the KGB had become suspicious of Penkovsky and placed him under tight surveillance.

Finally, in mid-October, McCone obtained the proof he needed from the National Photographic Interpretation Center (NPIC), an office jointly operated by the CIA and the Defense Department. While examining film from a U-2 overflight, the center's photo interpreters pinpointed unusual activity in a clearing in the Cuban countryside. When they compared the photos with a description of SS-4

A photo taken by a U-2 spy plane and labeled by NPIC provides proof of the existence of medium-range nuclear missiles in Cuba. The advanced state of construction at this site near San Cristóbal created an added sense of urgency in Washington.

CONSTRUCTION

TIMELINE:
APRIL 1962-
OCTOBER 15, 1962

APRIL 1962
U.S. Jupiter missiles in Turkey become operational; Khrushchev conceives the idea of deploying similar missiles in Cuba.

AUGUST 27, 1962
Last material received from Penkovsky.

FIRST WEEK OF SEPTEMBER 1962
Soviet troops begin arriving in Cuba; more continue to do so until mid-October.

SEPTEMBER 4, 1962
Attorney General Robert Kennedy and Soviet ambassador Anatoly Dobrynin (above) hold the first of several meetings; Dobrynin denies Soviets have offensive weapons in Cuba.

SEPTEMBER 27, 1962
U.S. Tactical Air Command presents a plan of attack on Cuba to air force chief of staff Curtis LeMay (above). LeMay approves the concept and orders the air force to be ready to implement it by October 20.

OCTOBER 14, 1962
U-2 flight over suspected Soviet missile sites in Cuba.

OCTOBER 15, 1962
National Photographic Interpretation Center (NPIC) finds evidence of medium-range ballistic missiles at San Cristóbal, Cuba.

MRBM LAUNCH SITE 1
SAN CRISTOBAL, CUBA
23 OCTOBER 1962

MISSILE ERECTOR

CABLE

MISSILE SHELTER TENT

TRACKED PRIME MOVERS

FUEL TANK TRAILERS

At a meeting of the Executive Committee, or ExComm, Defense Secretary Robert McNamara is seated at President Kennedy's right; CIA director McCone, at the far end of the table, is obscured from view.

At right, a follow-up photograph of the same San Cristóbal site shown on pages 96-97, taken nine days later by a low-altitude reconnaissance plane, shows unmistakable evidence of offensive missile components.

Below, a top-secret NPIC map shows targets that could be reached from Cuba. Robert Kennedy wrote that if the missiles had been fired, "80 million Americans would be dead" within minutes.

EXCOMM DELIBERATES

On October 16, President Kennedy convened a special group of top advisers within the National Security Council. Over the course of the next two weeks this Executive Committee, or ExComm, would meet frequently to determine a response to the developing crisis in Cuba. At the first session the group reviewed the U-2 photos. The experts, Attorney General Robert Kennedy later wrote, "told us that if we looked carefully, we could see a missile base being constructed." He added, "I, for one, had to take their word for it." About the only good news to come out of the meeting was one interpreter's assertion that he didn't think the missiles were ready to fire. Nevertheless, the information Penkovsky had previously supplied spelled out clearly the devastation that SS-4s could inflict should they become operational.

medium-range missile installations in a manual that Penkovsky had provided earlier, the site's purpose was clear.

Next, ExComm wrestled with the sticky question of how to force the Soviets to remove the missiles from Cuba. The two best options seemed to be either a naval blockade of the island or an air strike on the installations, possibly followed by a full-scale invasion. Although they left the matter unresolved at the meeting, two days later they would be forced to make a choice. By October 18, detailed information from reports and photographs, along with the missile specifications supplied earlier by Penkovsky, was providing a clear picture of Soviet intentions in Cuba. That day the CIA presented a memorandum to ExComm stating that at least 16 ballistic missiles with a range of more than a thousand miles had been deployed to two sites. "These mobile missiles," the memo stated, "must be considered operational now and could be launched within 18 hours after the decision to launch." In addition, two more sites were being readied to accommodate SS-5 missiles, which had a range of 2,200 miles. If construction continued, 16 SS-5s could be ready to fire within two months.

McCone promptly told the American intelligence community of ExComm's decision to impose a blockade,

TIMELINE:
OCTOBER 16-23, 1962

OCTOBER 16, 1962
In response to the crisis, President Kennedy creates an Executive Committee (ExComm) of high-level advisers, including McCone; ExComm meets at least once a day for the duration of the crisis.

OCTOBER 18, 1962
President Kennedy meets with Soviet foreign minister Andrey Gromyko at the White House (above); Gromyko continues to deny the presence of missiles, and Kennedy does not reveal he knows about them.

OCTOBER 22, 1962
Unknown to his CIA/SIS handlers, Penkovsky is arrested in Moscow.

OCTOBER 22, 1962
7:00 p.m.
In a speech to the nation, President Kennedy announces U.S. military forces are at a heightened alert status in anticipation of war. He sends Khrushchev an advance copy of the speech and the first of several letters exchanged during the crisis.

OCTOBER 23, 1962
First low-level reconnaissance flights over Cuba. A total of 158 flights occur between this date and November 15.

OCTOBER 23, 1962
10:00 a.m.
ExComm decides to attack and destroy any Cuban surface-to-air missile site that shoots down a U-2.

OCTOBER 23, 1962
7:06 p.m.
In a White House ceremony, President Kennedy signs a proclamation to enforce a blockade against Cuba.

OCTOBER 23, 1962
8:35 p.m.
In a televised speech, Fidel Castro announces a combat alarm, with Cuban armed forces placed on highest alert.

warning that "Soviet reactions are expected to be severe" and might involve a reciprocal action against West Berlin. "More extreme steps" on the U.S. side, he added, "such as a limited air strike, comprehensive air strike, or military invasion would be withheld awaiting developments."

On October 22, U.S. military forces worldwide were placed on alert, and the CIA sent another urgent message to Penkovsky, requesting "all concrete information about military and diplomatic moves being planned by the Soviet Union either in Cuba itself or elsewhere in the world"; once again, there would be no reply. In a television address, President Kennedy informed the nation of the presence of Soviet missiles in Cuba and his intention to blockade the island. Khrushchev, in a later response, threatened to sink any U.S. vessel that tried to interfere.

BACK FROM THE BRINK

The world held its breath as the first Soviet ships approached the blockade line on the morning of October 24. At about 10:00 a.m., naval intelligence reported that

a Soviet submarine had moved into place between two Soviet ships, the *Gagarin* and the *Komiles,* only a few miles short of the blockade. As ExComm members anxiously awaited developments, a messenger arrived with a note for McCone. "We have a preliminary report," McCone announced, "which seems to indicate that some of the Russian ships have stopped dead in the water." Kennedy ordered U.S. forces to avoid confrontation until the situation could be clarified. After three days of agonizing suspense, a formal missive from Khrushchev arrived at the White House. "You are disturbed over Cuba," he wrote, "because it is ninety miles by sea from the coast of the United States of America." But, he pointed out, "you have placed destructive missile weapons, which you call offensive, in Turkey, literally next to us." He proposed that both sides remove those missiles.

ExComm could not agree to that proposal but would accede to an earlier Soviet proposal which asked only for a pledge of no U.S. invasion of Cuba; secretly, Kennedy also sent private assurances that the missiles in Turkey

Opposite page: Secretary of Defense McNamara and President Kennedy share a quiet moment on the White House portico on October 29, shortly after the crisis was resolved. McNamara had urged Kennedy to plan an attack on the missile bases but to exercise the option only as a last resort.

OXIDIZER TRAILERS
OXIDIZER TRAILER
2 MISSILE TRANSPORTERS
6 MISSILE TRANSPORTERS
PROB IRBM PROPELLANT TRAILERS
ERECTOR
3 MISSILE TRANSPORTERS

At left, an aerial-reconnaissance image of Mariel, Cuba, shows missile equipment being loaded onto ships on November 5, 1962. Five days later, near Puerto Rico, the USS Barry (inset, lower ship) escorts the Soviet freighter Anosov on its way.

would be removed later as well. On October 28, Khrushchev reported via Radio Moscow that the USSR had ceased work on the Cuban missile sites and "issued a new order on the dismantling of the weapons which you describe as 'offensive' and their crating and return to the Soviet Union." Both sides drew back from the verge of war to begin working out the details of the settlement.

The facts Oleg Penkovsky had provided since he first allied himself with the West had been vital to U.S. intelligence in detecting the missiles and determining the threat they posed at each stage of installation, as well as the true strategic balance, which was heavily in the U.S. favor. But the Soviet agent was never able to receive his allies' thanks and praise. On October 22, the same day Kennedy made the missiles' existence public, the KGB had arrested the ill-fated informer. Although his CIA handlers urged the U.S. government to negotiate his release, the mistrust and hostility stemming from the crises in Berlin and Cuba precluded bargaining for his life. Convicted by a Soviet military court, Penkovsky was executed in May 1963.

TIMELINE:
OCTOBER 24, 1962–
MAY 11, 1963

OCTOBER 24, 1962
On the first day of the U.S. blockade of Cuba, Soviet ships approach but later stop or retreat. For the first time in history, the U.S. Strategic Air Command is placed on DEFCON 2 alert, one level short of nuclear war.

OCTOBER 26 AND 27, 1962
Late-night secret meetings between Robert Kennedy and Dobrynin near agreement that missiles in Turkey will be withdrawn if Soviet missiles in Cuba are taken out first.

OCTOBER 27, 1962
The CIA reports all but one of 24 medium-range ballistic-missile sites in Cuba are operational.

OCTOBER 27, 1962
The FBI reports Soviet diplomats in New York are destroying sensitive documents.

OCTOBER 27, 1962, noon
U.S. Air Force major Rudolf Anderson Jr. (above) is shot down piloting a U-2 over Cuba.

OCTOBER 28, 1962
9:00 a.m.
A message from Khrushchev to Kennedy broadcast on Radio Moscow effectively ends the missile crisis.

JANUARY 1963
Turkey announces that Jupiter missiles on its soil are to be phased out; by April all are removed.

MAY 11, 1963
Penkovsky (above) is sentenced to death; his execution is announced six days later.

TURBULENT
YEARS

 illiam Colby could not have arrived in the South Vietnamese capital of Saigon at a better time. When he was posted there as the CIA's deputy chief of station in February 1959, a wonderful calm prevailed. Vietnam's successful rebellion against the French colonialists was long over, the nation having been divided into a Communist North and a non-Communist South five years before. The battle in the countryside against the Vietcong, the guerrilla force backed by North Vietnam and the Soviet Union, was only just beginning to heat up. Colby felt comfortable in bringing along his wife Barbara and their four children.

"The short drive from Tan Son Nhut Airport was remarkably peaceful," he was to write in his memoirs. "Saigon was a gracious colonial city with treelined boulevards, bustling marketplaces, pedicabs racing to and fro, and wonderfully pretty women." The Colby family's new residence was equally inviting: a villa from the colonial era that came with "spacious rooms, high ceilings from which graceful fans whirred, a well-manicured garden, and the appropriate number of charming Vietnamese servants."

A year and a half later, Colby was chief of station, and the countryside brimmed with rebellious Vietcong and agents infiltrated from North Vietnam, seeking to reunify the country under Communism. In response, the United States had stepped up efforts to bolster the South, providing aid, military advisers, and intelligence data. Yet the unrest was already taking a toll. In November 1960 a South Vietnamese army colonel who believed President Ngo Dinh Diem was lax in the fight against subversion attempted a coup in which paratroopers besieged the presidential palace. In their villa nearby, Colby's family received a "baptism of fire," he recalled. "Bullets whined through our windows, and I barricaded Barbara and the children in a hall on the top floor." That afternoon, during a lull in the fracas, he sent his family off to the safety of a neighbor's house. The CIA, uncertain of the affair's outcome, maintained contact with both the rebels and government until Diem smashed the revolt.

At left, a helicopter owned by the CIA's Air America transport firm takes on refugees at a CIA evacuation point in Saigon, South Vietnam, during the city's fall on April 19, 1975. CIA involvement in both Vietnam and neighboring Laos was extensive during the busy 1960s and early 1970s, although agency missions continued elsewhere as well.

For Colby and the CIA—and for the United States—an event-filled era was under way. During the 1960s and early 1970s, the agency, led first by CIA director John McCone and later by Richard Helms, would help wage a military and political war in Southeast Asia, while its analysts provided some of the more accurate analyses of enemy strength and intentions. At the same time, the CIA's broader struggle against the Soviet Union would lead both to technological innovations *(pages 116-117)* and to a relent-less, ultimately self-destructive search for KGB moles within the agency. In the mid-1970s the CIA would face trials of a different kind, as revelations about its prior actions exposed the secretive organization for the first time to wide-ranging public scrutiny—and thrust Colby himself, as CIA director, into the center of the maelstrom.

MISSION TO VIETNAM

Those complexities still lay ahead during Colby's first posting to Vietnam. When he arrived in Saigon after an assignment in Rome, William Colby was 39, short and lean, his round glasses giving him an owlish appearance. He had the clandestine operative's knack of staring without emotion and, colleagues said, of lying with a straight face. After his wartime service with the OSS, Colby had returned to civilian life as a student at Columbia University Law School, then worked for the law firm of former OSS chief William Donovan. In a subsequent stint as a government labor lawyer, the future CIA director defended striking California grape workers.

A few years after the CIA was founded, Colby himself signed on. He had been with the agency almost nine years by the time he reached Vietnam. While there, one of his many tasks was to help plan a resistance operation in North Vietnam. Starting in early 1961, small teams of South Vietnamese volunteers were secreted into the North, often by parachute, in order to build intelligence-gathering and resistance networks. Had they succeeded, the three- to seven-man squads might have helped even the score with the North for its stepped-up infiltration of Vietcong into the South. But the North Vietnamese captured almost every one of the 20 or so teams that were sent. Years later, the CIA abandoned the effort, transferring responsibility to the U.S. Army.

Colby's efforts in the South met with greater success, at least for a time. South Vietnam continued to face a growing guerrilla war as the Vietcong executed village leaders and forcibly recruited young men into their armed bands. As CIA station chief, Colby became a prime advocate of fending off the Vietcong at the local level.

To put that approach to the test, his team worked with U.S. and Vietnamese Special Forces on the strategic-

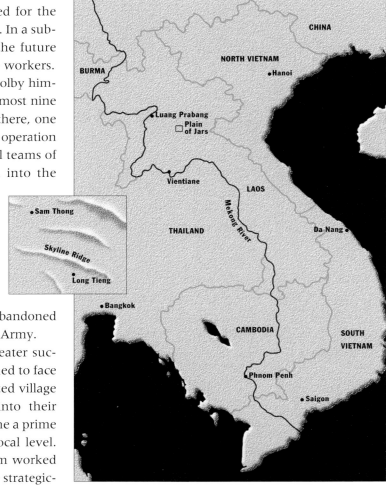

A focus of U.S. and CIA concern since the late 1950s, both Laos and North Vietnam bordered on Communist China. A key CIA stronghold in Laos was at Long Tieng (inset), a military headquarters located near the hotly contested Plain of Jars.

CIA station chief William Colby (above, far right) confers with senior South Vietnamese military officers in the A Shau Valley near the Laotian border in 1962. In order to see how the strategic-hamlets strategy was working, Colby went on several such farewell trips before his return to headquarters that year.

hamlets program to relocate peasants to areas cleared of Communist units. There the residents were trained to shoot carbines, string barbed-wire perimeters, and patrol the surrounding land. In a complementary effort, the Agency for International Development (AID) taught basic medicine, laid water and sewer lines, and constructed schools and markets. The initiative sought to make thousands of villages throughout South Vietnam self-reliant in defense and daily life.

In the fall of 1962, Colby was reassigned to Washington. He later recalled taking his family to pay a farewell call on President Diem, who expressed satisfaction with the war effort. But on November 1 of the following year, Diem was murdered in a generals' coup. Although U.S. decision makers and the CIA knew about the impending overthrow, they neither sponsored it nor tried to stop it. By then, the strategic-hamlets program was crumbling due to a combination of factors, including Communist attacks, its association with the Diem regime, and rampant corruption. Siphoning off U.S. funds and construction materials from the initiative, the South Vietnamese government herded people into fortified villages but reneged on promised social services.

In subsequent years, the U.S. military took over the main thrust of the struggle in Vietnam as the old emphasis on small-scale defensive action gave way, starting in 1965, to a reliance on large numbers of American troops and an intensive air bombardment of North Vietnam. By then, however, the CIA was already heavily engaged in the neighboring country of Laos, which proved to be the agency's primary stage in Indochina.

Like South Vietnam, the kingdom of Laos was a former French colony locked in a struggle against indigenous Communists aided by North Vietnam and the Soviet Union. Laos, too, was seen as crucial to the fate of the region. As outgoing president Eisenhower told President-elect Kennedy in January 1961, "If Laos is lost to the Free World, in the long run we will lose all of Southeast Asia." Eisenhower, who had already thrown U.S. support behind pro-Western factions in the Laotian government, was determined to avoid sending U.S. ground troops, but he saw an alternative. In one of his last official acts, he approved a CIA plan to greatly expand a small, existing effort to mobilize anti-Communist Laotian guerrillas.

That January, accordingly, CIA officer James William Lair helicoptered into the village of Ta Vieng. Located in Laos's mountainous northeast, Ta Vieng was the home base of a rugged, fiercely independent mountain people numbering about 250,000. Although they were known to outsiders as the Miao, a word derived from the Chinese for barbarian, they called themselves the Hmong—"the free people."

Bill Lair had come to Ta Vieng to meet a leading Hmong military commander, a Royal Laotian Army officer named Vang Pao. Not yet 30, Vang Pao had been a teenage courier for French colonial troops during World War II and had subsequently served as a colonial police lieutenant as France tried to hold on to Vietnam. Lively and keenly intelligent, he was also hot tempered, at times foulmouthed, and in combat remorseless to the point of cruelty.

Vang Pao quickly sized up his visitor as very different from the stereotype of the aggressive, bossy American. Bill Lair, to be sure, had the credentials to be a CIA "cowboy." For nearly a decade he had been training Thailand's national police in guerrilla warfare. But with his slicked-back hair and glasses, he seemed more like a mild-mannered clerk. He spoke Thai with a Texas drawl and had adopted the deferential Thai manner of lowering his gaze when addressing someone. Thai officials thought very highly of Lair—not least because he had married into a prominent Bangkok family—and had made him a police colonel. For the CIA, the police assignment provided the perfect cover.

James William Lair

Seen here in his Thai police colonel's uniform, CIA officer Bill Lair was a Texas A&M geology graduate who spent the 1950s training Thai policemen in paramilitary skills. In 1961 he cemented the CIA's alliance with Hmong tribesmen in Laos.

Lair greeted Vang Pao respectfully, according to local custom, holding his hands prayerfully before his face, and then gradually got down to business. He asked Vang Pao about the indigenous Communists—the Pathet Lao—who were being supplied by Soviet airdrops. Having taken the offensive, they had recently driven back the Hmong from the strategic Plain of Jars. "We have only two choices," Vang Pao replied. "We fight them or we leave." He added, "If you give us the guns, we will fight them."

WAGING A SECRET WAR

Within days, planes from the regional flying service Air America, secretly owned and operated by the CIA *(pages 130-139),* parachuted weapons to the Hmong. The World War II-vintage arms were reliable enough and, because they were easily available around the world, difficult to trace. With Pathet Lao forces closing in on the Hmong training base, Lair then set up an extraordinary crash course that was to last just 72 hours—the time it would take enemy troops to reach them. The instructors were Thai, members of Lair's elite CIA-trained group. The trainees consisted of three Hmong companies of 100 men each. On the first day, they learned to fire rifles; on the second day, they worked with machine guns, mortars, and bazookas; on the third day, they were taught ambush tactics, including the use of trip-wired grenades. The day after that—January 21, 1961—20 Hmong graduates of the course staged an ambush, cutting down 15 surprised members of the Pathet Lao.

The secret war in Laos was moving into gear. In the years that followed, the CIA would run the burgeoning war in this small country of about three million inhabitants, operating clandestinely through the Hmong with the aid of U.S. Special Forces. Over time, the agency would also support fighters from other indigenous cultures— among them, the Lahu, Shan, Yao, Tai, and ethnic Lao—as well as fielding some 18,000 hired soldiers from Thailand. The conflict would continue through the assassination of President Kennedy and the terms of Lyndon Johnson and Richard Nixon, as the far more visible war in Vietnam dominated America's TV screens and public debates. It would be fought behind a thin layer of neutrality, without a formal

> "We have only two choices. We fight them or we leave. If you give us the guns, we will fight them."
>
> —Vang Pao, Hmong leader

In an undated photograph, Vang Pao (below, front), followed closely by Bill Lair, in sunglasses, strides past a throng of Hmong villagers. Charismatic and energetic, Vang Pao marshaled Hmong support for the CIA in northeast Laos.

Nestled in the mountains of north-east Laos at an elevation of 3,100 feet, the remote village of Long Tieng expanded as shown at left as it became a regional military headquarters and CIA staging area. Pilots using the foggy, bowl-shaped air base with its dirt airstrip called it the "dreaded valley."

declaration of war and under the official command of whoever happened to be U.S. ambassador in the Laotian capital of Vientiane. Above all, it would be war on the cheap, waged at a fraction of the cost of the Vietnam engagement, with a final CIA combat death toll of four field advisers and a peak CIA strength of only 225 officers.

What the French-speaking Hmong called their Armée Clandestine, or "Secret Army," soon grew to 9,000 men. But then in the summer of 1962 the United States and the Soviet Union concluded an accord in Geneva for "a neutral and independent Laos." In line with the agreement, Washington pulled out 666 advisers and staff from the U.S. military there. Two CIA officers and less than two dozen Thai police remained to advise the Hmong. Meanwhile, Bill Lair and other CIA officers moved south across the Mekong River to Thailand and flew, like commuters, into Laos every morning aboard Air America.

Back at headquarters, CIA managers—including Bill Colby, now chief of the Far Eastern division—fought for renewed aid to the Hmong. The CIA estimated that nearly 7,000 North Vietnamese troops were still in Laos; only 40 had bothered to exit through internationally monitored checkpoints. At length, assistance resumed, in increasingly larger amounts.

The force in Laos now grew steadily in actual size and strength. Within five years of Bill Lair's first meeting with Vang Pao, the secret army had surpassed its former size, now numbering over 15,000. Its nerve center was the Hmong headquarters situated at the bustling town of Long Tieng in a high mountain valley. On busy days Air America planes landed on a paved runway every few minutes to swiftly disgorge their cargo. Supply-laden helicopters and single-engine aircraft then took off for small satellite airfields carved out of the slopes of Laos's fog-draped mountains.

The Hmong flocked to Long Tieng, building bamboo and sheet-metal shacks far up the jagged limestone hillsides and swelling its population to

40,000—second only to Vientiane. In the thriving open-air market, old men sold vegetables, textiles, and raw opium, a popular Hmong medicine, stuffed into old whiskey bottles. Up to 100 Americans—CIA officers, Air America crews, and U.S. military advisers—were in residence.

Six miles away by air was Sam Thong, the operations center for AID. Under the direction of Edgar "Pop" Buell, a retired Indiana farmer, AID workers closely supported the CIA effort by supplying the Hmong with food. They set up thatched-roof hospitals, dug and stocked fishponds, and established pig-breeding programs. Buell began building schools with the revolutionary notion that all Laotians, girls and boys, should be educated, and he had Hmong women trained as nurses. His labors coincided with CIA thinking on "nation building," which stressed civilian development along with military preparedness.

The secret war assumed a pattern. In the dry season, from October to May, the Communists pushed forward, retaking control of the Plain of Jars, a grassy, 50-square-mile plateau northeast of Long Tieng that took its name from scores of huge jar-shaped rock structures that may have served as ancient burial urns. Throughout the war battles raged back and forth over this flat expanse, with its rudimentary but vital network of roads. Then, in the

Below, Edgar "Pop" Buell, U.S. AID adviser in Laos, poses with three Laotian guerrilla leaders behind a vegetable-laden table. An Indiana farmer who had joined the Swiss-run International Voluntary Services when his wife died, Buell was hired by AID after his volunteer service in Laos ended. His economic development work helped confirm the Hmong's positive view of their U.S. allies.

spring monsoon, the Hmong went on the offensive, using Air America to leapfrog units into position.

One of several dynamic Hmong military leaders was Soutchay Vongsavanh—an energetic, Fort Benning-trained commander with the Laotian army, whose airborne troops made up in courage what they lacked in equipment. Upon landing, it was said, their heads rang from the crack of the uncushioned helmets on their skulls. But they jumped in fair weather or foul, and they were the only soldiers to stand fast in the defense of the key north Laotian town of Nam Tha when Communist forces on the commanding heights rained down machine-gun fire from above.

AN ENIGMATIC GUERRILLA CHIEF

Meanwhile, CIA officers based at Long Tieng continued to work most closely with Vang Pao. Perpetually restless, he slept only a few hours a night. Vang Pao would race to a firefight in an Air America helicopter to personally fire a 105 mm howitzer or would order in propeller-driven T-28 attack planes flown by the CIA's Thai contract pilots. In Long Tieng he strode about followed three paces behind by one of his half-dozen wives. He lived with all six spouses and a score of children in a new two-story stone house, under which he stocked a large supply of opium.

The drug was legal in Laos, where it was a traditional cash crop and medicine. Vang Pao did not smoke opium nor allow his soldiers to indulge. But he kept the stash as insurance; if the United States abandoned him, he could sell it to keep up the fight. To maintain their allegiance, he let top subordinates market the harvest, which they smuggled to Thailand on Air America or openly loaded aboard a pair of old CIA-supplied C-47 transports, dubbed Air Opium by American observers.

Air America's supposed associations with the narcotics trade would later engender considerable controversy. In 1972 the CIA inspector general investigated the agency's role in Laos's drug trafficking; his report found there had been no official sanction for the trade, although some individuals had taken part in smuggling. Far more visible than Vang Pao's involvement in drugs was that of Laotian general Ouane Rattikone, whose fighter-bombers smashed rival opium traders and whose helicopters ferried 55-gallon drums of ether to local heroin refineries.

At his stone house Vang Pao held nightly feasts for his people, and when they died in battle, he openly wept. He was a tactical genius in fighting the Pathet Lao and North Vietnamese and was brutal in his treatment of them. He summarily executed some prisoners, keeping others in large metal barrels fastened together in the ground. When a CIA man asked him how he knew his men had been killing North Vietnamese, Vang Pao showed him a set of ears from dead enemy soldiers.

At left, villagers gather around an Air America plane parked near a Laotian poppy field along the Thai-Burmese border in 1973. In this area, known as the Golden Triangle, trade in unrefined opium was an accepted condition of economic life.

The generals who commanded the Royal Laotian Army considered the hill people inferior and sought, ineffectively, to undermine Vang Pao. King Savang Vattana, however, became the first government official to visit the mountain tribesman's Long Tieng base; he promoted Vang Pao to general and, later, commander of the region's government troops.

One of the few CIA men failing to share that high opinion of the Hmong leader in the early days of the war was Anthony Poshepny, who called himself Tony Poe. An experienced officer who was named senior adviser to Vang Pao in 1963, Poe mapped out battlefield strategy and organized the Hmong into regular units.

Poe was a CIA cowboy in the classic mold, with a flamboyant personality just the opposite of mild-mannered Bill Lair, now running the Hmong operation from Thailand. A hulking, hard-drinking former Marine who carried a boxer's mouth guard in his pocket, Poe was in the CIA lexicon a "knuckle dragger"—a paramilitary specialist a world away from the desk-bound analysts at headquarters. Wearing a Marine drill instructor's flat-brimmed hat, he roared boot-camp style at Hmong trainees and paid a bounty for enemy ears. In his spare time, he brewed up batches of homemade napalm by carefully stirring detergent in hot gasoline. "I'm an obnoxious bastard," Tony Poe liked to say. "That's one of my biggest faults."

Poe quarreled bitterly with Vang Pao, griping about the traditional practice whereby Vang Pao and his subordinates skimmed an extra share off the CIA payroll, leaving some enlisted men short of pay. For his part, Poe angered Vang Pao by marrying an attractive local woman whom the commander himself had an eye on. She was from a prominent Hmong family, and the marriage cost Poe a dowry of water buffalo and goats.

Poe repeatedly defied standing orders that CIA men stay out of combat. Perhaps his most notable exploit came during Operation Triangle in the summer of 1964. In May the enemy had seized the Plain of Jars. Operation Triangle was intended to retake a key junction of the routes that linked the plain to the governmental capital of Vientiane and to the separate, royal capital of Luang Prabang. Approval had come all the way from President Lyndon Johnson, who wanted to show that Laotian factions could work together. The Royal Army was supposed to capture the road nexus while the Hmong played supporting roles. But Tony Poe radioed in helicopters ferrying two Hmong companies. Poe and his band took the junction, upstaging the Royal Army and infuriating his superiors.

Poe's unauthorized appearances in combat became legend among his peers—and anathema to his bosses. In one firefight, he killed 17 North Vietnamese. Then, severely wounded and using his M-1 rifle for a crutch, he hobbled to a helicopter. Once airborne, he forced the pilot to evacuate 13 badly injured Hmong. In 1965 Poe was sent off to northern Laos to drill Yao tribesmen. He was finally exiled to a training camp in Thailand after a newspaper article blew his cover in 1970.

By that time the high point of the Laotian struggle was already past.

Anthony "Tony Poe" Poshepny

CIA officer and paramilitary specialist Anthony Poshepny, usually known as Tony Poe, smoothed over ethnic hostilities among the many Hmong tribes. His outspokenness, impulsive behavior, and raw bravery gave him a larger-than-life reputation within the covert community in Laos.

"I'm an obnoxious bastard. That's one of my biggest faults."

—Tony Poe

In 1968 Vang Pao's army reached its peak strength of 40,000 men. Increasingly, it resembled a conventional army. Men who once dressed in thread-bare clothes and went barefoot wore camouflage pants and combat boots. They entered battle in battalion-sized units, backed by regular Laotian troops, helicopters, and Thai-based U.S. fighter jets, which flew hundreds of sorties. The trend toward conventional warfare was a reaction to North Vietnam's growing deployment of regular troops to Laos, and it paralleled the Johnson administration's buildup of U.S. troops in South Vietnam. Yet the change deeply distressed Bill Lair. "We got away," he later commented, "from what was their greatest capability—which was to hit and run and use the country which they knew so well." Disillusioned about the abandonment of his guerrilla strategy, he transferred out in 1968.

Lair still harbored a fondness for Vang Pao, however, and escorted the Hmong leader later that year during a secret tour, at CIA invitation, of the United States. On a White House visit, Vang Pao panicked the Secret Service

Silhouetted against the sunlit scene outside, soldiers of the Communist Pathet Lao meet in a cave at the edge of the Plain of Jars, the largest expanse of open ground in northern Laos. By the early 1970s the Pathet Lao and North Vietnamese held the region securely.

Triumphant troops from a special Laotian strike force flank a CIA case officer standing in the hatchway of a recently captured enemy tank in November 1972. By that point in the Laos conflict, North Vietnamese forces outnumbered the Pathet Lao; this tank was seized in south-central Laos, near the village of Moung Phalane.

by arriving with an antique muzzleloader rifle, a gift for President Johnson. Several months after his return, over CIA objections, Vang Pao mounted Operation About-Face, an audacious large-scale conventional offensive, in August 1969. A smashing success, it reclaimed the entire Plain of Jars.

That was the high-water mark. The North Vietnamese now fielded 67,000 troops inside Laos. Their next dry-season offensive was pounded by American B-52 bombers—a development that essentially ripped the veil of secrecy off the U.S. role in Laos—but to no avail. By early 1970 Communist forces had shattered Vang Pao's army. Pop Buell's AID center at Sam Thong was overrun, and the headquarters at Long Tieng imperiled. Vang Pao had to replace his mounting casualties with middle-aged men and boys as young as 10. "Where were the ones in between?" asked Pop Buell. "I will tell you, they are all dead." In response, the CIA recruited more Thai mercenaries and regular troops, who grew to outnumber the Hmong fighters. At the end of 1971, the population of Long Tieng shrank to 5,000 troops and a handful of CIA officers as Communist 130 mm shells slammed into town. Hmong refugees streamed south, and tribal elders denounced Vang Pao to his face as a power-mad lackey of the Americans.

Back in the United States, congressional support for the secret war was also waning; use of the B-52s led to demands for a full accounting. A month after three American reporters visited Long Tieng in early 1970, President Nixon publicly acknowledged U.S. involvement in the war. By then, domestic unrest over the U.S. role in Southeast Asia had undercut remaining political support for the Laotian operation. In 1973 the Paris peace accords mandated a cease-fire and withdrawal of U.S. troops from South Vietnam and prescribed a coalition government in Vientiane. The agreements ended U.S. air support for the war in Laos and pulled the CIA's advisers out of the country. A final outflux of U.S. planes radioed to the ground, "Good-bye and see you in the next war."

The Laotians were now on their own, and the Communists made

steady gains. In May 1975, three months before the Communist seizure of Vientiane, Vang Pao agreed to leave. As thousands of Hmong seeking evacuation swamped the Long Tieng runways, Vang Pao had to be secretly airlifted by chopper to ward off assassination by his own people. The CIA later flew him to America and helped him buy a modest house in Missoula, Montana, where the mountains occasionally reminded him of home. The secret conflict had failed at a cost of some 30,000 Hmong dead, more than one out of every 10 of those living at the start of the war. Tens of thousands of Laotians would flee the country.

A PHOENIX RISES

For all the CIA's attention to Laos during the 1960s and early 1970s, the U.S. government for the most part had remained largely preoccupied with Vietnam. Even while stationed at headquarters, Bill Colby had often visited the country, and in 1968 he was assigned there again. At the request of the White House, and under official cover as Vietnam's AID program chief—a position that carried the rank of ambassador—he took over as deputy chief of a new "pacification program" aimed at winning the loyalty of the South Vietnamese. It was known in the acronym-heavy war effort as CORDS—for Civilian Operations and Revolutionary Development Support.

The architect of CORDS, and Colby's new boss, was Robert W. Komer, a brilliant, hard-driven former CIA analyst and National Security Council staffer. Komer had caught the eye of President Johnson, who gave him the task of energizing "the other war"—the fight for the hearts and minds of the people. Sent to Saigon in May 1967, Komer shrewdly cut through old rivalries by making CORDS a joint civilian-military venture. The military, he realized, could give him the requisite logistical support and manpower. Colby later described Komer, his new boss, as "abrasive, statistics-crazy and aggressively optimistic" but added, "I also thought he was about the best thing that had happened in the Vietnam war to date."

By the time Colby joined him in March 1968, Komer had CORDS up and running with a staff of 3,800 soldiers and civilians. Colby's primary responsibility became a CORDS program named Phoenix—or, in Vietnamese, Phung Hoang, a mythical bird of peace. Phoenix was intended to identify and take out the Vietcong cadres, who fueled the Communist insurgency by

In a colorful U.S.-produced propaganda poster, self-reliant South Vietnamese villagers guard their community against the Vietcong. The CIA-linked CORDS effort, established in 1967, used similar means to rally grass-roots support for the war effort; it also took the reverse approach by targeting suspected members of the Vietcong.

SPY SATELLITES AND
A SUNKEN SUBMARINE

During the 1960s and 1970s, the CIA made great strides in collecting intelligence through cutting-edge technical methods. Among the most remarkable of these was the Corona, the world's first spy satellite. Tested in the late 1950s, the Corona began photographing Soviet sites in August 1960. In 17 orbits at an altitude of 100 miles, it zoomed in on 1.5 million square miles of Soviet territory. Although those early images did not have the same resolution as photographs from the agency's U-2 spy plane, the area surveyed was greater than that covered by all 24 U-2 missions flown over the Soviet Union in the previous four years.

After U-2 Soviet overflights were banned later in 1960, the satellite program became all the more essential. In the next 12 years, Corona missions captured everything from weapons ranges to airfields and uranium mines. By the time the Corona program ended in 1972, a host of covert satellites, both American and Soviet, were in orbit.

Two years later, CIA intelligence gathering took a unique twist with the Hughes Glomar Explorer. Supposedly designed for deep-sea research, the 36-ton ship was actually built to retrieve a Soviet submarine that had

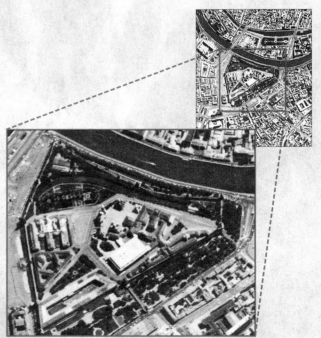

Above, a detail from a May 1970 Corona photograph of Red Square and its surroundings faintly reveals, at far left, a right-angled line of tourists outside Lenin's tomb.

At left, technicians prepare a KH-4A Corona for launch. First used in the mid-1960s, this version of the satellite had two cameras focused 30 degrees apart, allowing analysts to create stereoscopic images that gave more detailed information.

sunk northwest of Hawaii in 1968. Soviet search teams had failed to locate the sub, which held three nuclear missiles, code books, and radio gear, but the CIA, thanks to the U.S. Navy, knew exactly where it was.

In 16,000 feet of water and at an estimated dead weight of 4,000 tons, nothing so big had ever been hoisted to the surface from such a great depth before. For help, the CIA turned to secretive billionaire Howard Hughes, of Hughes Aircraft Company. The company quickly built the 618-foot Glomar, complete with eight giant claws, beneath a huge roof, erected to conceal

its special features from Soviet spy satellites. After taking to sea, the Glomar arrived over the sub's position on July 4, 1974.

Days later, it lowered its claws and grasped the sub. At first, all went well. Then, halfway to the surface, the sub broke in two; the portion containing the missiles and encryption gear slipped away. The Glomar managed to salvage a small forward section. Its contents remain uncertain, but the Glomar is known to have recovered the bodies of several Soviet crewmen. In a moment that transcended nationalities, all six were given a formal burial at sea.

Reclusive billionaire Howard Hughes, shown at right in a portrait from the 1940s, had his company build the Hughes Glomar Explorer for the CIA. Among the salvage ship's most visible features (below) were a helipad at the stern, a towering derrick, and two tall, submersible docking legs.

collecting taxes and spreading propaganda. Entire hamlets might be cordoned off and searched for suspects. Once identified, the cadres would be neutralized—captured, killed, or converted to the government's side. With its direct tactics, Phoenix differed starkly from other pacification programs in agriculture and education. "When you got 'em by the balls," read a sign hanging in Phoenix offices throughout the countryside, "their hearts and minds will follow."

In November 1968 Komer left Vietnam, and Colby took over CORDS. A CIA colleague, Evan Parker Jr., whom Colby had met in the OSS, now directed Phoenix. The CIA had a peak roster of 700 operatives in South Vietnam, and many of them served Phoenix in Saigon or in the field before military advisers took over by the end of 1969. The agency worked with the Vietnamese Police Special Branch to gather information about the people to be targeted. With CIA help, the South Vietnamese government alerted villagers to Vietcong suspects through wanted posters or through psychological warfare teams that announced suspects' names from loudspeakers mounted on trucks and sampans. One broadcast encouraged an individual to defect in this way: "We know you, Nguyen Van Nguyen; we know where you live! We know you are a Communist traitor. Soon the soldiers and police are coming for you. Rally now while there is still time!"

Among the most potent performers on the Phoenix team were the elite strike forces called Provincial Reconnaissance Units (PRUs). Each

Above, an American soldier nails up wanted posters identifying known or suspected Vietcong insurgents. The Phoenix program found that naming alleged Vietcong cadres often led them to flee the area; others, when caught, were either converted to the South Vietnamese cause, imprisoned, or killed.

province had its own PRU of up to 100 men, recruited, paid, and advised by the CIA. They were hard-bitten fighters: Many had lost family members to the Communists and were eager for revenge. Others had defected from the Vietcong and could not legally serve in the regular army.

The PRUs adopted techniques of terror usually attributed to the Communists. On occasion they roared into a village in helicopters to browbeat inhabitants into shunning the Vietcong. They had a reputation for sneaking into a suspect's home at night and taking their target dead or alive. During one 10-month period, the PRUs reported killing 4,406 of the enemy and capturing 7,408, while suffering only 179 fatalities.

"Sure we got involved in assassinations," Charlie Yothers, the CIA's chief of operations in the northern part of the country, later said. "That's what PRUs were set up for—assassination. I'm sure the word never appeared in any outlines or policy directives, but what else do you call a targeted kill?"

Indeed, many CIA and army personnel felt that the slaying of Vietcong cadres was inevitable in a brutal wartime setting where they were often armed and accompanying Communist military units. "Some guy's running around with a gun and you're not going to shoot him?" asked one U.S. offi-

Below, a dapper-looking William Colby, head of the CORDS program that included Phoenix, visits an open-air market in the city of Hue in central Vietnam in January 1969. Seized by the Vietcong in 1968, Hue was briefly abandoned by its residents after being recaptured; the bustling market scene meant life was returning to normal.

cial skeptically. "You don't just sneak up and tap the guy on the shoulder and say, 'Stop. We're the police, and we just want to capture you, Mr. VC.' "

Colby himself, however, would vehemently deny charges by the growing U.S. antiwar movement that Phoenix was an assassination program. The Vietcong, he pointed out, were "of more value to us alive than dead," especially if they could be wooed to the anti-Communist side. In 1969, however, he felt compelled to issue a directive to all Phoenix staff prohibiting "assassination and other equally repugnant activities."

Colby later conceded that government forces committed "excesses." Phoenix dossiers might contain what one CIA inspector called "trash"—hearsay or malicious gossip. Local officials sometimes targeted political rivals, pursued personal vendettas, or engaged in gangster-style shakedowns.

Because the suspects were technically civilians, the Geneva Convention rules on prisoners of war did not apply. A defendant had no recourse to legal counsel nor the right to review his dossier. He could be detained for two years without trial. At the notorious Con Son Island prison, visiting U.S. congressmen in 1970 found three to five inmates apiece in "tiger cages," shackled to the floor in tiny stone compartments, beaten, begging for meals and mercy. In jails overflowing with Phoenix captives, moreover, the Vietcong mixed freely with hardened criminals, recruiting them for the cause.

For both the Vietcong and the South Vietnamese, physical abuse was a routine method of eliciting intelligence. CIA adviser Orrin DeForest, assigned to the southern region around Bien Hoa, later wrote that South Vietnamese officials "beat the hell out of suspects." Yet many CIA personnel realized information extracted under torture was notoriously unreliable, and other tactics proved effective. In a country with abysmal medical care, for example, some wounded Vietcong prisoners gladly cooperated in exchange for treatment by highly regarded American doctors.

Phoenix set a numerical quota of 1,800 neutralizations a month, something both Komer and Colby had regarded as a practical way to measure progress. Yet the quotas gave district officials an incentive to inflate results. Civilians and enemy soldiers who were killed during normal military operations might be identified, falsely, as Vietcong cadres. "All of it went into the Phoenix hopper," wrote DeForest, "the guilty, the innocent, the enemy killed in action, the casual bodies along the roadside. They'd carry them in and count them up."

But Colby was not content to idle in Saigon and pore through statistics. At a moment's notice, he would order up a helicopter to inspect a Phoenix outpost. He also wrote later of safely motorcycling across the Mekong Delta with CORDS adviser John Paul Vann to celebrate the 1971 Tet, or New Year, concluding that some degree of stability was returning to daily life.

In Colby's mind, what he had observed on his rambles was confirmed by the numbers on Phoenix and other pacification programs. By the end of 1970, the CIA's computers reported more than 90 percent of the population of South Vietnam lived in secure or relatively secure areas. By 1971 Phoenix headquarters asserted that precisely 67,282 Vietcong had been neutralized, of whom 20,587 were killed; the remainder had been imprisoned or con-

Getting It Right

"This troubled essay proceeds from a deep concern that we are becoming progressively divorced from reality in Vietnam," wrote a CIA analyst in April 1965, adding the United States might be "proceeding with far more courage than wisdom—toward unknown ends." He was not alone. From the start of American involvement in Vietnam, many CIA analyses told a more pessimistic—and often, in hindsight, more accurate—story than policymakers wanted to hear.

In 1964, as President Johnson considered whether to escalate America's role, CIA reports disputed the domino theory, the main justification for doing so. Instead, they noted there was little evidence to suggest losses in South Vietnam and Laos "would be followed by the rapid, successive communization of the other states of the Far East." After Johnson moved forward with bombings of the North in 1965, reports by the CIA showed the campaign had not affected North Vietnam's ability to wage war.

In 1967 the CIA was again an unpopular truth teller when its estimates of the size of enemy forces exceeded lower, more palatable figures put forward by the military. The same year, another report stated that the risks of defeat might be "more limited and controllable" than was generally believed. After the late 1960s, CIA analyses on such larger issues were few, as the agency focused on tactical intelligence during the war's last years.

This "wanted poster" featuring the likeness of William Colby began appearing in Washington, D.C., in the spring of 1973, shortly after his nomination to head the CIA. An obvious reference to the posters used in Vietnam by the Phoenix program, it stated that Colby was wanted for "crimes in connection with the Phoenix Murder Plan."

verted to the government cause. More than 85 percent of the deaths, however, had occurred in combat actions by regular or paramilitary forces—not in the kind of targeted operations envisioned for Phoenix.

Colby would later cite the North Vietnamese shift from guerrilla to conventional tactics, in their large-scale offensives of 1972 and 1975, as proof of U.S. victory in the war at the grass roots. After the war was over, prominent Communists confirmed that Phoenix, together with the drastic losses of the 1968 Tet offensive, had helped cripple the Vietcong.

Bill Colby left Vietnam for the second time in 1971 to become the agency's executive director-comptroller. In 1973 he was put in charge of clandestine operations; at his own suggestion, however, the traditional—and deliberately vague—title deputy director of "plans" was now replaced by the more straightforward one of deputy director of "operations." Later that year, he became CIA director. Yet the specter of Phoenix followed him to the very top of the CIA. It became, in his words, "a shorthand for all the negative aspects of the war." In the summer of 1973, during his Senate confirmation hearings for CIA director, posters mimicking those circulated by Phoenix appeared around the nation's capital, featuring an unflattering image of Colby and the accusation that he was responsible for the assassinations of 20,000 people.

THE GRAY GHOST OF LANGLEY

During Colby's tenure as CIA director, the agency would be riven by controversy, a result of its widely publicized role in an unpopular war, combined with growing public distrust of government. But from the outset Colby also confronted a longstanding internal problem. For almost two decades, James Jesus Angleton, the former Rome station chief, had been the agency's chief of counterintelligence, responsible for thwarting the work of hostile intelligence services. It was his job to suspect everyone—and he did, to a fault. Angleton had become increasingly convinced, to the point of obsession, that the KGB had recruited CIA officers as "moles" within the agency. For years, his relentless hunt for these alleged, but elusive, moles had ruined careers, frozen the recruitment of Soviet agents, and all but paralyzed the agency's critical Soviet division.

By 1973 Angleton was a 57-year-old veteran of the spy business. Tall and slightly stooped, he was so gaunt that someone remarked he looked "like his ectoplasm has run out." A lover of things English, he favored an old-fashioned black homburg and dark three-piece suits, never removing the jacket when playing poker. Despite his long tenure, he was still such a shadowy presence that colleagues called him the Gray Ghost. Practically unknown to the public, he was a legend in intelligence circles, having developed tactics that even the KGB used.

Angleton shared his views, including a rigid Cold War ideology, with a hard core of CIA staffers and friends from allied intelligence services known

AGE — 48
HEIGHT — 6'1"
WEIGHT — 160
EYES — Hazel
HAIR — Gray

SIGNATURE

FOR IDENTIFICATION ONLY
This is to certify that
JAMES ANGLETON
whose photograph, signature and description appear hereon, is an employee of the United States Government
CENTRAL INTELLIGENCE AGENCY
No. 12319
EXPIRES: 30 Nov. 1967
FOR THE DIRECTOR OF SECURITY

The back of a 1967 CIA identity card shows counterintelligence chief James Angleton several years after he took that position. Even within the CIA, Angleton was such a shadowy figure that one coworker later said he had mistakenly thought another employee was Angleton for more than 15 years.

as the Fundamentalists. They often gathered for lunch with Angleton at a Georgetown restaurant, La Niçoise. There he routinely downed so many bourbons and martinis that his companions marveled he could stand upright. But no matter how much he drank, he was always security conscious, going to his tailor shop next door to borrow its phone for sensitive conversations.

His grand obsession, the Soviet mole hunt, traced its roots in part to the revelation that Kim Philby, a leading British intelligence officer, was a Soviet agent. Philby, who had secretly helped doom CIA-British efforts in Albania, among other things, had been stationed in Washington from 1949 to 1951. While there, he had become Angleton's lunchtime drinking companion. He and Angleton had also held 36 meetings together at the CIA, and Angleton had been thoroughly duped by the charming British officer. Philby's betrayal, wife Cicely Angleton later remarked, "was a bitter blow he never forgot."

It was much later, in 1962, that Angleton's intense suspicions about hidden traitors took on new life, when he met Soviet defector Anatoli Mikhailovich Golitsyn. A squat, 35-year-old former KGB major, Golitsyn had turned up the previous December, seeking asylum, on the doorstep of the CIA station chief in Helsinki. Golitsyn quickly supplied solid information, revealing that a Frenchman in the NATO press department was a Soviet spy. But he also proved abrasive, asking at one point for over $10 million to fund his own organization to subvert the Soviet government. After some months, the CIA's warm welcome cooled. "There was no question in my mind that Golitsyn was paranoid, no question that he was mentally ill," recalled the CIA psychologist who gave the defector a routine mental-health exam.

To Angleton, however, Golitsyn was a soul mate. Apparent schisms in the Communist world, Golitsyn insisted, were merely part of the Soviet master plan to gull the West. The split between Yugoslavia's Tito and the Soviets was a charade, the Chinese-Soviet breakup a sham. A CIA colleague noted that Golitsyn's ideas exerted "a hypnotic effect" on Angleton, who even let Golitsyn carry top-secret files out of CIA headquarters.

Soon Angleton and Golitsyn teamed up to name prominent figures in friendly nations who they alleged were Soviet agents. In 1963 Golitsyn singled out none other than Sir Roger Hollis, the director general of MI-5, Britain's security service. A five-year inquiry found no evidence to support his charge. Golitsyn also asserted that KGB moles had penetrated France's military and counterintelligence services, leading President Kennedy to write a personal letter of warning to French president Charles de Gaulle. When Angleton felt France was moving too slowly, he led CIA and FBI agents in a burglary of the French embassy, where they stole secret ciphers. De Gaulle was so incensed by the interference that he suspended joint intelligence operations.

At the same time, Golitsyn asserted that virtually every Soviet defector besides himself was a false agent, a "dangle" deliberately planted by the Soviets to befuddle the CIA and its allies. The most notorious result of these accusations was a case that began just months after the assassination of President Kennedy on November 22, 1963.

The president and his wife had been riding in a motorcade through downtown Dallas, Texas, when shots rang out. Kennedy was pronounced dead half an hour later at Parkland Memorial Hospital. His apparent murderer, Lee Harvey Oswald, was arrested that day but was slain during a jail transfer two days later, before he could be fully interrogated. Stunned by the assassination, a shocked nation could only speculate as to whether Oswald had truly acted alone or had been encouraged or even paid for his role *(page 125)*. Perhaps the most horrifying possibility of all, in that Cold War era of nuclear brinkmanship, was that the Soviet Union could have been involved. If proven, such a connection could have led to an open confrontation.

It was in this context, then, that the CIA greeted Soviet defector, Yuri Nosenko, a 36-year-old KGB captain who arrived in the United States in February 1964, just three months after Kennedy's death. Lee Harvey Oswald was known to have resided in the Soviet Union from 1959 to 1962; Nosenko told the CIA that he had personally handled Oswald's case. The files showed, he said, that the KGB had routinely monitored Oswald in Minsk, where he worked in a factory, but had no other connection with him. In short, the Soviet Union had nothing to do with the assassination.

The news, if true, was very significant. Yet Nosenko's credibility came under question when he lied about his KGB rank. More important, Golitsyn insisted that Nosenko was not to be trusted. Soon after Nosenko's

KGB defector Anatoli Golitsyn (below, far left) and James Angleton (below, far right) dine with Sir Charles Spry, director of Australian intelligence, and his wife, Lady Spry, at a 1967 conference in Melbourne. Although Golitsyn had actually had little access to critical intelligence, he became Angleton's most trusted source on Soviet penetrations and often traveled with him.

arrival, Golitsyn rushed into Angleton's office. "This is the one I warned you about," he declared. "This is the man who has come to discredit me."

Nosenko's hoped-for new life in the United States soon lapsed into nightmare. Angleton persuaded Tennent "Pete" Bagley, the chief of counterintelligence within the Soviet division, that the newcomer was a plant. A government committee approved locking him up as a "cooperating source," a nonresident without right to an attorney. Angleton's allies blocked Nosenko from testifying about Oswald before the Warren Commission, which was investigating the Kennedy assassination.

In April 1964 the CIA began a "hostile interrogation." For 1,277 days Nosenko was held in 10- by 10-foot rooms without heat, ventilation, or visitors. He was forbidden radio, television, or reading matter. Guards even confiscated a chess set he had improvised from pieces of thread. Pete Bagley and others grilled Nosenko relentlessly, at times keeping him in the same chair for 24 hours without a break. But Nosenko stuck with his story.

In 1967 CIA director Richard Helms intensified an internal review of the case and moved Nosenko into a milder form of detention. Helms was one of Angleton's key supporters within the agency and as deputy director of plans had even approved the defector's harsh treatment. But he also realized the case had crippled further recruitment of Soviet agents. In 1968 the review cleared Nosenko. It also noted that Angleton and his allies, in their zeal, had suppressed at least six solid leads on Soviet agents in Europe. Nosenko now provided leads for nine new cases, and his erstwhile interrogators were transferred out. Much to Angleton's disgust, the CIA even hired the defector as a consultant.

Nosenko aside, however, the principal preoccupation of Angleton's 200-man staff remained the search for traitors within the CIA itself. Here, Golitsyn offered tantalizing hints. He vaguely remembered seeing something in the KGB files about a CIA operative of Slavic background. The person's KGB code name was Sasha; his actual surname probably ended in "ski" and began with the letter *K*. On this fragmentary foundation, Angleton built his mole hunt. Some unlucky CIA officers with names starting with the wrong letter were suspected of being Sasha or his accomplice.

In the summer of 1964, Angleton assigned to the chase a super-secret team called the Special Investigations Group. He gave it the code name Honetol—based on Golitsyn's first name, Anatoli, and the last name of J. Edgar Hoover, the FBI director. Angleton needed Hoover because by law the FBI was responsible within the United States for collaring enemy spies—even those at CIA headquarters. Hoover, however, cooperated only briefly and then pulled out. He so distrusted Golitsyn he refused to allow him inside the FBI.

During the 1960s Angleton's mole hunters listed as suspects more than 40 senior CIA officials in the CIA's Soviet division. Between 100 and 200 CIA officers were investigated. Although perhaps only 15 or so were placed under intense surveillance, all had a two-inch-high *H*, for Honetol, stamped on their personnel folders. In many cases, this brand led to dismissal, transfer, smeared reputation, or resignation. Richard Kovich, the CIA's most experi-

"This is the one I warned you about. This is the man who has come to discredit me."
—Golitsyn, on Yuri Nosenko

Yuri Nosenko

Yuri Nosenko (above), a KGB captain who defected in 1964, struggled to convince the CIA that Kennedy assassin Lee Harvey Oswald had no link to Soviet intelligence—a task made more difficult by Golitsyn's skepticism. Nosenko may have been inspired to defect after a 1957 visit to England gave him a taste of life in the West.

enced recruiter of Soviet agents, found his career abruptly stalled. The same thing happened to Paul Garbler, a Moscow station chief. Years later, both were cleared and, in 1981, awarded $100,000 each in compensation. Serge Peter Karlow of the agency's technical division, a decorated OSS veteran who had lost his leg during a World World II mission, was fired outright. For Karlow, too, decades would pass before vindication; in 1988 he was finally compensated with almost $500,000. Every suspect, in fact, turned out to be innocent—but the damage was done. Said a CIA investigator, "Angleton's attitude emasculated a generation of counterintelligence officers."

The Soviet division was so weakened that in 1968, when Red Army tanks massed on the Czechoslovakian border, the CIA had scarcely any well-placed agents to assess Soviet intents. The new head of the division, Rolfe Kingsley, flew to New York to consult with Golitsyn. There would be no Soviet invasion, Golitsyn told him, explaining that the Czech crisis was simply a Communist ruse. By the time Kingsley returned to Washington, Soviet tanks were rolling into Prague's bloodied streets.

The out-of-control mole hunt also shelved promising information about real spies. The FBI sent Angleton a rich lode of leads about penetrations, obtained from a senior Soviet military intelligence officer code-named Nicknack. The moles in question included a British researcher in missile guidance and a huge ring of spies in France. There were

Oswald, the KGB, and the CIA

Within a week of John F. Kennedy's death, a poll showed that only 29 percent of Americans believed the accused assassin, Lee Harvey Oswald, had acted alone. Nor were those doubts put to rest by the report of the government's Warren Commission, which placed the blame solely on Oswald. One major reason for suspicion was Oswald's own murder two days after the assassination. Equally disturbing for many was Oswald's 1959 defection to the Soviet Union, where he wed Marina Nikolayevna Prusakova (above) before returning to the United States in 1962. Over time, assassination buffs wove that fact and many others into countless conspiracy theories, none ever proved.

In 1999 a groundbreaking book on the KGB's archives, *The Sword and the Shield,* revealed that a few of the conspiracy theories had had some unsuspected encouragement from Soviet intelligence. Tasked with discrediting the U.S. government, the KGB had often tried over the years to link the CIA to the assassination. During the mid-1960s, for example, it made anonymous donations to an American author who believed that parts of the U.S. government had plotted Kennedy's death. Although the writer never knew the source of the money, it helped him continue his work.

Another attempt to implicate the CIA came in 1975, with a letter created by KGB forgers. Dated just before the assassination, the note was supposedly written by Oswald to E. Howard Hunt, the one-time CIA officer best known by the mid-1970s for his role in the Watergate affair. Its words implied, vaguely, that Oswald was waiting to hear from Hunt before proceeding. Handwriting experts later hired by a congressional committee cast doubt on the document, however, and the elaborate ruse had little effect.

20 such leads—all of which later turned out to be fruitful. But believing that Nicknack, too, was a Soviet dangle, Angleton stuffed everything into an office safe, where it lingered for years until acted upon by his successor.

On the world stage, meanwhile, the roster of possible Soviet agents compiled by Angleton and Golitsyn continued to grow. At one time or another it included Golda Meir of Israel, Olof Palme of Sweden, and Willy Brandt of West Germany.

No matter how outrageous Angleton's claims, however, scarcely anyone dared challenge him. An agency institution, he enjoyed the friendship and support of successive directors. He could overwhelm any doubters with a shower of arcane knowledge or abruptly end the conversation by suggesting the matter was too hush-hush to discuss. "If someone was difficult to deal with," recalled one former CIA officer, "Angleton concluded he was under Soviet instructions to frustrate the mole investigation."

By the early 1970s, matters were so surreal that one of Angleton's own investigators surmised that Angleton himself might be the mole, citing the case of Project Honetol, which had wrecked so many CIA careers. (After a careful review the agency dismissed his findings due to a complete lack of hard evidence.) Meanwhile, the counterintelligence czar was showing strain. His chronic insomnia worsened and he was drinking more than ever. Some colleagues feared Angleton had become lost in his own "wilderness of mirrors"—a phrase Angleton himself had borrowed from a favorite poet, T. S. Eliot, to describe how a counterintelligence officer's suspicions resemble images reflected endlessly back and forth.

In an ironic twist, it would not be the mole hunt and its consequences that led to the climax of the Angleton affair. Instead, it would be repercussions from a domestic espionage scandal—uncovered in the new investigative era that followed the Watergate affair—that finally took Langley's Gray Ghost out of the intelligence game.

WATERGATE INTERVENES

In June 1972 a group of burglars broke into Democratic National Headquarters at the Watergate luxury apartment complex in Washington, D.C., immediately raising suspicions about the agency because of the culprits' previous CIA ties. Among the five arrested were James McCord, a former high-ranking CIA security officer, and Eugenio Martinez, a Bay of Pigs veteran with a long record of service to the agency. Later implicated was none other than E. Howard Hunt, the former CIA officer who had participated in both the Guatemala operation and the Bay of Pigs invasion of Cuba. Indeed, the Cuban-Americans arrested at the Watergate were among Hunt's contacts in Miami's exile community.

Facing the storm with characteristic calm was 59-year-old CIA director Richard Helms, who had led the agency since 1966. A specialist in intelligence gathering, Helms had, like so many other ranking agency officers, served in the OSS. Always impeccably dressed, he had an acerbic wit and a very low tolerance for fools. Colleagues considered him the ultimate professional, who knew when to keep his own counsel and was tough, sharp

Although the CIA played no role in the Watergate break-in, four of the five arrested at the scene had previous ties to the agency. James McCord was a former employee of the CIA's Office of Security, and Bernard Barker had been involved in the Bay of Pigs invasion. Like Barker, Eugenio Martinez and Frank Sturgis were from Miami; both had worked informally for the agency in the past. Over time, the reason for the connection emerged; White House operative E. Howard Hunt, no longer with the CIA, had recruited old associates from his agency days.

James McCord

Bernard Barker

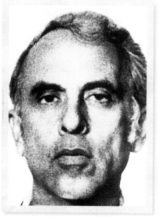

Eugenio Martinez

Frank Sturgis

witted, and doggedly loyal to the CIA. Faced with the incipient Watergate scandal, he did his best to distance the agency from the controversy.

Helms told the FBI and federal prosecutors as little as possible and kept mum about his strong suspicions as to a White House cover-up on Watergate. All the same, he stood up to the White House when it really counted, balking when President Nixon asked the CIA, on shaky national security grounds, to block an FBI investigation of Watergate.

After his 1972 reelection, Nixon wanted more of his loyalists in top positions. This desire extended to the CIA, an agency the president had long viewed as a hostile Washington bureaucracy. Presumably the "disloyalty" Helms had displayed over Watergate was also a concern. In February 1973 Nixon replaced the CIA director, who left to become ambassador to Iran.

Helms's successor was James Schlesinger, the tweedy-looking, 44-year-old former chairman of the Atomic Energy Commission. Schlesinger came to the CIA with a mandate to shake up an agency he himself viewed as overstaffed. Colby, now deputy director of operations, urged his new boss to jettison Jim Angleton. Like many others, he was bothered by Angleton's paranoid world view. Further, Colby and Angleton were longtime foes, and their hostility had deepened during Colby's Vietnam tours. Angleton had blamed Colby for neglecting counterintelligence—with some reason. While Colby ferreted out Vietcong cadres in the countryside, he gave short shrift to some 40,000 enemy loyalists who had infiltrated the South Vietnamese army and government. With his typically strident suspicions, Angleton thought there was blood on Colby's hands, that he had in effect done North Vietnam's bidding. Colby, for his part, found Angleton's complicated theories about a KGB master plan baffling.

Schlesinger did not fire Angleton, but he did dismiss or force into retirement some 1,000 staff members—about seven percent of the CIA. Then, in May 1973, he was named secretary of defense. His replacement as CIA director was Colby, who immediately determined, among other items, "to get rid of Angleton, but in a dignified way."

At first Colby tried to ease Angleton out by whittling his staff and duties. He also terminated Angleton's Lovestone project, which since the 1950s had spied on trade unions at home and abroad. But Angleton still hung on. Then, in December 1974, Colby received a call from Seymour Hersh, a Pulitzer Prize-winning *New York Times* reporter. In the era ushered in by Vietnam and Watergate, a new style of investigative reporting had become increasingly common, and Hersh was among its leading stars. He told Colby that he had unearthed massive and illegal domestic spying by the CIA. The CIA director agreed to meet with him.

In their encounter, Colby confirmed some problematic incidents—including the fact that one project, code-named Chaos, operated by Angleton's counterintelligence shop, had gathered thousands of files on U.S. antiwar protesters and others. Hersh's impending news story was bad news for the agency, but it also gave Colby the impetus to resolve the festering situation in counterintelligence. "This story is going to be tough to handle," he told Angleton. "We've talked about your leaving before. You will now leave,

Former CIA director Richard Helms (standing) is sworn in by North Carolina senator Sam Ervin, chairman of the Senate Watergate Committee, before he testifies on August 2, 1973. During the mid-1970s, Helms was called to testify before different congressional committees more than 30 times.

period." Angleton's supporters would be especially angered by that timing. When the *Times* article was followed by Angleton's resignation, it was widely assumed that Angleton had been primarily responsible for Chaos. In fact, Richard Helms had set it up in 1967 on President Johnson's orders.

In the year following Angleton's departure and the revelations on domestic spying, the CIA endured a harsh and unprecedented public examination *(pages 140-151)*. Colby later wrote of being summoned to Capitol Hill every week, where he faced "hours of hostile questioning." Some of the grist for the hearings was a long, internally generated list of questionable activities that CIA insiders referred to archly as "the family jewels." President Ford, who had become president after Richard Nixon resigned in the wake of Watergate, inadvertently helped leak the most sensitive matter. At a meeting with *New York Times* editors in January 1975, Ford hinted that some controversial actions were still undisclosed. "Like what?" an editor asked. "Like assassination," the president reportedly replied, referring to plots against foreign leaders.

Colby eventually turned over the entire list, which included mind-control experiments, to investigators. The once proud agency was stuck with Senator Church's label—"a rogue elephant rampaging out of control"— regardless of the fact that Church later regretted the phrase. That the White House had ordered many of the CIA's most disturbing acts was generally ignored. Colby's testimony, meanwhile, angered many CIA veterans. Former director Helms commented to an acquaintance, "Colby's not only telling all,

> ## "Colby's not only telling all, he's telling more than all."
>
> —Richard Helms, reported comment on William Colby

> ## "The agency's survival could only come from understanding, not hostility, built on knowledge, not faith."
>
> —William Colby

he's telling more than all." Friends of the recently retired Angleton remarked that Colby's behavior was "consistent" with that of a Soviet mole.

The director himself, however, felt that he had no alternative. The mid-1970s were a time of government scandals and antiwar sentiment, of an increasingly powerful Congress and a newly aggressive press. Colby was convinced his agency could be saved only by talking openly about its successes and failings. Helms had once said, "The nation must to a degree take it on faith that we too are honorable men devoted to her service." Colby saw the agency as honorable as well, but in the climate of the mid-1970s, he felt that the CIA's survival depended on "knowledge, not faith."

To the White House, however, he was expendable. The end came in the fall of 1975 after Colby dropped another bombshell in congressional testimony. An employee had discovered in a CIA vault possible assassination tools: quantities of shellfish toxin, cobra venom, and a dart gun. The new disclosure, in Colby's words, "blew the roof off."

He was summoned to the White House on Sunday morning, November 2, 1975. A presidential election was in the offing, and several changes were under way. President Ford wanted a fresh face for the CIA, longtime Republican Party leader George Bush, then the ranking U.S. diplomat to China. Bush—who would later become the first CIA director to rise to vice president and then president of the United States—had none of the baggage Colby carried from the ordeal of the hearings, and so he was better positioned to help the agency recover from a troubled time. For Colby, however, the battle was over. The meeting in the Oval Office "lasted about fifteen minutes," he later wrote, "and in those fifteen minutes my thirty-year career as an intelligence officer had been brought abruptly to an end."

Idaho senator Frank Church (at left), chairman of the Senate select committee on intelligence, confers with CIA director William Colby prior to committee questioning in September 1975.

AIR AMERICA: CIA LINCHPIN IN LAOS

I was subjected to greater hazard during my time with Air America than at any time I was in combat in any of the three wars I was in," recalled veteran pilot Bob Dawson. "And I was a fighter pilot." The hazards to which he referred faced every pilot who worked for Air America, the CIA-owned flight charter company. Operating in Southeast Asia since 1950—the year the CIA first purchased the firm, then known as Civil Air Transport—Air America became the linchpin of the CIA-backed war in Laos in the 1960s and early 1970s.

Supplying arms and ammunition, transporting troops, and dropping food to refugees, pilots for Air America flew as many as 68 missions a day—much of the time in the cross hairs of Communist gunners. "Every landing, every takeoff, every departure and every letdown and every flight was a risk," Dawson recalled, using the pilots' term *letdown* for landing. A privately owned, civilian company on paper, Air America was contracted for work by the U.S. Agency for International Development (AID) and the State Department, and even by commercial clients. Drawn to the job by high salaries and high adventure, its airplane pilots, like Dawson, were typically veterans of World War II and Korea; the younger men were often helicopter pilots with prior service in South Vietnam.

After a successful delivery, Air America helicopter pilot Fred Sass (right foreground) poses with Vang Pao, leader of irregular Hmong forces fighting the Pathet Lao and North Vietnamese.

Air America pilot Joseph Butler plays with a pet panther outside his quarters in Thailand, where the airline maintained extensive facilities to support operations in Laos.

From the cockpit of his plane, Butler took this photo of the Laotian countryside, a peaceful scene whose beauty belies the war raging below.

Butler's Caribou cargo plane stands beside a destroyed C-130 transport on the runway at Kontum, South Vietnam. Pilots "usually kept the engines running" at Kontum, he wrote, because of enemy mortar fire.

PILOT IN A SECRET WAR

Typical of the seasoned pilots who flew for Air America, Joseph Butler was a former U.S. Air Force pilot who had flown a total of 138 combat missions in World War II and in Korea, where he shot down a Chinese MiG-15. Like many flyers, he also kept scrapbooks of his experiences in the Laos war. The resulting images and memorabilia, some of which are shown here, offer a look at the life of an Air America pilot, both on and off duty.

Butler loved to fly; his résumé proudly states, "Never turned down a flight, no matter the destination, weekends, or weather." He maintained a home in Saigon with his wife but spent much of his time at a residence in Bangkok, Thailand, ready for the next mission. He survived every one and later returned to the United States.

Like all Air America pilots, Butler carried an ID card and a Laotian pilot's license, which lists his qualifications. His heavy silver ID bracelet bears the airline's insignia.

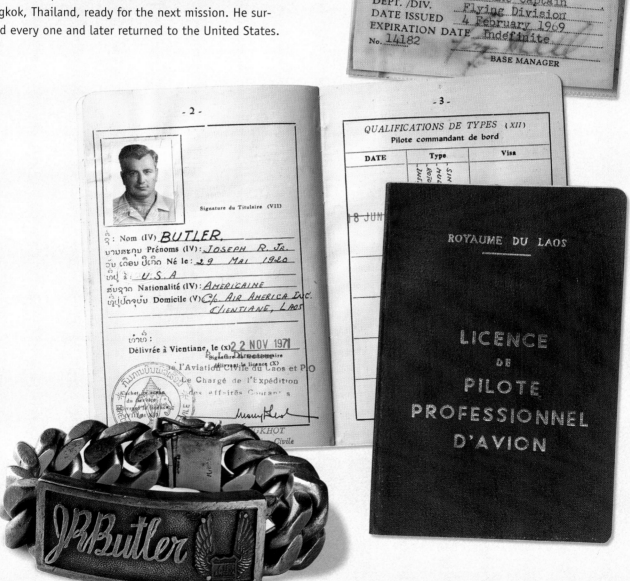

On a mountainside overlooking the Plain of Jars, an Air America helicopter delivers supplies to Hmong fighters during a 1969 offensive against the Pathet Lao and North Vietnamese. Pilots and fighters sometimes had to use the emergency codes below to communicate.

At right, an Air America kicker sends a pallet of rice out of the rear of a cargo plane as earlier loads plummet toward an isolated Hmong village.

MOVING MEN AND SUPPLIES

In early 1972 a young CIA case officer arrived in Laos. Eager to reach his unit, he asked an Air America chopper pilot, "Frenchy" Smith, to take him to a remote hilltop currently taking fire. Frenchy agreed, but warned, "I will be skids down for only three seconds on that pad," just enough time for the officer to jump out before the chopper took off. As the helicopter approached the mountaintop, it hovered to one side of the landing pad so a crewman could lean out the door and help guide the pilot to a safe landing. Thinking the copter had already landed, the CIA officer jumped out, fell 50 feet, and rolled partway down the mountainside, all without serious injury. Frenchy, as the story goes, asked, "Where'd that sumbitch go?"

Fortunately, Air America pilots usually delivered their cargo without such mishaps. Irregular warfare like that in Laos often requires the quick movement of troops, and since the rugged terrain made ground transport impractical, airplanes and helicopters were the only means at hand. With its ability to land in tight places, the helicopter was an excellent means of transporting small numbers of men and supplies. Multiengine airplanes worked better for larger groups and much heavier loads of supplies and were more practical for the transport of food.

Because the war prevented the hill tribes from farming or tending livestock, their survival depended on refugee assistance. The AID provided rice and livestock—pigs, in particular—for the Hmong people and contracted with Air America to deliver it. "It gave you a good feeling to go to some little mountain peak and drop 12,000 pounds of rice almost into their cooking pot," one pilot recalled.

Although the cargo planes would deliver food to landing strips when possible, airdrops were often necessary to supply those villages located in inaccessible regions. From an altitude of 800 to 900 feet, a crewman known as a kicker pushed the supplies out the plane. The villagers would be waiting for the bags of food to fall from the sky, and if some broke open, there would often be a mad scramble to claim the contents before the village pigs beat them to it. Pigs too were sometimes part of the supply drops, their descent toward earth slowed by parachute.

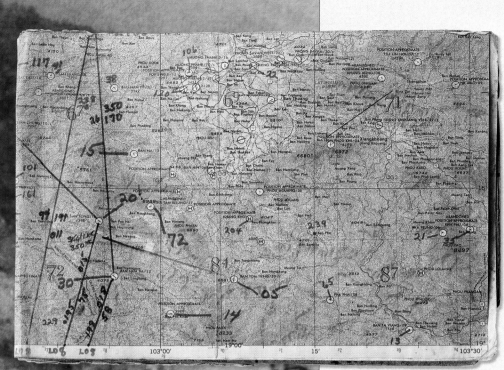

On a pilot's map of the Plain of Jars and surrounding mountains (left), landing strips are identified by circles; slashes in the circles indicate runway lengths and orientations. The handwritten red numbers identify landing strips; for example, Long Tieng, headquarters for Hmong fighters in northeast Laos, is labeled 30.

"THE RAGGED EDGE OF NOTHING"

Carved into the sides and tops of mountains, the landing strips used by Air America in Laos ranged in length from just 300 to 600 feet and were as likely to be slightly curved as they were to have an upgrade of 45 degrees. "Landing up the mountain is the easiest once you have become psychologically adjusted," said one pilot; gravity stopped the plane "even without a reverse, brakes or anything else."

The turboprop PC-6 Pilatus Porter, designed by Swiss engineers to operate in the Alps, was ideally suited to these conditions. Known as a short takeoff and landing (STOL) aircraft, it could fly as slowly as 40 miles an hour, a necessity when landing on short runways. In certain conditions, an STOL aircraft could land in 75 feet, said Air America senior pilot George Calhoun, "if you want to go all out and operate the bird on the ragged edge of nothing."

If the short airstrips were a hazard, so were the flying conditions. Pilots claimed there were only three: fog, wind, and rain. When winds were treacherous or visibility dropped, a pilot could easily fly into the side of a mountain, something the crews called "rock-filled clouds."

At left, a Pilatus Porter airplane is unloaded after a mountaintop landing. A rise at one end of this airstrip made takeoffs easier.

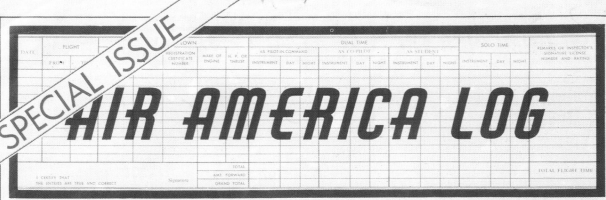

AIR AMERICA LOG

AIR AMERICA'S LAOS AIRLIFT

At the request of and with the assistance of the U. S. Agency for International Development Laos, Air America's Lao headquarters at Wattay Airport, Vientiane, the administrative capital of Laos, was responsible for three mass air evacuations of North Lao (mostly of the various Meo tribes) from insecure areas of North Central Laos to more secure villages. The three airlifts took place between January and April, 1970.

In the first two airlifts, 100 percent of the flight crews involved were Air America's; in the third airlift, AAM supplied a majority of the airlift with Company STOL-type aircraft.

In the first refugee movement, in January, some 5,000 North Lao tribespeople were airlifted from Moung Soui to Ban Xon (Air America Log, Vol. IV. No. 2).

In the second airlift — the most massive of the movements — 16,720 refugees were whisked from the Plaines des Jarres to Ban Keun and Vientiane. This airlift was accomplished in six days in February.

The third evacuation, which occured in April, involved moving some 3,500 refugees from Phou Sam Soun to Phu Cum in several days; in some cases Phou Sam Soun was under attack while the airlift was being accomplished. There were no casualties to Air America personnel nor damage to Company aircraft engaged in the operation.

Air America was commended by the customer for its Quick Reaction Capacity (QRC) during these evacuations.

Types of planes used in the various airlifts were: C-130s bailed to USAID, C-123Ks, C-7As, and PC-6Cs.

NOTE: Because of Air America's outstanding performance in these vital airlifts, we are publishing this first Special Issue of the AAM LOG which shows these evacuations on pages 1 through 7 plus page 12.

Pages 8 and 9 show Sam Thong, an important USAID logistics base 77 miles north of Vientiane, which was temporarily taken by hostile forces in late March.

Pages 10 and 11 show Ban Xon, the USAID base 58 miles north of Vientiane, to which many of Sam Thong's inhabitants were evacuated. (Two AAM Lao Utilitymen demonstrated their loyalty by walking from Sam Thong to Ban Xon—some 20 miles).

Pix by: J. A. Cunningham, BM/VTE; Ed Ulrich, CP/L; B.F. Coleman, Captain/VTE; G.L. Christian, DPRA/TPE—ED.

A blurred C-130 streaks past camera as it carries a load of refugees from the Plaine des Jarres.

A young refugee and baby await evacuation from the Plaine des Jarres.

An old refugee is helped to an evacuation aircraft at the Plaine des Jarres.

Five women, carrying their worldly possessions, walk to airlift site at the Plaine des Jarres.

"AIR AMERICA'S MOTTO: 'ANYTHING, ANYTIME, ANYWHERE—PROFESSIONALLY'"

*This cover page of a special is-
sue of Air America Log (left),
an internal periodical aimed
mainly at employees, high-
lights the evacuation of thousands of Laotian civilians
from the war zone in 1970.*

*At right, former Air America
pilots depart from the airfield
at Long Tieng in a C-46,
owned by the Continental Air
Service, in May 1975.*

FLIGHTS TO SAFETY

Flying in a country ravaged by war, Air America pilots
and crews were sometimes sent to perform mercy flights,
ranging from the evacuation of wounded Hmong soldiers
to the airlift of thousands of civilians. Over the course of
two years, from 1968 to 1970, more than 37,000 refugees
were evacuated, many with their livestock in tow.

Each airlift was a model of efficiency—in February
1970, nearly 17,000 Hmong civilians were flown to safety
in just one week. To assist on this massive operation,
U.S. Air Force crews flew C-130 transports into the
Hmong base at Long Tieng and turned the aircraft over
to Air America pilots.

Most other flights were simply a day's work to the
pilots, but the refugees' plight troubled more than one
crewman. "We moved them from one Communist taken-
over village to another," remembered one pilot. "You got
to feel real sorry for the people." The aircraft
would land and the refugees "would be herded together like cattle with their dogs and
sick kids," he continued. "We'd run them
into the plane until they were so
squashed together we couldn't close
the doors."

As the course of the war in Laos turned, Air America's
operations also drew to a close. In 1972, CIA director
Richard Helms ordered the agency to begin plans to
divest itself of Air America; it would exist only until the
end of the war in southeast Asia.

In early 1973 a cease-fire took effect in Laos. By the
end of the year, three-quarters of Air America's aircraft
had been eliminated from service and the rest were
based in Thailand. The last aircraft flew out of Laos on
June 3, 1974.

Some former Air America pilots remained behind, however, and continued to fly with another air charter company, Continental Air Service, which was owned by Continental Airlines *(above)*. Among the last missions of these
veterans was the rescue of Hmong civilians endangered
by the Pathet Lao takeover of Laos in 1975. For the
few pilots who stayed with Air America, the
fall of Saigon, and some final, frenzied
evacuation flights out of that city,
closed the book on America's
involvement in Southeast Asia—
and on Air America, which officially
ceased all operations in June 1976.

~~TOP SECRET~~

May 1963

A FLOOD OF REVELATIONS

It began with a leak, when highly classified information about the CIA's involvement in illegal domestic spying reached investigative reporter Seymour Hersh. Then on December 22, 1974, Hersh's report was splashed across the front page of the *New York Times (page 142)* and the floodgates opened.

Hoping to quell public suspicion without disclosing secrets vital to American security, President Gerald Ford appointed his vice president, Nelson Rockefeller, to head a commission on CIA activities inside the U.S. But Congress quickly launched several of its own, far broader, inquiries. Chief among them was an investigation by the Senate's select committee on intelligence, led by Frank Church, which focused on CIA actions both at home and abroad. Most of the resulting revelations were already contained in the CIA's own so-called family jewels memo, a long list of questionable activities compiled by agency staff in 1973 at the request of then-CIA director James Schlesinger.

During the next several months, emerging stories of incidents large and small suggested that the CIA had gone far beyond domestic spying. The agency had also plotted assassinations and conducted drug experiments on unwitting victims. New details about its work in toppling some foreign governments also caused concern. Even though many of the newly uncovered actions did not violate the law and often had been conducted at the direct request of the White House, the range of revelations made conspiracy theorists of Americans already reeling from the Watergate scandal. For the next year and more, the secretive government agency would be thrust into the glare of public scrutiny.

~~TOP SECRET~~

SPYING ON THE PEOPLE

Hersh's *New York Times* exposé pulled no punches. The CIA, he claimed, had "conducted a massive, illegal domestic intelligence operation during the Nixon administration against the antiwar movement and other dissident groups in the United States," engaged in "break-ins, wiretapping and the surreptitious inspection of mail," and kept "intelligence files on at least 10,000 American citizens." If the allegations were true, the CIA was violating the 1947 act that created it, which specifically barred it from most actions within the United States, denying it "police, subpoena, law enforcement powers or internal security functions."

Before the story broke, CIA director William Colby met with Hersh in an effort to contain the damage. In that meeting and later before the investigating committees, Colby confirmed the gist of what Hersh had unearthed but added that all questionable activities had been terminated by 1973. Denying that they amounted to a "massive, illegal" operation, he described them merely as "missteps."

Americans were in no mood to accept this and similar characterizations. As disclosed in the family jewels memo and subsequent inquiries, domestic spying by the CIA

LYNDON JOHNSON TOLD THE CIA TO INVESTIGATE ANTIWAR PROTESTERS IN 1967, THE YEAR OF THE DEMONSTRATION SHOWN HERE.

The newspaper clipping at the top of the page reads:

was hardly restricted to the Nixon years. It had gotten under way as long ago as 1952, when the CIA began monitoring mail moving between the United States and the Soviet Union in hopes of learning more about events behind the Iron Curtain and of fingering Americans who might be passing information to the Soviets; a similar program handled mail to and from mainland China. Although the operation yielded meager results, by the time it ended in 1973 a whopping 2.7 million envelopes had passed under the CIA's lens; more than 200,000 were actually opened, in clear violation of federal statutes.

In its domestic intelligence forays, as in most of its activities, the CIA was hardly playing a lone hand; much of its direction came

from the White House. In 1967 another domestic operation was launched at the insistence of President Lyndon Johnson. The project, later code-named Chaos, grew out of Johnson's stubborn conviction that student antiwar demonstrations were funded by North Vietnam and other Communist nations. A study by the CIA found

no such links, but then-director Richard Helms did as Johnson requested anyway. The CIA, as Helms later put it, was one of "the president's bag of tools."

Helms established a special unit in James Angleton's counterintelligence division to spy on dissidents and the antiwar press. Angleton chose CIA officer Richard Ober to lead the Chaos project, instructing

FORMER COUNTERINTELLIGENCE CHIEF JAMES ANGLETON, WHOSE OFFICE HANDLED THE CHAOS PROGRAM, TESTIFIES BEFORE THE CHURCH COMMITTEE IN 1975.

Ober to give it the highest priority, to keep it top secret, and to state, if necessary, that Chaos was justified because its targets received "foreign funding." Ober was alarmed. "I had a bear by the tail," he later testified before the Rockefeller Commission. He was convinced, he added, that the project would eventually be uncovered, with "explosive results."

While files accumulated on thousands of American dissidents, Chaos gathered momentum during the Nixon presidency that followed, even though CIA analysts repeatedly concluded that protest activity was free of foreign influence and hence should be off-limits to agency probing. By 1971 the Chaos staff had burgeoned from two full-time professionals to 54. Colby later testified that "about a dozen" of these agents had infiltrated protest groups. While the sole purpose, he said, was to gain "access to foreign circles" with which the dissidents might be linked, he acknowledged that reports solely on their domestic activities had been submitted to the CIA.

As more instances of domestic spying poured out, Americans were appalled to learn that the CIA was keeping tabs not only on dissidents but also on journalists and a few members of Congress. Among the latter was Congresswoman Bella Abzug.

Abzug, as it happened, chaired the House Subcommittee on Government Information and Individual Rights. Bristling over the discovery that the CIA had had its sights trained on her for more than 20 years, in March 1975 the outspoken Abzug hauled Colby in to testify. Their exchange fully dramatized the political damage caused by what the director called simple missteps. Wearing her signature hat and holding up her CIA dossier in full view of the cameras, Abzug declared, "To find myself in your files is outrageous!" The folder, begun in 1953, contained what she called a heap of "trivia and inaccurate information." It included letters written to the Soviet government when she was an attorney representing clients in estate cases and information on her representation of a client before the House Committee on Un-American Activities. More

controversial were details of her meeting in Paris in 1972 with delegates from the Provisional Revolutionary Government of South Vietnam, a puppet government created by North Vietnam.

In the face of her fiery attack, an unsettled Colby drummed his fingers on the witness table and finally conceded that in compiling such files on private citizens, the CIA had engaged in intelligence overkill. In Abzug's eyes it was much worse, "a violation of privacy," she said, as well as of "individual constitutional rights and the law." Put on the spot, the director promised to end the CIA's "questionable" surveillance of U.S. citizens.

Three months later, portions of the Ford administration's Rockefeller Commission report were made public. This report, too, condemned many of the agency's domestic ventures and labeled some of them "plainly unlawful." At the same time, it concluded that the majority complied with statutory requirements. These cautious conclusions failed to answer the public's concerns. Americans wanted further disclosures. Unwilling to have more spilled, President Ford felt it sufficient to implement several commission recommendations, putting an end to wiretaps and mail opening, and destroying some Chaos files. It would be up to the congressional committees to eke out more of the truth about CIA misdeeds beyond the commission's limited domestic-spying mandate.

DIRTY TRICKS IN CHILE

PRESIDENT SALVADOR ALLENDE, TARGET OF A LONGSTANDING CIA CAMPAIGN, SAVORS HIS ELECTION AS PRESIDENT OF CHILE IN 1970.

ON A VISIT TO AGENCY HEADQUARTERS, RICHARD NIXON GREETS CIA DIRECTOR RICHARD HELMS; NIXON LATER ORDERED HELMS'S AGENCY TO WORK AGAINST ALLENDE IN CHILE.

One subject area of great concern to the Church Committee was a topic that the CIA desperately wanted to keep under wraps: covert actions aimed at influencing political events abroad. This practice dated back to the agency's earliest days and the Italian election of 1948. For much of the public in 1975, however, the details of CIA meddling in foreign affairs came as a shock. Colby agreed to submit information on interventions in six different countries on the condition that only one be made public. And so, in its public hearings, the committee focused its attention on covert action in Chile, details of which had already leaked to the press.

The committee learned that between 1963 and 1973, under White House direction, the CIA had lavished some $13 million on a campaign to set the course of politics in South America's oldest democracy. During Chile's 1964 presidential election, the agency had poured funds into Eduardo Frei's Christian Democratic Party, underwriting at least half of its expenditures, and waged a massive propaganda campaign to blacken the reputation of Frei's opponent, self-professed Marxist Salvador Allende Gossens. In part because of this aid, Frei won a majority.

In 1970 Allende ran again, and the CIA funneled to his opponents money from several Chilean-based U.S. companies sweating over Allende's desire to nationalize industry. International Telephone and Telegraph Corporation alone slipped $350,000 to the most conservative candidate in the three-way race. CIA operatives also produced scores of anti-Allende broadcasts, editorials, cartoons, and street posters—so many, in fact, that the State Department had to be repeatedly tipped off in order not to be confused by false or distorted reports planted by the CIA.

The CIA's efforts became more sinister and entangled after Allende led the three-way balloting with 36 percent of the vote. President Nixon now feared an Allende victory could spread Communism elsewhere in Latin America. With the Chilean Congress poised to choose between Allende and a conservative runner-up, CIA director Richard Helms, at Nixon's express order, launched a hypersecret operation to kindle a military coup. When Chilean army chief General René Schneider opposed military intervention, the CIA began talks with factions plotting to assassinate

GENERAL AUGUSTO PINOCHET, WHO LAUNCHED A REIGN OF TERROR AGAINST PERCEIVED OPPONENTS, ATTENDS MASS ON THE DAY OF HIS 1973 COUP.

Schneider. On October 22, 1970, he was cut down by one of these groups. But after the Chilean Congress voted Allende in, the army made no further effort to stop him from taking office on November 3.

The White House then requested the CIA to work to unseat the new president, primarily by destabilizing the economy. Soon Chile was awash in laundered CIA money. The nation's largest newspaper, *El Mercurio,* received $1.5 million to

beat its anti-Allende drums; CIA funds found their way into the hands of truckers whose strikes helped cripple the economy; and other laborers were paid to fumble in their jobs, helping to bring Chile's economic crisis to a head. Meanwhile, the CIA exploited its ties with Chilean army officers, stirring them up with false stories about left-wing plots.

The long-awaited military coup finally took place in September 1973, although, as the Church Committee concluded, without CIA involvement. During the hoopla of an independence day parade, General Augusto Pinochet Ugarte's forces wrested control of the government from Allende. In the ensuing confusion, Allende

died, reportedly by his own hand. Within days, Pinochet launched a campaign of severe repression against dissidents. Between 1973 and 1978, some 3,000 Chileans died or disappeared at the hands of his brutal forces; tens of thousands were detained and many tortured.

In its final report of April 26, 1976, the Church Committee recommended a statute outlawing both the subversion of democratic governments and clandestine support for repressive regimes, but the proposal did not become law. The Senate and the House did, however, each set up a permanent intelligence oversight committee. Congressional hearings would henceforth become a routine part of agency life.

ESCORTED BY ARMED GUARDS, PRESIDENT ALLENDE *(CENTER, IN GLASSES)* WATCHES REBEL PLANES FLY OVERHEAD DURING THE 1973 COUP.

TAKING AIM AT FIDEL CASTRO

Perhaps the most sensational topic taken on by the Church Committee was that of political assassination. Day after day, the committee sorted through allegations of planned political murders at hearings that filled America's public discourse with the seamy details of a real-life James Bond world.

The committee focused on plots to murder three leading political figures. Late in 1960 the CIA had targeted socialist Patrice Lumumba, the first leader of the newly independent Congo. The agency ordered its station chief in Léopoldville to arrange for Lumumba's disposal by means of a lethal biological agent prepared by CIA scientists. But local foes got to Lumumba first, killing him in early 1961. A few months later, CIA agents in the Dominican Republic supplied a few small arms to local conspirators already planning to assassinate dictator Rafael Trujillo Molina. The deed was done in May 1961—possibly with pistols provided by the CIA.

The CIA's longest-running campaign to assassinate a foreign ruler, however, was waged against Cuba's Fidel Castro. The effort began in 1960, when Eisenhower was still president, and continued for five years under Kennedy and Johnson. By the Church Committee's count, at least eight plots were cooked up, ranging from bungling to bizarre. One idea was to load Castro's favorite cigars with poison. Cuba's leader also harbored a passion for

FIDEL CASTRO'S PASSION FOR SCUBA DIVING INSPIRED SEVERAL CIA DEVICES INTENDED TO BRING ABOUT HIS DEMISE, INCLUDING A POISONED WET SUIT AND A SEASHELL RIGGED WITH EXPLOSIVES.

scuba diving, and a scheme was hatched to plant explosives near where Castro liked to dive. In still another scheme, the CIA briefly became a bedfellow of the Mafia. In late 1960 a CIA case officer got in touch with former FBI agent Robert Maheu about the Castro problem. Maheu brought in veteran mob lieutenant John Rosselli, who in turn enlisted Chicago mafia chief Sam Giancana and Florida crime boss Santos Trafficante, whose Havana gambling interests

had been seized by Castro. The CIA offered the men $150,000 if the racketeers took out Castro, preferably before or during the Bay of Pigs invasion it was planning.

Since a hit man probably could not survive a gangland-style shooting in Cuba, the agency set its technical staff to work preparing pills carrying a deadly toxin. Rosselli

THE CASTRO PLOT MADE STRANGE ASSOCIATES OF JOHN KENNEDY, HERE WITH BROTHER ROBERT, AND MOB FIGURE SAM GIANCANA (INSET).

then smuggled the pills to Castro's private secretary, Juan Orta Cordova, who was to doctor the leader's drink. Apparently the would-be assassin lost his access to Castro before the job could be finished, and another plot collapsed.

After the Bay of Pigs fiasco, the CIA came under intensified pressure from President Kennedy and his brother, Attorney General Robert Kennedy, to topple the Castro regime. The agency responded in late 1961 with a project called Mongoose. The main thrust of Mongoose was to depose Castro indirectly, through a program of economic sabotage and paramilitary harassment. But several new assassination plots accompanied Mongoose as well. One high-level CIA effort was made to recruit a disaffected major in the Cuban army, Rolando Cubela, as the assassin. Cubela was in close contact with Castro and felt that he had betrayed the revolution. To do the job, the CIA supplied Cubela with a ballpoint pen designed to inject Castro with poison. Distinctly

unimpressed, the major told his case officer that surely the agency could recommend a "more sophisticated" scheme.

No plot was going to solve the CIA's real problem: gaining access to Castro without exposing its involvement. After the Kennedy assassination in November 1963, the Cubela plot lost steam, and by 1965 the CIA dropped its attempts to engineer the Cuban leader's demise.

For all the stranger-than-fiction details it uncovered, however, the Church Committee cleared the CIA of blame for any actual assassination. As CBS news correspondent Daniel Schorr later reported, "no foreign ruler was directly killed by the CIA, but it wasn't for want of trying." At the time of the hearings, the question of just who had authorized the plots to kill Castro bedeviled the committee. Although CIA officials were tight-lipped on the subject, few observers believed the agency would have gone ahead without some direction from the White House. To prevent future in-

cidents of the same type, President Ford—who had been shocked on first hearing news of CIA assassination plots—signed an executive order in 1976 forbidding federal employees to engage in such activity.

Inevitably, questions also later arose about the link between John Kennedy's apparent role in pressing for Castro's removal and the president's own assassination, especially since the CIA's anti-Castro activities were not well explored by the Warren Commission set up to investigate Kennedy's death. Some conspiracy theorists asked whether Castro, or his supporters, might have been behind the killing. The Mafia connection also stoked rampant speculation, especially when Giancana was shot in the head in June 1975, days before Rosselli testified before the Church Committee; the committee had planned to question Giancana as well.

In later years, however, newly released records suggested that the CIA's motive in keeping evidence from the Warren Commission was much simpler than the tortured motives suggested by all of this. With the advantage of hindsight, it appeared that after the death of President Kennedy, those involved had simply wanted the Castro assassination plots kept hush-hush.

AT THE HEARINGS, MEDIA ATTENTION FOCUSED ON EXOTIC WEAPONS, INCLUDING A MYSTERIOUS CIA DART GUN WIELDED HERE BY ARIZONA SENATOR BARRY GOLDWATER, AS MARYLAND'S SENATOR MATHIAS LOOKS ON.

MIND CONTROL'S HAUNTING SPECTER

One potentially explosive revelation about the CIA received only passing mention by the Rockefeller Commission: the fact that the agency had slipped a "behavior-influencing drug" to an unnamed employee of the U.S. Army, who later plunged to his death from the window of a New York hotel. Little information about the incident was available; most records of the CIA's mind-control experiments had been destroyed. After the commission's report came out, however, details began to emerge through the efforts of congressional committees and investigative journalist and author John Marks, who used the Freedom of Information Act to gain access to documents that had escaped the CIA shredder.

The CIA had become interested in mind control in the early 1950s, when stories circulated about a new science called brainwashing allegedly being practiced in China, eastern Europe, the Soviet Union, and Korea. In response, the CIA set out to investigate ways of mastering the human will. Under a program known as MK Ultra, the agency both conducted its own experiments and secretly funneled millions of research dollars to universities, research centers, prisons, and mental hospitals. Over the years human guinea pigs—both volunteers and unwitting subjects—were exposed to assaults on the psyche ranging from hypnosis to mind-altering drugs to sensory deprivation, electroshock, and psychological harassment.

The man chosen to lead MK Ultra was Sidney Gottlieb, a well-liked agency chemist who lived in the country and milked goats each morning before heading off to his CIA laboratory.

Gottlieb was particularly intrigued by a then-little-known synthetic substance called lysergic acid diethylamide, or LSD. Discovered during the war by a Swiss research chemist, LSD was still relatively obscure in the early 1950s, when MK Ultra began. Its apparent ability to alter consciousness fascinated Gottlieb. Colorless, odorless, and tasteless, the drug was easy to slip to subjects in food or drink.

The CIA's most notorious experiment with LSD took place at a government meeting. One of the unwitting subjects on that occasion was Frank Olson, a 43-year-old biochemist who worked at the U.S. Army's biological research center at Fort Detrick, Maryland. Specializing in germ warfare, the center included a "special operations" group that collaborated closely with CIA scientists in developing chemical and biological agents for use in covert action, including assassination.

testimony by Olson's boss, Lieutenant Colonel Vincent Ruwet, the biochemist was still agitated. On his return home, he seemed unusually withdrawn. "Something was terribly wrong," his wife, Alice, later recalled. "The entire weekend he was very melancholy and talked about a mistake he had made."

Over the coming days Olson grew worse, persisting in the notion that he had done something wrong. Alarmed, Ruwet and Gottlieb's deputy, Robert Lashbrook, hustled Olson to New York to talk with Dr. Harold Abramson, an immunologist with no formal psychiatric training who had a high-level security clearance. By the time Abramson met his patient, Olson no longer trusted Ruwet and Lashbrook. The CIA, he said, was out to get him. That was on the Tuesday before Thanksgiving; on Thursday morning, with Abramson's permission, Olson and his escorts took a plane back to Maryland for the holiday. But before reaching home, Olson told Ruwet he was too unstrung to face his family. So back to New York Olson flew—this time with Lashbrook alone. Abramson saw Olson again, concluded that he was psychotic, and recommended hospitalization.

Friday night Olson and Lashbrook booked a room in New York's Statler Hotel. Hours later, Olson's body lay on the sidewalk, 13 stories below. According to the account the CIA first gave Olson's family, Lashbrook woke up to witness Olson crashing through the window glass. Lashbrook's own written report said he woke up

Olson was a high-ranking member of the special operations team.

In November 1953 some top men from the CIA's technical staff and the Fort Detrick special operations unit, including Sidney Gottlieb and Frank Olson, met for a retreat at a lodge in the remote wooded highlands of western Maryland. After dinner on November 19, Olson and several others were served an after-dinner round of Cointreau. About 20 minutes later, Gottlieb told them he had laced the liqueur with LSD. The discussion became increasingly confused and soon ended. By the next morning, according to later

to find the window shattered and Olson gone.

In the immediate aftermath, the CIA presented the incident as the suicide of a man who had struggled with depression. Neither the police nor the Olson family was told about the spiked Cointreau. Then, 22 years later, the Rockefeller Commission issued its findings—and there it was, that brief mention of a nameless, drug-induced suicide that soon turned out to be Frank Olson. Within a month, President Ford invited Olson's widow and her three children to the White House and apologized for an action he called "inexcusable and unforgivable." The family was given certain relevant CIA documents and $750,000 in compensation.

But the matter continued to haunt some in the Olson family. Frank's son Eric, a clinical psychologist, doubted that a single dose of LSD could have driven his stable, easygoing father to take his own life nine days later. In 1994, the year after Alice Olson passed away,

Frank Olson's body was exhumed and studied by a team of forensic scientists. The results included evidence of an apparent blow to the head and a lack of facial lacerations from the window glass. Already suspicious, Eric Olson now speculated that his father had been killed by the CIA, perhaps because

his intake of LSD, rather than triggering psychosis, had loosened his tongue, perhaps leading him to reveal ugly secrets related to biological weapons research.

The CIA and many historians of the agency continued to believe that Olson's death was not a homicide, but rather the unintended result of a careless, shamefully reckless experiment. Yet the new findings did persuade the New York district attorney to open a homicide investigation in September 1997. That investigation was still going on less than two years later, when Sidney Gottlieb, a key witness, passed away. For his family, the final word on Frank Olson's death would remain elusive.

CIA DIRECTOR ALLEN DULLES WROTE THIS MILD REBUKE TO GOTTLIEB BUT KEPT IT OUT OF HIS PERSONNEL FILE.

SECRET

CENTRAL INTELLIGENCE AGENCY

WASHINGTON 25, D. C.

OFFICE OF THE DIRECTOR

FEB 10 1954

PERSONAL

Dr. Sidney Gottlieb
Chief, Chemical Division
Technical Services Staff

Dear Dr. Gottlieb:

I have personally reviewed the files from your office concerning the use of a drug on an unwitting group of individuals. In recommending the unwitting application of the drug to your superior, you apparently did not give sufficient emphasis to the necessity for medical collaboration and for proper consideration of the rights of the individual to whom it was being administered. This is to inform you that it is my opinion that you exercised poor judgment in this case.

Sincerely,

Allen W. Dulles

A COVER BLOWN

As the CIA came under scrutiny in the 1970s, certain publications began revealing the identities of CIA officers overseas in hopes that the agency would cease its interventions abroad. In 1975, the magazine *Counterspy* issued a list that included the name Richard Welch, inaccurately placing him in Peru; he was now station chief in Athens. On November 25, 1975, the *Athens News* ran a letter identifying Welch as a CIA officer and giving his address. Four weeks later, as he returned from a Christmas party, he was shot dead. Greek terrorists later claimed responsibility.

While genuinely shocked, the CIA and the White House took the opportunity to counter bad press about the CIA by making a martyr of the slain officer. His body was flown home to a hero's welcome,

and President Ford attended the funeral. The same horse-drawn caisson used for President Kennedy's funeral conveyed Welch to Arlington National Cemetery.

CIA officials and others at first blamed Welch's death on *Counterspy*. The issue revealing his name had run a piece by a member of the magazine's board, disaffected former CIA officer Philip Agee, calling for the "neutralization" of CIA employees abroad. But neither *Counterspy* nor Agee could be faulted in this case. Welch's name had been spilled several times before, first in a 1967 East German book, *Who's Who in the CIA*. Moreover, his CIA affiliation was no secret around Athens, and Welch had chosen to live in a house known as the residence of previous CIA station chiefs.

A public impression persisted, however, that the recent exploration of CIA secrets had somehow contributed to Welch's death. William Colby later attributed the murder to "the sensational and hysterical way the CIA investigations had been handled and trumpeted around the world." Welch's death dampened the investigative zeal of the media and of the congressional committees as they drafted their final reports, and the torrent of revelations trickled to a halt. Years later, Congress passed the 1982 Intelligence Identities Protection Act, making it a crime to reveal the identity of covert agents currently working for the United States.

DIRECTOR WILLIAM COLBY AND RICHARD WELCH'S WIFE HONOR THE SLAIN CIA OFFICER ON HIS RETURN HOME.

ENTERING THE
END GAME

On January 28, 1980, six American diplomats and two CIA officers waited nervously in the departure lounge of Iran's Mehrabad Airport. Just three months before, Iranian zealots had seized the U.S. embassy in Tehran and captured its occupants; 13 of those seized had been released two weeks later, but 53 Americans were still held hostage. At the time the embassy fell, and in strictest secrecy, six other American diplomats had avoided capture. Since then they had been hiding at the Tehran homes of the Canadian ambassador and one of his top subordinates. But the situation in Iran was volatile and dangerous. The CIA had been asked to get the six safely home.

Antonio Mendez, of the agency's Office of Technical Service, and a former chief of disguise, had gotten the assignment in December. The 39-year-old agency veteran immediately realized the problem. He needed a cover story to account for the six Americans, who would have to travel under assumed identities. But how could any story explain why a group of Westerners would be in Iran at such a dangerous time? Then the perfect explanation came to him. He would camouflage the escapees as location scouts for a Hollywood picture.

For background information on the movie industry, Mendez contacted his friend John Chambers, a Hollywood makeup man who had won an Oscar for his work on *Planet of the Apes*. To add believability to the scheme, the CIA rented offices at Columbia Pictures in Hollywood for its imaginary film company, named Studio Six in honor of the six diplomats. *Star Wars* was a smash hit that year, so Chambers supplied a real, but never produced, script he had received for a science-fiction movie based on Middle Eastern myths. It made the perfect excuse for a production company scouting out film locations in Tehran. "They'd have to believe if we were crazy enough to write this script, we'd be crazy enough to be looking for locations in a place like Iran," Mendez later recalled. They titled the movie

At left, American-backed Nicaraguan rebels known as Contras march in formation at the Centro de Instrucción Militar in Honduras. Nine miles from Nicaragua, the clandestine jungle boot camp ran thousands of recruits through CIA-designed training programs between 1985 and 1989. In the Cold War's last decade, the White House and CIA gave strong support to anti-Soviet rebels in Afghanistan as well.

Argo, after Jason and the Argonauts, and took out ads for it in *Variety* and the *Hollywood Reporter*, the industry's trade publications. So successful was the ruse that the company received 26 additional scripts—including pieces by other writers submitted by directors George Lucas and Steven Spielberg.

The next step was to devise cover stories for the diplomats. Mendez felt strongly that they should pose as Canadians, whom the Iranians viewed with far less hostility than Americans. The Canadian government offered to help, supplying six false passports as well as fake birth certificates; the Royal Canadian Mounted Police chipped in with false drivers' licenses. All six of the diplomats were provided with a "legend"—a detailed cover identity that included their job within the movie team.

ROBERT SIDELL AND ASSOCIATES
PRESENT
A STUDIO SIX PRODUCTION

ARGO

A COSMIC CONFLAGRATION
FROM A STORY BY TERESA HARRIS
COMMENCING PRINCIPAL PHOTOGRAPHY
MARCH 1980

Promoting a make-believe movie, the ad at left ran in Variety to supply added cover for six American diplomats fleeing Iran. Tony Mendez, the CIA officer who orchestrated their escape, carried the fake business card below.

studio 6
STUDIO SIX PRODUCTIONS
SUNSET GOWER INDEPENDENT
STUDIOS   SUITE 300
1420 NO. BEECHWOOD DR.
LOS ANGELES, CALIFORNIA 90028
TELEPHONE (213) 465-2101 - 2102

KEVIN COSTA HARKINS
PRODUCTION MANAGER

The CIA's technical shop went to work. Forgers crafted Iranian visas as well as such items as dry-cleaner chits, called "pocket litter" by intelligence experts. A portfolio with a promo package and set designs for the movie was put together. Some of the material was sent into Iran by Canadian diplomatic pouch. Meanwhile, as Mendez later explained, "We were working against time." By matching the list of hostages with the embassy's roster, certain reporters had figured out some diplomats were missing and were presumably in hiding. Canada persuaded journalist Jean Pelletier, who knew about the six, to sit on his story.

On January 25, 1980, Mendez and another CIA officer fluent in Farsi flew into Mehrabad Airport and met with Canadian ambassador Ken Taylor. That same night they met with the six diplomats and explained the plan. Because the six had no experience in such matters, Mendez and the other officer would lead them through the escape in person; Mendez would pose as the team's "production manager," while his colleague would be the "associate producer."

Swiftly, the diplomats were told about their new identities and provided with the forged credentials and some very simple disguises. Mark Lijek, who was to pose as the "transportation coordinator," darkened his blond beard with mascara. His wife, Cora-Amburn Lijek, turned into Teresa Harris, screenwriter, by changing the part in her hair. Consul general Robert Anders, a conservative-looking man who was well known in Tehran, was transformed into location manager Robert Lee Baker. With his white hair pulled back in a blow-dried pompadour, he wore skintight, flared jeans, a thick gold medallion, and an open-necked silk shirt. In a practice run, Roger Lucy, Ambassador Taylor's number two at the Canadian embassy, then "interrogated" the envoys after dressing as a Revolutionary Guard, complete with swagger stick and jackboots. "Where you get visa?" he badgered in a thick Farsi accent. "Mother's name. Father's birthday. You liar, you spy." Their cover stories held up.

Finally all was ready. The six fugitives and their two CIA minders arrived at the airport at the carefully chosen hour of 5:00 a.m. "The officials," Mendez later explained, "might still be sleepy, and most of the Revolutionary Guards would still be in their beds." They made it through customs and immigration. Suddenly, loudspeakers announced, "SwissAir Flight 363 delayed due to mechanical problems." Mendez was worried; he knew that with each extra minute the operation could be blown. After an hour in the bleak, crowded departure lounge, the P.A. system finally announced the flight was ready for boarding. Trying to appear casual, the eight climbed onto the plane, which by chance was named "Argau," after a region in Switzerland. In reaction to the coincidence, one member of the party exclaimed giddily, "You guys arrange everything, don't you?" As the plane ascended, their spirits rose still further.

A few days later word of their successful exit hit the press. But the excited stories included not a word about Mendez, or even about the CIA. As had been planned all along, Ambassador Taylor of Canada—who had, of course, helped conceal the diplomats all this time—took full public credit for the escape. It was feared that if the agency's role were known, Iran would take out its anger on the embassy hostages. For the Iranians, recalled Mendez in 1998, "the true Satan is the CIA. So it comes down to how mad do you want to make them. We didn't want to make them that mad." It was not until September 1997, on the 50th anniversary of the CIA's founding, that Mendez, now retired, was permitted to reveal his secret role in the affair.

For President Jimmy Carter and the American public, the return of the Canada Six, however mysteriously it had been accomplished, was a rare bright spot in a difficult time. The continuing hostage crisis was only the most visible of several frustrating signs of American impotence abroad. In July 1979 Nicaraguan dictator Anastasio Somoza Debayle, a longtime ally, had fallen to the Marxist-leaning Sandinistas, who then ousted the more moderate elements of their coalition. To many observers, Nicaragua under its new Sandinista leader, Daniel Ortega Saavedra, represented a disturbing new expansion of Soviet influence abroad—especially after Ortega began backing leftist guerrillas from El Salvador who sought to topple their government and supplying them Soviet-bloc weapons that arrived by way of Cuba.

In a secret 1980 Oval Office meeting, President Jimmy Carter congratulates Mendez on his safe recovery of the Americans, as CIA director Stansfield Turner looks on. Although memoirs by Carter and others hinted at a CIA role in the affair, the escape was generally credited to the Canadian government until 1997, when Mendez was publicly honored.

Even more alarming was an unprecedented move by the Soviet Union itself on December 27, 1979. Faced with an anti-Soviet regime in the nearby state of Afghanistan, the USSR suddenly embarked on a full-scale military occupation of the country, including the murder of its head of state by the KGB. The Carter administration and the West were caught flatfooted. The invasion was the Soviets' first use of troops to expand their empire since the 1948 seizure of Czechoslovakia, and their first ever outside of Eastern Europe. Locally, it threatened the vital, oil-laden Persian Gulf.

In response, Carter clamped an embargo on grain shipments to the Soviet Union and vetoed U.S. participation in the 1980 Moscow summer Olympics. Secretly, he also began arranging covert aid through the CIA to anti-Soviet Afghan rebels known as the mujahedin, already waging a burgeoning guerrilla war. In conjunction with the CIA supply effort, his administration lined up help from several nations, including Egypt, Saudi Arabia, and China, the Soviets' great rival in central Asia. Supplies and arms would be funneled through Afghanistan's neighbor Pakistan.

On January 20, 1981, the day that Jimmy Carter's successor, Ronald Reagan, was sworn in as president, the Iran crisis finally ended with the hostages' safe return. But the troubles in Nicaragua and Afghanistan remained, shaping up as major new battlefields in the decades-long Cold War.

CASEY TAKES COMMAND

Several weeks before taking office, Ronald Reagan had selected his campaign manager, William J. Casey, as director of the CIA. A lawyer and former head of the Securities and Exchange Commission, Casey was also an aggressive risk taker. As a young OSS officer, he had managed the insertion of more than a hundred agents into the Third Reich late in the war. Now,

A seemingly endless line of Soviet personnel carriers crowd an Afghan highway near the capital of Kabul in early 1980. Within a month of the December 1979 invasion, the Soviet army had secured most major cities and highways but faced growing resistance in the rural areas.

President Ronald Reagan and CIA director William Casey confer in 1984, with Vice President George Bush—himself a former CIA director—at far left. A successful businessman, Casey managed his agency with confidence; he once replaced 130 pages of covert-operations guidelines with a memo that told employees to use common sense.

entrusted with Reagan's confidence, he became the first CIA director accorded full cabinet rank. Fueled by a generous budget that soared during the 1980s to an estimated $30 billion, Casey would reinvigorate the CIA—and especially the operations directorate—for the last major stage of the Cold War struggle.

Casey's can-do spirit would spur his deputies into daring ventures in Nicaragua, Afghanistan, the Middle East, and elsewhere, but it would also prove to be a double-edged sword, as some in the agency pushed past the boundaries of the law. Years later, the resulting Iran-Contra scandal, which to some extent involved the CIA, would stun Langley. It would also help distract top CIA leaders from detecting a treacherous mole hidden deep within the agency itself.

The missionary zeal that Casey brought to the job in 1981 was not immediately apparent, however, as he walked through Langley in his ill-fitting business suit, shoulders slumped, pale eyes remote above his sagging jowls. He also tended to mumble. In his senior year in high school, Casey, a skinny kid, had taken up boxing. Making up in energy what he lacked in weight, he was nicknamed "Cyclone." But one day he took a hit in the throat that caused life-long muscle damage.

Looking every bit his 67 years, Casey would lean back in his office chair and listen with half-closed eyes to the reports of deputies. Then suddenly his body would stiffen and his eyes shoot open. He would fire off a volley of questions about the details at hand—a covert war's cost, rebel enlistment rates, whether fighters were getting the right weapons. Whatever the answers, Casey always ended with an exhortation to do more.

In Central America, in particular, Casey was determined to do a great deal more. The Sandinistas had now been in power two years, and their hold on Nicaragua—and interventionist efforts in El Salvador—had only strengthened. An impatient Casey, with the support of the White House, decided it was time to get tough. The man he chose for the job was Duane "Dewey" Clarridge, a veteran operations officer who was then the Rome station chief. The flamboyant 49-year-old had a penchant for expensive cigars and elegant restaurants. He would snap his suspenders as he reclined, the jacket of his Italian-cut white silk suit wide open, set off with a colorful handkerchief and an equally vivid tie. But Clarridge was also known as someone who would get the job done.

Robert Gates, Casey's deputy director of intelligence and a future CIA director himself, later wrote that the shoot-from-the-hip Clarridge was "one of our best operations officers. Just make sure you have a good lawyer at his elbow." He added, "Dewey's not easy to control." When Casey asked for his prescription on Central America, Clarridge offered two-pronged advice, according to his own memoir: "Take the war to Nicaragua," and "start killing Cubans." The CIA director made Clarridge head of Latin American operations.

The agency set out to recruit a force of 500 Nicaraguan exiles who would form the core of a far larger resistance force known as the Contras, from the Spanish *contrarrevolucionarios*. The CIA built a main base camp for them in Honduras and leased an airport from the Honduran military. Although ultimately aimed at toppling the Sandinistas, the Contras' first objective was to stop the flow of Cuban arms from Nicaragua to the Salvadoran guerrillas. Soon Contra fighters crossed the border at night, hitting bridges and supply dumps.

As the force expanded, it came to include several distinct groups. One element consisted of indigenous Miskito tribesmen unsettled by Sandinista land seizures and forced relocations. Another, the largest, was the Nicaraguan Democratic Force (FDN), led by Enrique Bermúdez, a former colonel in Somoza's notorious National Guard.

Eager to broaden support for the movement, Clarridge sought out a guerrilla leader who had fought against the old Somoza dictatorship, a key credential that could appeal to moderate and socialist elements abroad. One charismatic warrior seemed to fit the bill: Edén Pastora Gómez, whose nom de guerre was Commander Zero. During the Somoza period, Pastora had once seized the National Palace with only a few dozen guerrillas. He and his band took 1,500 hostages, including 50 legislators, and demanded the release of jailed rebels. Three days after the takeover, Pastora marched out in triumph, having secured the release of his comrades, a half-million dollars in cash, and a hostage's Rolex watch.

Within the Contra force, however, Pastora's troops soon proved feeble, putting little pressure on the Sandinistas. Those dealing with Pastora also found him hot tempered and unpredictable. And on September 8, 1983, he and his followers nearly undid the Contra venture altogether when they undertook a mission that Clarridge later described as "one of the great stupidities of all time."

That Thursday at 8:00 a.m., a U.S. Air Force C-140 was heading toward the airport in Managua, Nicaragua's capital. On board to look into the Central American situation were Senator William Cohen of Maine, a Republican, and Senator Gary Hart of Colorado, a Democrat. Suddenly the pilots received a radio message that the airport was closed, so they landed the plane in Honduras. That afternoon, the Managua airport reopened and the two senators finally flew in. They found the center of the terminal a wreck. Shattered glass littered the ground; the room scheduled for their press conference had been hit hard. A worker had been killed.

Adolfo Calero
Duane Clarridge

Reunited years after the Contras disbanded, former Nicaraguan Contra leader Adolfo Calero and CIA officer Duane Clarridge pose for a snapshot. Calero, a key civilian figure among the rebels, had spent 25 years managing a Coca-Cola bottling plant before actions by the Sandinista government pushed him into exile and then rebellion.

As the debris suggested, Cohen and Hart had barely missed a bombing raid. A propeller-driven twin-engine Cessna carrying 500-pound bombs had done the damage before being downed by antiaircraft fire. Local, pro-Sandinista reporters attributed the assault to the Contras, but Cohen scoffed, "the CIA is not that dumb." Then the Nicaraguans produced the Cessna pilot's briefcase, which contained not only a Florida driver's license but also CIA code words identifying the operation, and the name and phone number of a CIA officer at the U.S. embassy in Costa Rica.

At midnight the senators met with the local CIA station chief, who gamely defended Pastora's "new air force," which had bombed the airport on its first mission. The strike would demonstrate the Contras had the power to carry the fight to Nicaragua's capital, he told them. Hart angrily asked why anyone would choose a civilian airport as a target. "This is bad politics, bad diplomacy, and bad operations," he exclaimed.

The episode was particularly ill timed because a congressional ban on CIA efforts to overthrow the Sandinistas had been passed less than a year before. Since 1981, when he asked for $19 million for the Contras, Casey had

His features hidden behind a thick beard, Edén Pastora stands beneath a concealed helicopter at a Contra base camp in Costa Rica. Duane Clarridge helped sign up the popular revolutionary leader for the Contra side but found Pastora to be an unpredictable ally.

been pressing a wary Congress to support the growing guerrilla force. Yet legislators in both parties worried that too powerful a threat from the Contras would only frighten Nicaragua into closer ties with Cuba. Casey had then tried casting the Contras as a mere harassing force, despite its true aim of ousting the Sandinista regime. It was a typical Casey ploy. Under reforms passed in the wake of the 1975 Church Committee hearings, congressional committees now provided real oversight of the agency. Casey, however, had his own formula for testifying before the lawmakers. As he told Senator David Durenberger, he encouraged agency staff to "tell you everything we think you ought to know."

Despite Casey's best efforts, congressional mistrust over the Contras' intentions had grown. In late 1982, Massachusetts congressman Edward Boland, House Intelligence Committee chairman, successfully put forward the so-called Boland amendment, which stated that funds from the CIA and other government agencies could not be used to overthrow the Sandinistas. The 1983 airport raid seemed, on its face, to go against that law.

A few months after Hart and Cohen's close call, Congress placed a cap on funding for the Contras. Yet by the spring of 1984, the Contras had swelled to a force of 10,000. Casey, unrelenting, now asked Capitol Hill for $21 million more. The funding debate continued, muddied by excesses on both sides in Nicaragua. Among other acts, the Sandinista government had censored the press and collectivized the farms of peasants, who then flocked to join the rebel Contras. The Contras, on the other hand, had killed nurses, doctors, and government officials, as Clarridge himself had acknowledged in earlier congressional testimony. In the months ahead, startling events off Nicaragua's coasts would help determine which side prevailed.

Clarridge later wrote that these new developments originated in early 1984, when he arrived home after a grueling day at CIA headquarters in Langley, Virginia, poured himself a glass of gin on the rocks, and lit up his accustomed cigar. He leaned back, not to relax but to ruminate. The

At a secret Contra training camp inside Nicaragua, an instructor guides a group of raw recruits in the use of firearms. Like the troops fielded by Nicaragua's Sandinista government, the Contra force was mainly composed of teenagers from poor families; both sides also used cheap, Soviet-style AK-47s like those seen here.

Contras had to find a way to push the Sandinistas into negotiations—ideally, by weakening the Nicaraguan economy in some way. The answer that occurred to him was to deploy sea mines, which he referred to as firecrackers, since they made a lot of noise but did only modest damage. If a few firecrackers were planted in Nicaragua's harbors, Clarridge reasoned, shipping would dwindle and the economy would founder.

In February 1984, Clarridge's notion became a reality when a converted oil-drilling vessel moved into position in international waters just outside the Nicaraguan harbor of Puerto Sandino. Quietly, it launched so-called Q-boats—converted high-speed boats that the U.S. Customs Service had confiscated from drug smugglers—into the port, where contractors hired by the CIA dropped the firecracker mines and, for good measure, shot up oil tanks on the bluffs above before fleeing to the larger ship. At Langley, Clarridge monitored the operation via enciphered satellite communications.

Passing repeatedly through the Panama Canal, the CIA force went on to lay mines and target patrol boats in harbors along Nicaragua's Atlantic and Pacific coasts. And, at first, the effort paid off as intended, causing some real economic harm. Then the U.S. Congress found out.

Although 75-year-old Barry Goldwater, a Republican senator from Arizona, had always backed the Nicaraguan guerrillas, the senator loathed surprises. On April 5, 1984, Goldwater, then under heavy medication for a hip ailment, was addressing the Senate in support of renewed aid to the Contras. An irate Senator Cohen handed him a memo prepared by an intelligence committee staffer. Goldwater looked it over and, angrier even than Cohen, began reading it into the public record until Cohen cut him short. The message disclosed that CIA-hired personnel, rather than the local Contras, had planted 75 firecracker mines in three major Nicaraguan harbors. Seven ships, including British, Dutch, and Japanese vessels and one Soviet oil tanker, had been damaged. Goldwater wrote Casey a furious public letter decrying the action—and the lack of congressional notification—in the saltiest terms. The revelation sparked a storm of damning headlines.

In fact, Casey had informed the Senate about the mining effort the previous month, although without indicating that it was the CIA, rather than the Contras, that mined the harbors. "Magnetic mines have been placed" in Nicaraguan ports, he had stated to a busy, distracted committee in a 27-word passage. Senators now found this less than full disclosure, however, and Casey had to eat crow before the Senate Intelligence Committee. "I apologize profoundly," he said in testimony a few weeks later.

Casey was also forced to move Clarridge away from Contra matters, making him chief of the agency's vital European division. Two years later, at Casey's urging, Clarridge would go on to form the CIA's Counterterrorist Center (CTC), a new unit that drew together resources that were once compartmentalized among the agency's separate directorates. The CIA "damn near had a civil war" from the bureaucratic infighting, an official recalled, but as terrorism emerged as a key security issue in the years to come, the CTC would prove one of the more lasting legacies of the Casey era.

Meanwhile, on the Hill, Casey's reluctant *mea culpa* went unheeded. His sales pitch for continued aid to the Contras was further undercut by word of a CIA field manual, written for the rebels, which discussed how to "neutralize" ranking Sandinistas, an apparent euphemism for assassination, which the agency was supposed to have put behind it in the mid-1970s. Instead of forwarding more funds to the rebels, Congress passed a second Boland amendment in October 1984 barring all Contra military support for 1985.

Backed by President Reagan, who saw the Contras as heroic freedom fighters fully deserving American support, Casey never considered ending aid to his guerrillas. Since the Boland legislation forbade the intelligence agencies from sending the Contras cash, he looked to the National Security Council instead. Casey and Reagan exhorted NSC director Robert McFarlane to find a way to keep the Contras together "body and soul." In turn, the NSC chief looked to Oliver North, a ramrod-straight Vietnam veteran on his staff. North, with Casey's encouragement, then contacted arms dealer and retired air force major general Richard Secord. Secord was "a person who got things done," noted the CIA director. Secord quickly established "a series of organizations that would do what the CIA had done before," North later testified. The former general set up arms-purchasing corporations, located airplane crews, leased aircraft and warehouses, and arranged for landing sites and ammunition drops in Costa Rica, El Salvador, and Honduras. He called the operation "the Enterprise."

While Secord was setting up the Enterprise, North and McFarlane beat the bushes to pay for it, since direct government funding was barred. To solicit money from wealthy individuals partial to the Contras, fund-raisers were held, featuring notable speakers—including President Reagan himself—who were also available for private chats and photo opportunities. A tax-exempt organization accepted the millions raised, which was then laundered through the Enterprise network of companies and Swiss accounts. Even more cash rolled in from friendly foreign governments, including Saudi Arabia and South Korea. A stash of weapons Israel had seized during its 1983 invasion of Lebanon also found its way to the Contras. Through such improvisations, the Enterprise bridged the congressional funding ban and kept the Contras in business—at least for the time being.

RUSSIA'S VIETNAM

As official CIA funding for the Contras was suspended in 1984, the agency-supported war against the Soviet occupiers of Afghanistan was stalled. A large contingent of Red Army troops continued to hold the war-ravaged

"When we supported organized resistance against Hitler, it saved lives in the long run. It's the same thing in Afghanistan."

—William Casey, responding to a briefing on Afghanistan

Afghan rebels known as mujahedin rest briefly in the hills outside a village. Their bolt-action rifles, which date from the World War II era, would later give way to more modern arms, supplied in large part through the CIA.

country despite the best efforts of the mujahedin. Although fearless and sometimes fanatical, the Afghans were simply outgunned by the modern Soviet arsenal.

In the swift-moving guerrilla war, Soviet air power, particularly helicopter gunships, lent a decided edge. Especially dreaded was the Hind Mi-24, an armored helicopter and weapon of terror. It raked the ground with a complement of 128 rockets and cannon that could fire 1,000 rounds a minute, tearing apart military formations and civilian settlements alike. A half-dozen working together could—and frequently did—obliterate entire villages, some of which had existed for centuries. Uprooted by the war's destruction, three million Afghans had fled to Pakistani refugee camps.

All the same, the Soviets had as yet been unable to eradicate the Afghan resistance, which the CIA had continued to support as much as its resources permitted. To foil Soviet claims that the resistance forces were puppets of Washington and maintain "plausible deniability," the U.S. and other friendly nations supplied mostly Soviet-designed arms, and CIA officers generally kept out of Afghanistan itself. Instead, the agency maintained staffs within Pakistan at Islamabad and Karachi. In Peshawar, a rugged town some 10 miles from the Khyber Pass between Pakistan and Afghanistan, 60 CIA and U.S. Special Forces advisers instructed tribesmen how to scout Soviet positions and smuggle in arms through the wild border mountains.

Actual weapons training was left to Pakistani trainers who had themselves been instructed by CIA weapons officers. In an effort supervised by Pakistani military intelligence, seven training camps ultimately prepared more than 80,000 guerrillas for the holy war against the Soviets. The CIA paid the salaries of rebel leaders and sent in arms, intelligence, flour and rice, even packhorses and mules. Once a year, Casey himself slipped in secretly aboard a C-141 Starlifter transport plane for strategy sessions with Pakistani intelligence.

Given the Soviets' overwhelming air-power advantage, the mujahedin pleaded with the United States to send Stingers—shoulder-mounted, ultrasophisticated rocket launchers that fired heat-seeking missiles accurate

> "The Afghans control the ground. The Soviets control the air. Take the Soviets out of the air, and they lose."
>
> —1983 briefing by private researcher Jack Wheeler for the president, CIA, and NSC officials

Dressed like the Afghan rebels around him, U.S. congressman Charles Wilson travels on horseback during a covert visit to a mujahedin base in 1987. One of the rebels' staunchest supporters, Wilson wanted the conflict to be as draining for the Soviets as Vietnam had been for the United States.

up to 15,000 feet. But many in the U.S. government, including some in the CIA, feared losing control of such potent weapons, which could well end up in the hands of terrorists targeting civilian aircraft.

Among the American advocates for the Stingers was Democratic congressman Charles Wilson, a backslapping former naval officer from the wildcat oil country of Texas. Wilson, like many Americans, was still fuming over the Vietnam War. His district had observed 167 funerals of slain Vietnam veterans, and he vowed, "We owe the Russians." After three trips to Pakistan in the early '80s, he concluded the war in Afghanistan was winnable. As some in the CIA would later put it, Afghanistan could become the Soviets' version of Vietnam.

In 1984 Wilson pressed Casey for the Stingers, but Casey, preoccupied with Nicaragua, begged off. Unfazed, Wilson persuaded his colleagues to quadruple the CIA's budget for Afghanistan to $120 million and Casey to procure specimens of the Oerlikon, a Swiss antiaircraft cannon. The 1,200-pound guns, however, proved too cumbersome for the mujahedin's mules to tote up steep mountain trails.

Still trying to conceal the U.S. role, the CIA scavenged everywhere for effective but untraceable ordnance, with sometimes mixed results. Egypt sent boxes of rifles rusted together and piles of bullets in loose heaps. Pakistan, whose role in the arms pipeline was meant to be secret, furnished 30 million rounds of rifle ammunition stamped POF, for Pakistan Ordnance Factory; the bullets had to be restamped at considerable cost. China, meanwhile, continued to supply Soviet-type arms. It also set up, with CIA help, guerrilla training camps on its Afghan frontier.

As the aid expanded, theft of arms was a constant headache. Rebel groups often complained they never received U.S.-supplied rifles. CIA-furnished AK-47s became so common at Pakistani bazaars that officials spoke of a "Kalashnikov culture," a reference to the gun's Soviet designer. By some estimates, as much as half of U.S. military aid was pilfered. The money and goods pouring into the region also funded a massive expansion of the local drug trade. Warehouses' worth of narcotics, including enough opium for much of the U.S. heroin supply, moved back and forth across the mountain passes.

Meanwhile, the Pakistanis were delighted with America's high-tech wizardry. Especially prized were its space-based images of bomb damage and valley trails. "Nothing above ground was hidden from the all-seeing satellite," Pakistani general Muhammad Yousaf later commented admiringly. With every image tendered by CIA officers, "we would be supplied with recommended approaches, enemy dispositions, likely reactions to attack," he wrote. At one point, Pakistani-trained Afghans, aided by CIA-furnished satellite photos of targets, actually crossed the Soviet border to attack nearby factories and fuel dumps, before the agency, wary of Soviet retaliation, backed off.

CIA electronic interception gear also enabled the mujahedin and the Pakistanis to eavesdrop on Soviet radio traffic. After one battle, CIA transmitters allowed a guerrilla leader to break into the Soviet army's radio network to detail and deride Soviet casualties. The same hardware let Pakistan evaluate the validity of rebel boasts of Soviet losses and decide which groups to reward with better weapons. It turned out the best fighters belonged to the most fundamentalist bands—groups that passionately hated the Soviet invaders but often detested the antireligious influence of the West as well. During the war, such groups got an estimated 70 percent of the arms supplied. Later on, some who had fought the Soviets turned their training against other targets as they joined the ranks of anti-U.S. terrorists. Others formed part of the radical Taliban group that seized control of Afghanistan years later.

For all the high-tech satellite and signals intelligence help, however, the guerrillas were still kept at bay by Soviet air power, as a badly divided U.S. government withheld the Stinger missiles. The Defense Department argued that the Soviets, if they captured the rockets, could use the technology against NATO. Casey's men countered with evidence the Soviets had already obtained Stinger know-how through an intelligence leak. Clair George, the deputy director for operations, swayed minds in the Senate with testimony he was "absolutely convinced" the missiles "could make the difference" in the war. Opinions shifted further when heavy fighting on the Afghan border with Pakistan, coupled with incursions by Soviet aircraft, ignited fears of a Soviet invasion of that country too. In February 1986 the Stinger shipments were finally approved. The CIA was to furnish a thousand and instruct the resistance in their use.

At noon on September 25, 1986, 35 Afghan guerrillas crept through the underbrush a mile from Afghanistan's strategic Jalalabad airfield. Their commander, Ghaffar, spotting enemy soldiers guarding the runway, ordered his men to stop in the cover of a hillside. They crouched in the brush, waiting. At 3:00 p.m. their patient vigil was rewarded when eight of the death-dealing Mi-24 helicopters appeared in the sky, preparing to land.

At left, an Afghan fighter aims a Stinger missile-launcher supplied by the United States. Although the sophisticated, shoulder-mounted device debuted in 1981, its first use in combat was not until 1986 in Afghanistan.

In a mocking Afghan poster from the late 1980s, Soviet president Mikhail Gorbachev sits on a useless tank, surrounded by dead Soviet soldiers, damaged tanks, and crashed helicopters. In all, 15,000 to 20,000 Soviet troops and at least a million Afghans died in the decade of fighting.

Three of the mujahedin rose and hoisted missiles onto their shoulders. A fourth rebel lifted a video camera to record the historic moment of the first Stinger firing in Afghanistan.

As each Stinger-equipped rebel chose a helicopter through the launcher sight, the Iden-tification Friend or Foe system sensed the heat of the Mi-24, and a pinging sound indicated the missile had located a hostile target. Ghaffar shouted, "Fire!" With a cry of *Allah O Akhbar*— "God Is Great"—the men complied. Their in-frared, heat-seeking missiles, protruding from tubes atop the sighting mechanisms, shot into the sky at 1,200 miles an hour. Two of the gun-ships exploded into flames. A fast, frantic reload, another salvo, and another helicopter lit up the heavens. Later, President Reagan was shown the resulting videotape, which displayed blurred im-ages of sky and earth. The amateur cameraman had been too excited to hold his camera steady.

As Wilson and others had predicted, the Stingers helped turn the war around. The very accurate missiles had a "hit ratio" ranging from 50 to 80 percent. Less exotic weaponry, such as the Chinese-supplied Dashika 12.7-millimeter machine gun, brought down still more aircraft. Soviet pilots flew scared, high above the missiles' range, their bombing raids rendered far less ef-fective. Yet the foes of the Stinger deployment found their predictions coming true as well, to a degree. Nearby Iran man-aged to capture a number of Stingers, while others disappeared, with some later surfacing as far afield as the Philippines. After the war, the CIA ran a buyback program to purchase the stolen missiles at twice their original cost, but hundreds remained unaccounted for.

Still, the CIA operation overall was a grand slam. As early as 1986, So-viet president Mikhail Gorbachev had admitted to the 27th Communist Party Congress that "counterrevolution and imperialism have transformed Afghanistan into a bleeding wound." Three years later, on February 15, 1989, the last Soviet soldier left Afghanistan. At headquarters, the CIA's Afghan Task Force celebrated with champagne.

A COMPLEX WEB UNRAVELS

In 1986, the same year that Gorbachev began to acknowledge disaster in Afghanistan, the parallel struggle in Nicaragua resurfaced in the American press—to Casey and the CIA's great detriment. The story now in the head-lines had begun a world away from Nicaragua in the spring of 1985, when Casey began advocating a reopening of relations with Iran. Since the hostage crisis, Iran had faced a U.S. weapons embargo, a difficult burden given its ongoing war with its neighbor, Iraq. Now Casey was actively re-thinking this strategy. By denying aid to that nation, he reasoned, the U.S. might be pushing Iran toward the Soviet Union's embrace.

As CIA director, Casey also had a second agenda. His Lebanon station chief, William Buckley, had been kidnapped the year before and was now still held by terrorists from an organization known as Islamic Jihad. A CIA officer for many years, Buckley had worked on the Berlin tunnel intercepts, helped train Cubans for the Bay of Pigs, and led perilous missions into Laos during the Vietnam War. He had also more recently served in the Middle East, before becoming well enough known that he had withdrawn from active duty and later retired. It was only at Casey's personal request that he had gone to Lebanon at all. Casey knew the United States had no leverage with the hostage takers, but the Iranians had plenty. Iran's need for weapons, he reasoned, might give the United States a bargaining chip for Buckley and six other longtime American hostages in Lebanon.

Casey's proposal violated a basic intelligence maxim that one should never mix separate operations. It also flew in the face of a pledge by Presi-dent Reagan that "America will never make concessions to terrorists." And it faced opposition from Defense Secretary Caspar Weinberger and Secre-tary of State George Shultz—but not from national security adviser Robert McFarlane. McFarlane quietly met with Israeli officials, who argued the Ira-nians wanted missiles and in return might use their influence over radical groups to free the hostages. McFarlane and Casey pressed for secret negoti-ations with Iran, and the president went along.

At the National Security Council, Oliver North, already tasked by Mc-Farlane with transporting arms to the Contras, handled the complex nego-tiations, with Iranian businessman Manucher Ghorbanifar, a figure with a somewhat murky past, as middleman. The CIA asked Ghorbanifar to sub-mit to a polygraph test, one of the agency's favored tools for vetting its offi-cers and intelligence sources. He flunked 13 of 15 questions, getting only his name and nationality right. With Casey's support, he continued to broker the dealings anyway. By the end of 1985, the Israelis had sent Iran 504 TOW antitank and 18 Hawk antiaircraft missiles, all of which were then replen-ished by the United States. In December President Reagan signed a CIA-requested finding that authorized the shipments, after the fact. The trans-fers resulted in the release of a single hostage—the Reverend Benjamin Weir. Buckley, mistreated and sick, had died in captivity.

Early in 1986, this quiet arrangement took a dramatic new turn when North suggested adding a funds-diversion scheme to aid the Contras. The United States would now sell missiles directly to the Iranians, rather than through Israel. Iran's payments would be deposited into the Swiss bank ac-count of the Enterprise, and any profits would go to the Contras. Since the Iranians were willing to pay $10,000 for TOW missiles costing the Defense Department $3,700 each, these promised to be substantial. Later North would testify that Casey was "effusive" and enthusiastic about the plan. Casey, however, would deny it.

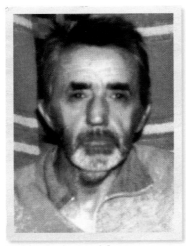

William A. Buckley

One of several longtime American hostages in the Middle East, Lebanon station chief William Buckley looks thin and weary in this picture issued by Islamic Jihad in October 1985, along with an announcement of his death at their hands. Lebanese CIA contacts, the FBI, and a covert U.S. Army unit had desperately searched Beirut for Buckley; it was later learned he had been sent to Syria for interrogation and probably died in June 1985.

More missiles, purchased from the Pentagon by the CIA, were delivered to Iran in the spring of 1986. In May, North flew to Tehran for secret negotiations accompanied by George Cave, a retired CIA officer who had helped Kermit Roosevelt during the agency's 1953 coup in Iran. In July another hostage went free. Casey wrote to McFarlane's successor as national security adviser, Admiral John Poindexter, that U.S. officials should "consider what we may be prepared to do to meet minimum requirements that would lead to the release of the rest of the hostages." But in September two more Americans were kidnapped off the streets of Beirut. Paying for hostages may have created a perverse incentive for boosting their supply.

By the end of 1986, the United States had shipped Iran 2,000 TOW missiles and an abundance of Hawk spare parts. Ultimately, more than $47 million would pass through the financial channels of the Enterprise in return, of which several million in "residuals" went to the Contras. Ironically, by then the elaborate funds-diversion scheme to help the Contras may no longer have been necessary. In October 1986 Congress had relented, passing a new, $100 million package in Contra aid. But that same October, a downed plane revealed the scheme.

Just after noon on October 5, 1986, a Sandinista surface-to-air missile shot down a U.S. C-123 cargo plane over Nicaragua. Everyone in the small crew died, with one exception: 45-year-old Eugene Hasenfus, a construction worker from Wisconsin who had temporarily left his wife and three children for a job paying $3,000 a month. Hasenfus had been hired as the "kicker," the one who pushed military supplies out of the plane's cargo door.

The pilot had told him the outfit was a "front" for "the CIA and the government" and was "being run directly out of the White House." And that is what Hasenfus told the Sandinistas when they captured him after he spent 24 hours stumbling through the jungle. Given the numerous docu-

"Don't worry. Everything is going to be okay, we haven't done anything illegal, you understand that?"

—Casey to Alan Fiers, CIA Central American task force chief

A charmed President Reagan receives an "I'm a Contra too" pin from Contra leader Adolfo Calero in a 1985 meeting arranged by Lieutenant Colonel Oliver North, visible in the background. After Congress barred the CIA from funding the Contras, North became the rebels' point of contact, helping them obtain weapons and providing intelligence from the CIA and Pentagon.

ments recovered, which linked the plane to an air base often used by the CIA, the Nicaraguans hardly needed his testimony.

Official Washington was flooded with denials; Secretary of State Shultz said the plane had been hired by unnamed "private people" with no connection to the government. That November the other side of the arrangement began to be exposed when a Lebanese publication disclosed the once secret Iranian arms shipments. Attorney General Edwin Meese confirmed later that month that some profits had been diverted to aid the Contras. By December 1996 Casey was telling a skeptical congressional committee, "All the activities were entirely properly conducted and fully authorized." But his old confidence before legislative foes was gone, sapped by mounting ill health. Four days after testifying, Casey collapsed in his Langley office from the effects of a brain tumor. He died the following May.

By that time, the commotion surrounding the Hasenfus shootdown and the newly revealed Iranian connection had helped bring the hidden ties among the arms shipments, the release of hostages, and the Contra supply pipeline into the public spotlight. In a six-year investigation that continued past the Reagan years and into the Bush administration, spanning the terms of several CIA directors, independent counsel Lawrence Walsh would prosecute prominent administration figures as well as a num-

Two days after his plane was shot down by a Nicaraguan missile, crew member Eugene Hasenfus is escorted through the jungle under armed guard. Although Hasenfus was later released, the revelation that the plane was carrying arms for the Contra forces helped set off the Iran-Contra scandal.

ber of CIA officers. The latter included three men—Duane Clarridge, Clair George, and Alan Fiers, head of the CIA Central American Task Force—who were charged only with perjury for false testimony, rather than with breaking the law as part of the Iran-Contra scheme itself. In December 1992 President George Bush pardoned all three—including Clarridge, who had yet to stand trial—along with Assistant Secretary of State Elliott Abrams, former NSC director Robert McFarlane, and Defense Secretary Weinberger, whose case, like Clarridge's, had not yet been tried. In a statement, Bush explained that he had pardoned the six because differences over policy were becoming criminalized.

By the time of that final twist in the Iran-Contra scandal, the world had changed dramatically since the old Casey days. In 1989 economic and political pressures had led Hungary and Poland to become the first Eastern European nations to slip from the grasp of a faltering Soviet Union, itself weakened economically, in part by the burden of the Afghan war. Later that year, the Berlin Wall toppled as the border between the two Germanys reopened. The following year, back in Nicaragua, the Sandinista government agreed to an election—and was quickly ousted. In 1991 the Soviet Union itself ceased to exist.

Created during the very early years of the Cold War against the Communist bloc, with the KGB as its seemingly perennial adversary, the CIA now faced a puzzling future in which terrorism, narcotics trafficking, and nuclear proliferation loomed as top items on the agenda. But before it could find its feet in this brave new era, the agency suffered a profound blow to its public image and internal morale. In 1994 the world and agency employees learned for the first time that the CIA had been harboring a Soviet agent within its own ranks for almost a decade. Blazoned in headlines and on television screens, the name of the traitor was Aldrich Hazen Ames.

THE TRAITOR WITHIN

In the spring of 1985, Rick Ames was nearing 44 years of age and feeling emotional and financial pressures. He had been employed by the CIA for almost 23 years, and his career was going nowhere. He was disillusioned with "the espionage business, as carried out by the CIA," he said later. If he felt cynical about the CIA, the agency did not care much for him either. Ames was regarded as lazy, a problem drinker, and a mediocre case officer who had been inept at recruiting agents while overseas. His annual performance reports even noted shortcomings of personal hygiene such as his slovenly clothing and rotting teeth.

Ames was also in financial trouble. He was getting a divorce and had agreed to provide his wife with $12,600 in future monthly payments; he was also paying off about $33,500 in debts, all on an annual salary of $60,000. Meanwhile, he was living with his future wife, Maria del Rosario Casas Dupuy, of a prominent Colombian family, whom he had met while stationed in Mexico. They planned a family, and he felt embarrassed that he might not be able to support her and any future children in a manner suited to her background.

Aldrich Hazen Ames

In a candid shot at upper left, CIA officer Aldrich Ames relaxes with future wife Rosario Casas on an Acapulco beach in 1983. Ames, shown above in an agency photograph, later became the CIA's most notorious traitor and probably the highest paid spy in history.

That spring, Ames began to perceive how he might attain the life he wanted. "Instead of robbing a bank," he later explained, "I decided to rob the KGB." Ames realized he had a valuable commodity to sell. Against all reason, this problem employee had been promoted to one of the most sensitive posts in the agency, chief of the counterintelligence group within the Soviet division. As such, he had access to information invaluable to the enemy. He knew, for example, the identities of every agent employed by the CIA inside the Soviet intelligence apparatus.

On the evening of April 16, 1985, Ames polished off his fifth vodka as he waited at the posh bar of Washington's Mayflower Hotel for Sergei Chuvakhin, first secretary of the Soviet embassy. Chuvakhin, who was running late, probably thought Ames was trying to recruit him. That was what Ames, in arranging the meeting, had told his Langley superiors. When Chuvakhin did not arrive, Ames, almost casually, took the fateful plunge, abandoning the hotel for the Soviet embassy two blocks away.

His approach to the graceful stone building was recorded by the FBI's hidden cameras across the street. Inside the reception room, he passed the security guard a sealed envelope addressed to the KGB resident. It contained a request for $50,000, a CIA directory with Ames's name and title, and a note listing two sources in the Soviet Union who had volunteered information to the CIA. Ames believed, he claimed later, that they were KGB plants and not real defectors at all; he thus rationalized the notion that the men he was exposing would not face a firing squad. Nevertheless, as he later admitted, "I had crossed a line; I could never step back."

At a follow-up meeting a month later, Chuvakhin met Ames and presented him with the $50,000 in cash. The next step, a few weeks afterward, came even more easily. In his fourth-floor Langley office, Ames packed hundreds of secret memos and dossiers weighing about six pounds into plastic bags and carried them to his car. To leave the building he simply had to punch his ID card into the turnstile exit. Ames was clutching the bags

"What I had done could never be undone."

—Ames, on accepting his first KGB payment, May 1985

Sergei Chuvakhin

While stationed at CIA headquarters in the mid-1980s, Ames passed agency secrets to Soviet diplomat Sergei Chuvakhin (above) during lunches in a Washington, D.C., restaurant. The shopping bags Ames walked away with never held less than $20,000.

when he entered Chadwick's, a Georgetown restaurant, to rendezvous with Chuvakhin once again.

Money was his motivation, yet, inexplicably, he gave away everything he knew that day without setting a price. The documents identified "virtually all Soviet agents of the CIA and other American and foreign services known to me," he would tell the FBI. "It was like a leap into the dark."

A grateful KGB "set aside for me two million dollars," he remembered. As an intelligence veteran, Ames knew the Soviets preferred cash payments to blackmail as a motivating factor; it made for happier, more cooperative spies. He would soon be receiving more than $300,000 a year.

The CIA had spent as much as 20 years working up its key Soviet contacts, who had literally risked their lives. In a flash Ames destroyed them. Ten of them were executed, many others sent to prison. In time over 100 intelligence operations were exposed.

"The KGB might as well have taken out an ad," Ames later griped. The executions, and the rapid disappearance of so many agents, made clear the Soviets had a direct pipeline to the CIA. "They were wrapping up our cases with reckless abandon," remembered one CIA officer. If anyone searched for a mole, Ames believed, the trail would lead to him.

As the grave losses of Soviet agents sank in, William Casey, still CIA director but immersed in other priorities, ordered an inquiry. The results were reassuring. The CIA's inspector general concluded in early 1986 that every instance of a spy's arrest could have been a separate failure, containing "the seeds of its own destruction," resulting from sloppy work by the doomed agent or a case officer.

In fact, many possible explanations of the leaks had been floated by the Soviets themselves in a clever disinformation campaign. At one point a KGB officer posing as a CIA sympathizer told the agency that its message relay center had been breached, leading to a fruitless investigation of 90 CIA employees. The KGB also took advantage of the fact that within days of Ames's first illicit contacts, former CIA officer Edward Lee Howard had betrayed a few agency sources in Moscow. The KGB, confident its story would leak to the West, informed thousands of its own employees that Howard was responsible for unmasking all the CIA's Soviet spies.

In October 1986 CIA counterintelligence did appoint a four-person investigatory team headed by 54-year-old Jeanne Vertefeuille, the former station chief of Gabon. The agency's old-boy network felt that such "little gray-haired old ladies" were best at screening for traitors; supposedly only they had the patience to sift for clues through mountains of files. For years Vertefeuille would doggedly stick to her inquiry with scant agency backing. In the wake of the devastating Angleton mole hunt of a decade ago, the agency knew the risks of uncontrolled suspicion. And, in an all-too-human impulse, at some level CIA veterans preferred any explanation other than that there was a traitor in their ranks.

In 1986 Ames, with considerable trepidation, faced a routine CIA lie-detector test. He asked the KGB for tips on passing it and was advised, "Get a good night's sleep, and rest, and go into the test rested and relaxed. Be nice

THE DOOMED

His greed fired by the KGB's initial payment of $50,000 in May 1985, CIA officer Aldrich Ames *(left)* wasted little time in demonstrating his enormous worth to his new masters. As a counterintelligence expert, he knew exactly what the Soviets would like most: the names of U.S. agents buried within their own intelligence network. In mid-June he began giving them just that information, ultimately identifying at least 30 of America's most valuable covert sources. For 10 of them—including those pictured at right—the cost of his revelations was a death sentence.

Two names that Ames made sure to include on the very first list were those of Valery Martynov and Sergei Motorin, KGB officers who had been recruited while stationed at the Soviet embassy in Washington, D.C. Because his own handlers were based at the embassy, Ames decided it was too dangerous for the two men to stay at large. "I didn't assume they would ever be involved or become knowledgeable," he later explained, "but accidents happen." Both were soon arrested and eventually shot.

The information that Ames passed along also condemned to death four more KGB officers, a Soviet defense researcher, and three members of the GRU, the Red Army's military intelligence service. By far the most valuable of the GRU sources was Dimitri Polyakov, a well-placed officer who had been providing information about Soviet weapons and strategy for more than 20 years. In return, Polyakov asked for an occasional modest present for his wife and once requested a shotgun he had taken a fancy to. Although he despised the Soviet system, he declined offers to defect because it would have meant leaving his family behind. "It was a bad day for us when we lost him," said one CIA employee when word of Polyakov's death finally reached the West.

Despite the rash of deaths and disappearances among Soviet operatives, few suspected Aldrich Ames. He would remain a trusted CIA officer—and secret KGB agent—for another 10 years.

ADOLF TOLKACHEV
CIA Code Name: GTSPHERE
Executed September 24, 1986

Seen here being manhandled by the KGB during his June 1985 arrest in Moscow, Tolkachev was a Soviet aerospace engineer who had been reporting to the CIA since the late 1970s on the design and testing of Soviet aircraft and missiles. By one estimate, his information on stealth technology alone saved the U.S. billions of dollars. Like several of the agents Ames named, he was held for several months, probably for interrogation, before his death.

DIMITRI POLYAKOV
CIA Code Name: GTBEEP
FBI Code Name: TOP HAT
Executed 1988

Polyakov first volunteered his services while in New York City in 1962. By the time of his arrest he had been promoted to lieutenant general, making him the highest-ranking GRU officer to work for Western intelligence.

GENNADI VARENIK
CIA Code Name: GTFITNESS
Executed 1985

A 32-year-old KGB officer, Varenik began working for the CIA in March 1985. He exposed several KGB operations in Germany, including a plot to plant bombs in bars frequented by Americans to stir up anti-German sentiment in the United States.

VALERY MARTYNOV
CIA Code Name: GTGENTILE
FBI Code Name: PIMENTA
Executed May 28, 1987

Tricked into returning to Moscow from Washington in 1985, Martynov told his wife and children he would be back soon. Ten days later they were brought home to find the KGB officer charged with high treason.

SERGEI MOTORIN
CIA Code Name: GTGAUZE
FBI Code Name: MEGAS
Executed 1986

A KGB major with a taste for high living, Motorin kept the FBI informed about KGB personnel working out of the Soviet embassy in Washington, D.C. When he moved back to Moscow, he began working for the CIA.

to the polygraph examiner, develop a rapport." The needle jumped when Ames was asked if he had been "pitched," or approached, by recruiters from a foreign intelligence service. He explained he feared being pitched by Soviet agents overseas. The polygraph operator rated Ames's responses as "direct" and "bright."

The test cleared the way for Ames's next posting, to Rome. In the Eternal City, the pattern of alcoholism, slipshod work—and betrayal—continued. At the U.S. embassy's Fourth of July party in 1987, he got into a public spat with a foreign diplomat, then staggered off drunk. Hours later Italian *carabinieri* picked the comatose officer out of a gutter. "You should be more careful," the station chief mildly advised him the next day. In a job review that fall, the chief complained Ames "handles no ongoing cases," and that his efforts to mine new Soviet contacts "have been desultory."

Ames earned high praise, meanwhile, from his Soviet handlers, experienced case officers who rarely criticized him even when he drank too much and forgot a meeting. Every six to eight weeks, Ames would stay late at the office and slip about a hundred secret reports into a shopping bag.

An FBI surveillance video camera captured this view of Ames as he walked through a Bogotá, Colombia, shopping mall to meet his Russian contact in November 1993. A reassembled note from Ames's trash (right) tipped off the bureau to the meeting, which helped convince the FBI that they had their man.

The documents identified CIA agents in Hungary and Czechoslovakia as well as others working for the U.S. Army and Navy. At a restaurant, Ames would pass the material to his Soviet contact in exchange for a cigar box stuffed with 200 to 500 one-hundred-dollar bills. Enjoying their new-found wealth, Rick and Rosario Ames began frequenting trendy bistros and going on expensive shopping sprees. Ames now sported expensive caps on his bad teeth.

When Ames attributed his sudden riches to marrying into wealth, he was readily believed; the agency employed other men and women with trust funds and inheritances. Rosario apparently swallowed her husband's yarn that an old friend was paying him handsomely to look after his Euro-pean investments. Supervisors also took little notice of Ames's alcohol-fueled binges. After all, heavy social drinking was part of the job of recruit-ing Soviets. "Thirty percent of the station went out and got drunk at lunch. It was a drunken culture," one Rome case officer later commented.

In 1989 Ames returned to headquarters, where he was handed a series of sensitive assignments. Ironically, he was one of the CIA officers given the job of debriefing Oleg Gordievsky, a former top British mole within the KGB who had defected to the West after his cover was exposed—unknown to Gordievsky, by Ames himself. "His face radiated gentleness and kindness," Gordievsky recalled of his interviewer. "Of course, I didn't know at that point that he had been trying to kill me."

The CIA began a low-key investigation of Ames after CIA officer Diana Worthen, a friend of the family, reported late that year that Rick and Rosario did not have the means to support their lifestyle, which by then included a $540,000 house, paid for in cash, and a flashy Jaguar. Worthen also noted that Ames had been privy to the compromised Soviet cases. Yet in 1990 Ames was assigned to a promotions panel, enabling him to pass along records of up-and-coming CIA officers. In October he was sent to the counterintelligence center to analyze KGB operations—but he was no longer unwatched.

At the end of 1990 the counterintelligence center pushed for a stepped-up inquiry of Ames. "There is a degree of urgency involved in our request," wrote the center's director. "We are quickly running out of things for him to do without granting him greater access." In September 1991 he was moved once again to the Soviet division, this time to a unit assigned to "put a stake through the KGB's heart."

Although the CIA and FBI had held meetings on the problem of trac-ing the apparent agency mole, a CIA-FBI team was not set up until April 1991. The joint operation first compiled a slate of 198 employees who had entrée to information on the executed spies, then narrowed the list to 29, including Ames.

As the net began to close without Ames's knowledge, he informed his wife of his relationship with the KGB in the summer of 1992. By her own account, Rosario spent the next few days in a panic. "What does one do when one's husband announces that he's a spy?" she remembered asking herself. For both husband and wife, the well-being of their son, Paul, born in 1988, was the paramount issue. Rosario chose to acquiesce in her husband's actions—even to take an active interest.

In 1993 an FBI team searched the Ames house while the family was on vacation and planted bugs in every room. Tapes revealed a husband and wife bickering about spying. "Why didn't you do it today, for God's sakes?" Rosario asked about a planned drop-off of secrets. "I should have," her spouse replied, "except it was raining like crazy."

Damning additional evidence came from a late-night action in which FBI agents removed the family trash can after substituting an exact duplicate. The contents of the original included a used printer ribbon that allowed the FBI to reconstruct a letter Ames had written to his new handlers in the Russian intelligence service that had replaced the KGB after the collapse of the Soviet Union. The letter was signed *K* for his chosen code name Kolokol, Russian for "Bell." Kolokol was also the password to Ames's home computer, which contained letters to his Moscow handlers downloaded by FBI agents who entered his house.

Under constant surveillance by a 50-person team, Ames was observed dropping off information and later picking up payments for it. In one instance he marked a Georgetown mailbox with chalk, signaling he had secrets to convey, then left a package of documents at an assigned footbridge. Four days later his Russian contact marked a telephone pole in Arlington, Virginia, indicating payment for services. That night Ames retrieved a package of cash from a drainpipe in a Maryland suburb, and he made $30,000 in bank deposits over the next two weeks.

Pulled over a few blocks from home on the morning of February 21, 1994, a disbelieving Aldrich Ames leans against his Jaguar as FBI agents put him in handcuffs (below). Shown at upper right in an arrest photograph, Ames was later sentenced to life in prison without parole; his wife Rosario, at lower right, was released in 1998.

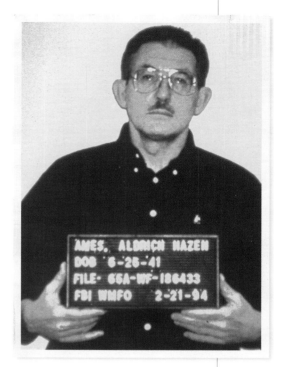

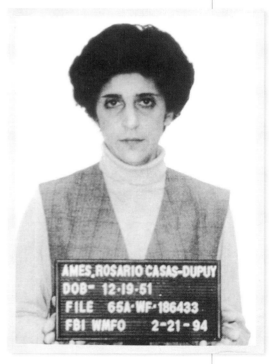

The CIA had by then moved Ames once again, this time to counternarcotics work. In the new, post-Cold War spirit of cooperation, he was directed to leave for Moscow on February 22, 1994, for a joint meeting on fighting drug trafficking. There Ames meant to ask his Russian paymasters for another $1.9 million. The day before he was to leave, however, his pursuers—fearing he would stay in the country he served so well—arrested the master mole on his drive to work.

"Espionage?" he bluffed. "You've got to be kidding." Informed that Rosario was also under arrest and the house was in FBI hands, he dropped his head and swore. For the sake of Rosario and their son Paul, he eventually cut a deal: His wife would be sentenced to a mere five years in return for his cooperation. She served three and a half and was released in 1998. Ames went to prison for life.

Director James Woolsey, who had been appointed CIA director just a year before by President Bush's successor, Bill Clinton, had to face a cyclone of criticism when the Ames story hit prime time. He asked the question on everyone's mind: Why did it take so long to find the mole? An investigation by the CIA's inspector general spat out a 486-page answer, which Woolsey summarized as "no one was watching," and "no one cared." It singled out 23 individuals for blame, including Woolsey's predecessors, the late Bill Casey and his successor, William Webster. In September 1994 Woolsey reprimanded 11 CIA officials, including Clair George and the polygraph operator who had vouched for Ames's veracity. In firing no one he infuriated agency critics, while the reprimands enraged agency officers. Beset on all sides, a frustrated Woolsey submitted his resignation at the end of 1994.

The CIA was battered by cartoonists, by furious congressmen—and by Ames, who gave a series of self-serving interviews that blasted everyone but himself. "These spy wars are a sideshow," he stated after his guilty plea, "which have no real impact on our significant national security interests." While Ames's bravado could be ignored, criticism by the press and other observers stung. Case officers left the agency by the score. President Bill Clinton directed that henceforth the head of the CIA's counterintelligence center be, of all things, an agent from the rival FBI.

On January 9, 1995, almost a decade after Ames had walked into the Soviet embassy, Woolsey bade farewell to the employees assembled in Langley's spacious lobby. His remarks sought to paint a broader picture of the work the agency was there to do. "You are in the job of stealing secrets," he told them. "We do our very best to hide these acts from all and sundry. That is what we are about." He added that this core task was a difficult one in an open society. In the aftermath of the Ames affair, and the wake of the Cold War, determining just what the CIA was "about" would be a challenge for Woolsey's successors, as the agency struggled to forge a new identity.

EPILOGUE:
NEW WORLD, NEW MISSIONS

It was fitting that after the Berlin Wall came crashing down in 1989, foreshadowing the collapse of the Soviet bloc, a section of the masonry was shipped off to Langley, Virginia. There, at CIA headquarters, this evocative fragment *(left)* was installed as a memorial to the end of the Cold War and to the agency's role in that epic East-West confrontation.

The wall, with its aura of spy-novel intrigue, embodied the CIA's original reason for being. Erected in 1961 to stop the flight of East Germans, it extended 28 miles across the city and 75 miles around the outside of West Berlin. As much as 15 feet high, topped with barbed wire and towers manned by armed guards, the wall was a glaring affront to freedom.

Yet through the 1990s, the agency's unusual souvenir also served as a symbol of a post-Cold War dilemma. Almost from the day of its creation in 1947, the CIA had served as an instrument in the growing struggle with the Soviet Union. In 1991 the end of the Soviet Union deprived it of that key target. Now began the struggle to come to grips with new challenges in a vastly changed world.

In the new era, tools and techniques honed on fighting the Communists had to be directed at more amorphous foes. Within the agency, "special centers" tackled not only the traditional problem of counter-intelligence but also terrorism, global narcotics traffic, and the spread of weapons of mass destruction. "The Cold War is over," President Bill Clinton cautioned the intelligence community in 1995, "but many new dangers have taken its place."

In handling these diverse missions, the agency was

A graffiti-covered souvenir of the Cold War, this section of the Berlin Wall stands at CIA headquarters in Langley, Virginia. Multilingual messages declare "finally free" in German and "peace" (mir) in Russian, written in Cyrillic characters.

plagued by fallout from the Aldrich Ames scandal. Morale in the directorate of operations, the agency's clandestine service, was devastated, and many veteran case officers quit in disgust. Then, in 1997, Harold Nicholson, branch chief in the counterterrorist center, confessed to spying for Russia in the years after Ames. He became the highest ranking CIA officer ever convicted of espionage.

COLD WAR LEGACIES

Less publicized than those counterintelligence failures was a success from the last days of the Cold War, code-named Rosewood. Only the barest details leaked to the public, but they outlined a major coup. Some time after the fall of the Berlin Wall, the CIA had spirited away the foreign-intelligence archives of the Stasi, the East German equivalent of the Soviet KGB. The CIA may have paid a Russian intermediary over one million dollars for the files, which contained code names, identities, and other critical information on tens of thousands of Stasi agents. Most were Germans or citizens of other European countries. But there were also Americans; in 1997 the files played a vital but secret role in the arrest and prosecution of three U.S. citizens for espionage *(below)*.

For several years, the CIA angered Germany by re-fusing to return the archives. After its reunification, Germany had set up a committee to review those Stasi files that it still had, which dealt mainly with East Germany's surveillance of its own citizens. Under German law, the committee publicly named former Stasi agents now active in politics, government, or the schools. Without the Rosewood files, however, its work was incomplete. Some observers speculated that the CIA may have refused to hand back the files because it might have hired some former agents itself.

In October 1999 the CIA finally agreed to return copies of some records, including a list of at least 30,000 Stasi agents and many more surveillance targets. Yet the agency reserved some key names, retaining for its own purposes information on former agents in the Middle East, Africa, the United States, and elsewhere in Europe.

Rosewood's quiet triumph contrasted sharply with a less palatable Cold War legacy. In its zealous crusade against Communism, the CIA had maintained close

In an artist's sketch, Kurt Stand, James Clark, and Theresa Marie Squillacote stand accused of spying for East Germany in the 1980s and, in the case of Stand and Clark, the 1970s. Files acquired by the CIA helped catch them.

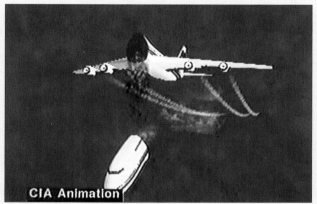

In an ingenious use of Cold War tools for civilian tasks, a CIA simulation re-creates the 1996 breakup of TWA Flight 800 off Long Island. Based on satellite data, these frames show how the back section briefly soared skyward, looking misleadingly like a missile.

director John Deutch appeared at a public meeting in Watts. Then the newspaper's own executive editor repudiated the series, and the controversy subsided.

SPIES FROM EARTH AND SKY

As it had during the Cold War, the agency relied for its new missions on updated space technology as well as old-fashioned earthbound agents. CIA analysts sitting at million-dollar microscopes studied images from billion-dollar Defense Department satellites originally devised to keep watch on Soviet weaponry. From 164 miles up, these orbiting watchdogs could snap sharp pictures of objects no larger than a paperback novel. They could pinpoint a cocaine-processing plant in Colombia, track signs of long-range missiles in North Korea, or detect apparent chemical-weapon preparations in Libya. But observant agents on the ground were still needed to determine where the eyes in the sky should look and to help interpret what they saw. "Spies tip off satellites," as director James Woolsey put it in 1994, "and satellites tip off spies."

In 1995 the satellites paid off handsomely when CIA analysts perusing imagery of India's northwestern desert spotted something suspicious. Thick cables snaked toward a deep shaft at Pokhran, where India had staged an underground nuclear test in 1974. U.S. diplomats confronted Indian officials with the evidence, persuading them to call off the planned test.

But India was determined to press ahead, and by the spring of 1998 it was making secret preparations for a new test. U.S. spy satellites on four different trajectories passed over the Pokhran test site at least once a day. Indian scientists learned the satellites' daily schedules—apparently, from a hacker's Web site on the Internet—and planned accordingly. Crews readied the test grounds only when the satellites were not overhead. Even so, satellite images were taken showing preparations six hours before the test, but they

ties with security forces in Latin America that had practiced assassination and torture on their own peoples. In the 1990s many of these links were more fully exposed than ever before. Other negative reports on the CIA's past, however, were far more debatable. In 1996, articles in the San Jose *Mercury News* alleged that the drug smugglers who had introduced crack cocaine to the black Los Angeles neighborhood of Watts in the 1980s had helped finance the CIA-backed Contras in Nicaragua. The charges stirred such anger that CIA

PRE-STRIKE

POST-STRIKE

← DESTROYED
← LIGHT DAMAGE

Aerial photographs show an Afghan terrorist training camp before and after U.S. missile strikes in 1998. Osama bin Laden (left) was linked to the camps by CIA analysts, who tracked him and his associates in the late 1990s.

were not processed in time. When three atomic devices exploded underground in May, the CIA got the news of the largest act of nuclear proliferation in 24 years from the media.

In Iraq, meanwhile, the agency resorted to cloak-and-dagger methods—with a new twist. CIA operatives infiltrated U.N. inspection teams charged with locating Iraq's biological and chemical weapons. The Iraqi government had long insisted the U.N. squads were riddled with American spies. In 1999 the *Washington Post* quoted American sources confirming the charge. Operating under U.N. cover, the article said, officers from the CIA and other agencies had installed gear allowing the U.S. to eavesdrop on Iraqi military communications.

TARGETING TERRORISTS

Late in 1995 President Clinton signed a top-secret order that directed the CIA to target a network of international terror. The ring was allegedly headed by Osama bin Laden, a 38-year-old Saudi multimillionaire. The agency's counterterrorist center set up a task force to disrupt bin Laden's loose-knit organization.

CIA information led to the arrest of a number of bin Laden's lieutenants and traced bin Laden himself to the Sudan, where he lived until 1996, and to terrorist training camps in Afghanistan.

The CIA was particularly intrigued by bin Laden's suspected links to the El Shifa pharmaceutical plant in the Sudanese capital of Khartoum. According to a later newspaper report, "highly reliable intelligence" indicated Sudan had allowed him to make chemical weapons there. Moreover, Iraqi chemical-arms specialists had made frequent visits to El Shifa. In the summer of 1998, a CIA operative from another Middle Eastern country dug up a soil sample outside the factory. Lab tests showed a high concentration of the chemical Empta, a key ingredient in the lethal nerve gas known as VX, but a CIA report cautioned the sample did not prove the plant was making nerve gas. To learn more, it recommended taking more samples.

Before that advice could be acted on, events intervened. On August 7, 1998, truck bombs exploded outside U.S. embassies in Nairobi, Kenya, and Dar es Salaam, Tanzania, killing 12 Americans and more than 200 Africans; an estimated 5,000 were wounded. Citing "convincing information," President Clinton tagged bin Laden as the mastermind behind the attacks and struck back. On August 20, U.S. warships unleashed Tomahawk cruise missiles, smashing the suspected terrorist camps in Afghanistan and leveling the pharmaceutical plant in Khartoum.

Doubts arose in the press, however, as to whether El Shifa was indeed the source of nerve gas. Contrary to earlier claims, it turned out that drugs for malaria and tuberculosis were manufactured there. In addition, bin Laden had no recent connection to the plant, which had changed ownership six months before. It also came out that in discussions leading up to the missile strikes, intelligence officials had downplayed the CIA report urging caution. The agency's job, said one veteran, ought to be "to put what you have on the table, and then someone else makes the decision."

NEW HIRES FOR A NEW ERA

Operating in the glare of publicity in the last decade of the millennium, the director of central intelligence clearly had one of Washington's toughest jobs. When George Tenet was appointed in 1997, he became the fifth director in six years. An energetic son of Greek immigrants, Tenet revitalized the agency's clandestine operations staff. In 1998 he played a role in U.S.-mediated talks between Israelis and Palestinians leading to the Wye River Accord. This agreement, which laid out a phased Israeli

withdrawal from the West Bank, gave the CIA an unprecedented public duty as a peacekeeper assigned to monitor terrorism. However, Tenet also had to take public responsibility for such snafus as the failure to predict the Indian nuclear tests, the bloody collapse of a CIA-directed Kurdish rebellion against Iraq's Saddam Hussein, and the inadvertent bombing of the Chinese embassy in Belgrade. The last was located at the only target site selected by the CIA during the 1999 NATO bombardment of Serbia; analysts had apparently relied on an out-of-date map.

In this new era, finding and retaining employees sometimes proved as hard as keeping directors. In the years after the Cold War, the CIA lost a quarter of its work force through attrition and early retirements. When it began recruiting vigorously again in the late 1990s, it faced a more onerous task than in the early Cold War, when young patriots rushed to join the agency's anti-Communist cause. Now recruits had to labor at more varied, and more subtle, missions, yet with the same anonymity that President Eisenhower described in 1959. "Success cannot be advertised; failure cannot be explained," he said of the CIA, in words that held true four decades later. "In the work of intelligence, heroes are undecorated and unsung, often even among their own fraternity."

Indian soldiers guard Prithvi missiles, able to deliver nuclear warheads like those India tested in 1998. The CIA failed to predict that test, but tracking the spread of nuclear weapons remains a priority.

ACKNOWLEDGMENTS & PICTURE CREDITS

ACKNOWLEDGMENTS

The editors wish to thank the following for their assistance in the preparation of this volume:

Tracey Bennett, Lapwai, Idaho; Chase Brandon, Office of Public Affairs, CIA, Washington, D.C.; Mary Caspari, McDermott Library, Univ. of Texas at Dallas, Richardson, Texas; Duane R. Clarridge, San Diego; Lauren Given, Henninger Media Services, Arlington, Va.; Gerald K. Haines, Center for the Study of Intelligence, CIA, Washington, D.C.; Toni L. Hiley, Center for the Study of Intelligence, Washington, D.C.; James Hill, John Fitzgerald Kennedy Library, Boston; Dean Love, Arlington, Va.; Roger McCarthy, Henderson, Nev.; John Marks, Search for Common Ground, Washington, D.C.; Antonio J. Mendez, Knoxville, Md.; James Morrison, San Antonio, Texas; Anna Nelson, American University, Washington, D.C.; Eric Olson, Frederick, Md.; Art Ronnie, Altadena, Calif.; Richard E. Schroeder, Center for the Study of Intelligence, CIA, Washington, D. C.; Jochen Staadt, Berlin; John E. Taylor, National Archives and Records Administration, College Park, Md.; Michael S. Warner, Center for the Study of Intelligence, CIA, Washington, D.C.; Charles L. Weldon, M.D., Chiang Rai, Thailand; David Wise, Washington, D.C.

BIBLIOGRAPHY

BOOKS

Ambrose, Stephen E. *Ike's Spies.* Garden City, N.Y.: Doubleday, 1981.

Andradé, Dale. *Ashes to Ashes.* Lexington, Mass.: Lexington Books, 1990.

Andrew, Christopher, and Vasili Mitrokhin. *The Sword and the Shield.* New York: Basic Books, 1999.

Barnes, Trevor. "Democratic Deception." In *Deception Operations,* ed. by David A. Charters and Maurice A. J. Tugwell. London: Brassey's, 1990.

Benson, Robert Louis, and Michael Warner (eds.). *Venona.* Washington, D.C.: National Security Agency/Central Intelligence Agency, 1996.

Berry, F. Clifton. *Inside the CIA.* Montgomery, Ala.: Community Communications, 1997.

Beschloss, Michael R.:
The Crisis Years. New York: Edward Burlingame Books, 1991.
Mayday. New York: Harper & Row, 1986.

Bethell, Nicholas. *The Great Betrayal.* London: Hodder and Stoughton, 1984.

Bissell, Richard M. *Reflections of a Cold Warrior.* New Haven, Conn.: Yale Univ. Press, 1996.

Blum, William. *Killing Hope.* Monroe, Maine: Common Courage Press, 1995.

Brown, Anthony Cave. *The Last Hero.* New York: New York Times Books, 1982.

Brown, Anthony Cave (ed.). *The Secret War Report of the OSS.* New York: Berkley, 1976.

Brugioni, Dino A. *Eyeball to Eyeball.* Ed. by Robert F. McCort. New York: Random House, 1991.

Burke, Michael. *Outrageous Good Fortune.* Boston: Little, Brown, 1984.

Chang, Laurence, and Peter Kornbluh (eds.). *The Cuban Missile Crisis, 1962.* New York: New Press, 1992.

Clarridge, Duane R., and Digby Diehl. *A Spy for All Seasons.* New York: Scribner, 1997.

Colby, William, and Peter Forbath. *Honorable Men: My Life in the CIA.* New York: Simon and Schuster, 1978.

Conboy, Kenneth, and James Morrison. *Shadow War.* Boulder, Colo.: Paladin Press, 1995.

Cullather, Nicholas. *Operation PBSuccess.* Washington, D.C.: History Staff, Center for the Study of Intelligence, Central Intelligence Agency, 1994.

DeForest, Orrin, and David Chanoff. *Slow Burn.* New York: Simon and Schuster, 1990.

Dickey, Christopher. *With the Contras.* New York: Simon and Schuster, 1985.

Dillon, Sam. *Commandos.* New York: Henry Holt, 1991.

Draper, Theodore. *A Very Thin Line.* New York: Hill and Wang, 1991.

Dulles, Allen. *The Craft of Intelligence.* New York: Harper & Row, 1963.

Epstein, Edward Jay. *Deception.* New York: Simon and Schuster, 1989.

Ford, Harold P. *CIA and the Vietnam Policymakers.* Washington, D.C.: History Staff, Center for the Study of Intelligence, Central Intelligence Agency, 1998.

Gelb, Norman. *The Berlin Wall.* New York: Times Books, 1986.

Gleijeses, Piero. *Shattered Hope.* Princeton, N.J.: Princeton Univ. Press, 1991.

Grose, Peter. *Gentleman Spy.* Boston: Houghton Mifflin, 1994.

Hamilton-Merritt, Jane. *Tragic Mountains.* Bloomington: Indiana Univ. Press, 1993.

Hamilton-Paterson, James. *America's Boy.* New York: Henry Holt, 1998.

Herda, D. J. *The Afghan Rebels.* New York: Franklin Watts, 1990.

Hersh, Burton. *The Old Boys.* New York: Charles Scribner's, 1992.

Hersh, Seymour M. *The Dark Side of Camelot.* Boston: Little, Brown, 1997.

Hinckle, Warren, and William Turner. *Deadly Secrets.* New York: Thunder Mouth's Press, 1992.

Hood, William. *Mole.* Washington, D.C.: Brassey's, 1982.

Immerman, Richard H. *The CIA in Guatemala.* Austin: Univ. of Texas Press, 1982.

Jeffreys-Jones, Rhodri. *The CIA and American Democracy.* New Haven, Conn.: Yale Univ. Press, 1989.

Kaplan, Robert D. *Soldiers of God.* Boston: Houghton Mifflin, 1990.

Keddie, Nikki R. *Roots of Revolution.* New Haven, Conn.: Yale Univ. Press, 1981.

Kennedy, Robert F. *Thirteen Days.* New York: W. W. Norton, 1969.

Kessler, Ronald. *Inside the CIA.* New York: Pocket Books, 1992.

Kinzer, Stephen. *Blood of Brothers.* New York: G. P. Putnam's, 1981.

Lansdale, Edward Geary. *In the Midst of Wars.* New York: Harper & Row, 1972.

Leary, William M. (ed.). *The Central Intelligence Agency.* University: Univ. of Alabama Press, 1984.

Lynch, Grayston L. *Decision for Disaster.* Washington, D.C.: Brassey's, 1998.

McAuliffe, Mary S. (ed.). *Cuban Missile Crisis.* Washington, D.C.: History Staff, Central Intelligence Agency, 1992.

McGehee, Ralph W. *Deadly Deceits.* New York: Sheridan Square, 1983.

McIntosh, Elizabeth P. *Sisterhood of Spies.* Annapolis, Md.: Naval Institute Press, 1998.

Mackenzie, Angus. *Secrets.* Berkeley: Univ. of California Press, 1997.

Mangold, Tom. *Cold Warrior.* New York: Simon & Schuster, 1991.

Marks, John. *The Search for the "Manchurian Candidate."* New York: W. W. Norton, 1979.

Martin, David C. *Wilderness of Mirrors.* New York: Harper & Row, 1980.

Melton, H. Keith:
CIA Special Weapons and Equipment. New York: Sterling, 1993.
The Ultimate Spy Book. London: Dorling Kindersley, 1996.

Mendez, Antonio J. *The Master of Disguise.*

New York: William Morrow, 1999.

Miller, Jay. *Lockheed Martin's Skunk Works.* Leicester, England: Midland, 1995.

Montague, Ludwell Lee. *General Walter Bedell Smith as Director of Central Intelligence.* University Park: Pennsylvania State Univ. Press, 1992.

Moyar, Mark. *Phoenix and the Birds of Prey.* Annapolis, Md.: Naval Institute Press, 1997.

Murphy, David E., Sergei A. Kondrashev, and George Bailey. *Battleground Berlin.* New Haven, Conn.: Yale Univ. Press, 1997.

North, Oliver L., and William Novak. *Under Fire.* New York: HarperCollins, 1991.

Olmsted, Kathryn S. *Challenging the Secret Government.* Chapel Hill: Univ. of North Carolina Press, 1996.

Parker, James E., Jr. *Codename Mule.* Annapolis, Md.: Naval Institute Press, 1995.

Pedlow, Gregory W., and Donald E. Welzenbach. *The CIA and the U-2 Program.* Washington, D.C.: History Staff, Center for the Study of Intelligence, Central Intelligence Agency, 1998.

Pelletier, Jean, and Claude Adams. *The Canadian Caper.* New York: William Morrow, 1981.

Persico, Joseph E. *Casey.* New York: Viking, 1990.

Philby, Kim. *My Silent War.* New York: Grove Press, 1968.

Phillips, David Atlee. *The Night Watch.* New York: Atheneum, 1977.

Polmar, Norman, and Thomas B. Allen. *Spy Book: The Encyclopedia of Espionage.* New York: Random House, 1998.

Posner, Gerald. *Case Closed.* New York: Random House, 1993.

Powers, Thomas. *The Man Who Kept the Secrets.* New York: Alfred A. Knopf, 1979.

Prados, John. *Presidents' Secret Wars.* New York: William Morrow, 1986.

Ranelagh, John. *The Agency.* New York: Simon & Schuster, 1986.

Rich, Ben R., and Leo Janos. *Skunk Works.* Boston: Little, Brown, 1994.

Richelson, Jeffrey T. *A Century of Spies.* New York: Oxford Univ. Press, 1995.

Robbins, Christopher. *Air America.* New York: G. P. Putnam's, 1979.

Roosevelt, Kermit. *Countercoup.* New York: McGraw-Hill, 1979.

Rositzke, Harry A. *The CIA's Secret Operations.* New York: Reader's Digest Press, 1977.

Ruffner, Kevin C. (ed.). *Corona* (CIA Cold War Records series). Washington, D.C.: History Staff, Center for the Study of Intelligence, Central Intelligence Agency, 1995.

Scheckter, Jerrold L., and Peter S. Deriabin. *The Spy Who Saved the World.* New York: Charles Scribner's, 1992.

Schlesinger, Stephen, and Stephen Kinzer. *Bitter Fruit.* New York: Doubleday, 1982.

Smith, R. Harris. *OSS.* Berkeley: Univ. of

California Press, 1972.

Srodes, James. *Allen Dulles.* Washington, D.C.: Regnery, 1999.

Sudoplatov, Pavel, and Anatoli. *Special Tasks.* Boston: Little, Brown, 1995.

Thomas, Evan. *The Very Best Men.* New York: Simon & Schuster, 1995.

Tourison, Sedgwick. *SecretArmy, SecretWar.* Annapolis, Md.: Naval Institute Press, 1995.

Turner, Stansfield. *Secrecy and Democracy.* Boston: Houghton Mifflin, 1985.

Valentine, Douglas. *The Phoenix Program.* New York: William Morrow, 1990.

Walsh, Lawrence E. *Iran-Contra.* New York: Times Books, 1994.

Warner, Roger:
  Back Fire. New York: Simon & Schuster, 1995.
  Out of Laos. Rancho Cordova, Calif.: Southeast Asia Community Resource Center, 1996.

Weldon, Charles. *Tragedy in Paradise.* Bangkok: Asia Books, 1999.

Weiner, Tim, David Johnston, and Neil A. Lewis. *Betrayal.* New York: Random House, 1995.

Winks, Robin W. *Cloak and Gown.* New York: William Morrow, 1987.

Wise, David:
  Molehunt. New York: Random House, 1992.
  Nightmover. New York: HarperCollins, 1995.

Wise, David, and Thomas B. Ross. *The Invisible Government.* New York: Random House, 1964.

Woodward, Bob. *Veil.* New York: Simon and Schuster, 1987.

Wyden, Peter. *Bay of Pigs.* New York: Simon and Schuster, 1979.

Yousaf, Mohammad and Mark Adkin. *The Bear Trap.* London: Leo Cooper, 1992.

PERIODICALS

Auster, Bruce B. "An Explosion of Indian Pride." *U.S. News & World Report,* May 25, 1998.

Barnes, Trevor:
  "The Secret Cold War" *The Historical Journal,* 1981, Part 1, Vol. 24, no. 2, and 1982, Part 2, Vol. 25, no. 3.

Bodirsky, Peter. "Canadian Caper in Iran Orchestrated by CIA." *London Free Press,* Feb. 28, 1998.

Braden, Tom. "The Birth of the CIA." *American Heritage,* Feb. 1977.

Branch, Taylor. "The Trial of the CIA." *New York Times Magazine,* Sept. 12, 1976.

Budiansky, Stephen, Erica E. Goode, and Ted Gest. "The Cold War Experiments." *U.S. News & World Report,* Jan. 24, 1994.

Chebium, Raju. "Iranians No Match for CIA's Top Agent of Disguise." *Washington Times,* Oct. 28, 1999.

"The CIA." *Time,* Sept. 30, 1974.

"CIA Agent Reveals Details of 1980 Rescue of U.S. Diplomats in Iran." *AP Online,* Mar. 2, 1998.

"CIA Also Deserved High Praise in Escape of Envoys from Iran." *Denver Rocky Mountain News,* Mar. 3, 1998.

"A CIA Scandal—and the Backlash." *U.S. News & World Report,* Jan. 6, 1975.*

"Damn the Leakers—Full Ahead!" *Time,* Jan. 19, 1976.

DeYoung, Karen, and Vernon Loeb. "Documents Show U.S. Knew Pinochet Planned Crackdown in '73." *Washington Post,* July 1, 1999.

"Donovan Upheld on Peace Spy Plan." *New York Times,* Feb. 13, 1945.

Drozdiak, William. "The Cold War in Cold Storage." *Washington Post,* Mar. 3, 1999.

Duffy, Bruce. "Journey." *Life,* Sept. 1997.

Evans, Joseph C. "Berlin Tunnel Intelligence." *International Journal of Intelligence and Counterintelligence,* Spring 1996, Vol. 9, no. 1.

Ford, Harold P.:
  "Revisiting Vietnam." CIA Studies in Intelligence, 1996, Vol. 39, no. 5.
  "Unpopular Pessimism." CIA Studies in Intelligence, Semiannual Edition, no. 1, 1997.

"General Donovan's Case for Unified Intelligence." *New York Times,* Sept. 21, 1945.

Hart, John L. "Pyotr Semyonovich Popov." *Intelligence and National Security,* Oct. 1997.

Hersh, Seymour M.:
  "Huge CIA Operation Reported in U.S. against Antiwar Forces, Other Dissidents in Nixon Years." *New York Times,* Dec. 12, 1974.
  "The Missiles of August." *New Yorker,* Oct. 12, 1998.

Hirsh, Michael, and Tom Masland. "The Deal Makers." *Newsweek,* Nov. 2, 1998.

Hood, William. "To the Manor Born." *International Journal of Intelligence and Counterintelligence.* Summer 1996, Vol. 9, no. 1.

Hosenball, Mark, and Sarah Van Bove. "Re-creating Flight 800's Final Seconds." *Newsweek,* Dec. 1, 1997.

Kornbluh, Peter:
  "NACLA Report on the Americas." *Declassifying U.S. Intervention in Chile,* May/June 1999.
  "The Storm over 'Dark Alliance.'" *Columbia Jounalism Review,* Jan./Feb. 1997.

Larsen, Douglas. "'Sulfato' Nemesis of Guatemalan Reds." *Flying,* July 1957.

Loeb, Vernon. *Washington Post:*
  "At Hush-Hush CIA Unit, Talk of a Turnaround." Sept. 7, 1999.
  "Bin Laden Still Seen as Threat." July 29, 1999.
  "CIA Still Recuperating from Mole's Aftermath." Feb. 22, 1999.
  "CIA Chief Takes 'Responsibility' for Bombing of Chinese Embassy." July 23, 1999.
  "A Dirty Business." July 25, 1999.
  "Key CIA Official to Step Down." May 7, 1999.
  "U.S. Wasn't Sure Plant Had Nerve Gas Role." Aug. 21, 1999.
  "Wanted." Nov. 27, 1998.
  "Where the CIA Wages Its New World War." Sept. 9, 1998.

McConnell, Malcolm. "Escape with the Master of Disguise." *Reader's Digest,* Apr. 1998.

McGeary, Johanna. "Nukes . . . They're Back." *Time,* May 25, 1998.

Mendez, Antonio J. "CIA Goes Hollywood." *Studies in Intelligence,* Spring 1999.

Miller, James E. "Taking Off the Gloves." *Diplomatic History,* Winter 1983, Vol. 7, no. 1.

O'Mahony, John. " 'Suicide' of LSD Guinea Pig Probed." *New York Post,* Sept. 21, 1997.

Phillips, Cabel. "The Shadow Army That Fought in Silence." *New York Times Magazine,* Oct. 7, 1945.

Pincus, Walter. *Washington Post:*
  "Berlin to Get CIA Copies of 320,000 Stasi Files." Oct. 27, 1999.
  "Cold War Footnote." Nov. 22, 1998.
  "Top Spy Retiring from CIA." July 29, 1999.
  "U.S. Won't Hand Over E. German Spy Files." Jan. 29, 1999.

"Props for Moscow's Puppet." *Time,* Jan. 28, 1980.

Roth, Melissa. "Frank Olson File: The CIA's Bad Trip." *George,* Oct. 1997.

Staadt, Jochen. "Harming the Regime." *Frankfurter Allgemeine Zeitung,* Jan. 10, 1998.

Stover, Dawn. "Was It Murder?" *Popular Science,* Apr. 1999.

Thomas, Evan, John Barry, and Melinda Liu. "Ground Zero." *Newsweek,* May 25, 1998.

Trohan, Walter. *Chicago Tribune:*
  "Army Submits Own Plans." Feb. 11, 1945.
  "Sleuths Would Snoop on U.S. and the World." Feb. 9, 1945.
  "Super-Spy Idea Denounced." Feb. 10, 1945.
  "U.S. Sets Up Gestapo." June 15, 1947.

"Truman Ends OSS." *New York Times,* Sept. 21, 1945.

"Urge Central Unit for Intelligence." *New York Times,* Feb. 10, 1945.

Waller, Douglas:
  "Coming in from the Cold." *Time,* Nov. 2, 1998.
  "Inside the Hunt for Osama." *Time,* Dec. 21, 1998.

Watson, Russell, and John Barry. "'Our Target Was Terror.'" *Newsweek,* Aug. 31, 1998.

"Wisdom about Intelligence." *Christian Science Monitor,* Apr. 14, 1947.

OTHER SOURCES

Central Intelligence Agency. "The Berlin Tunnel Operation." Clandestine Services Historical Paper, June 1968.

"Factbook on Intelligence." Washington, D.C.: Central Intelligence Agency, The George Bush Center for Intelligence, n.d.

Lowenthal, Mark M. "The Central Intelligence Agency: Organizational History." Congressional Research Service, The Library of Congress, Aug. 4, 1978.

Wyatt, Mark. Interview for CNN Cold War series, Feb. 2, 1996.

INDEX

Numerals in italics indicate an illustration of the subject mentioned.

About-Face (project), 114
Abrams, Elliott, 171
Abzug, Bella, *143*
Afghanistan: and bin Laden, *184,* 185; CIA in, 153, *156-157, 162-167, 164,* 166, 171
Agee, Philip, 151
Agency for International Development, 105, 109, 114, 115, 131, 134
AID. *See* Agency for International Development
Air America: insignia of, *131;* and Laos, 107, 108, 109, *110-111, 130-139;* precursor to, *29,* 131; and Vietnam, *102,* 139
Air America Log (periodical), *138*
Ajax (project), 58-61
Alabama National Guard, 87
Albania, 22-26, *24, 25*
Alfhem (freighter), 67-68
Allende Gossens, Salvador, *144, 145*
Ames, Aldrich, 171-*179, 172, 174, 176-177, 178,* 182
Ames, Rosario, 171, *172, 178, 179*
Anders, Robert, 154-155
Anderson, Rudolf, Jr., *timeline 101*
Angleton, Cicely, 122
Angleton, James Jesus, *122, 123;* and Italy, *18-*19; "mole" hunt by, 121-126, 127, 173; and Operation Chaos, 127-128, *142-*143; retirement of, 128, 129
Anosov (freighter), *101*
Arbenz Guzmán, Jacobo, *62-*71, 76, 78
Artime, Manuel, *78*
Athens News, 151
Auchincloss, Louis, 32
Audio surveillance equipment, *50-51, 52-53,* 165-166

Bagley, Tennent (Pete), 124
Balgar (ship), *84*
Barker, Bernard, 126, *127*
Barnes, C. Tracy: and Bay of Pigs invasion, 65, 78, 81, 89; and Guatemala, 64, *65,* 67, 69, 78
Batista, Fulgencio, 76
Bay of Pigs invasion: aftermath of, *89-91, 90,* 147; background of, 62, 76-78; buildup for, 78, 81-84; strikes in, *56,* 84-89, *84-85, 87, 88;* training for, 64, 65, 77, 79-81, *80*
Bentley, Elizabeth Terrill, *11-*12
Berlin. *See* Germany
Bermúdez, Enrique, 158
Bernays, Edward, 64, 71
BG Fiend (project), 22-26, *24, 25*
bin Laden, Osama, *184-*185
Bissell, Richard: appointed as deputy director for plans, 76; and Bay of Pigs invasion, 77-79, 82, 83-84, 87-89, 91; departure from CIA, 91; and Guatemala, 72, 76; and U-2 spy plane, *72-*74, 76
Blake, George, 33, 34, *38,* 41-42
BND (West German intelligence service), origins of, 39
Boland, Edward, 160, 162
Braden, Tom, 25
Braun, Wernher von, 9
Brigade 2506, *79-*91, *80, 84, 88, 90*
Britain, 69, 122. *See also* Secret Intelligence Service
Bross, John, 27
Buckley, William A., *168*
Buell, Edgar (Pop), *109,* 114
Building T-32, 41
Bundy, McGeorge, 83
Burke, Michael, 27
Bush, George, 129, *157, 170,* 171
Butler, Joseph, *132, 133*

Cabell, Charles, 84
Cabot, John Moors, 63
Cabot, Thomas, 63
Calero, Adolfo, *158, 169*
Calhoun, George, 137
Cameras, *44, 46-49*
Canada, 6, 11, 153, *154-155*
Carter, Jimmy, *155,* 156
Casey, William J.: and Afghanistan, 162, 164-166; and Ames, 173, 179; appointed as director of central intelligence, *156-157;* and CIA origins, *8;* and Iran-Contra affair, *167-*171; and Nicaragua, 157-162
Castillo Armas, Carlos, 65, 67-71, *68,* 77
Castro, Fidel, *timeline 99;* assassination plots against, 76, 77, *146-*147; Batista overthrown by, 76; and Bay of Pigs invasion, 57, 62, 76, 77-91; and Guatemala, 71
CAT. *See* Civil Air Transport
Cave, George, 169
Central Intelligence Agency: creation and mission of, *6-13,* 18, 35, 141, 171, 179, *181-*185; directorate functions, 37; employment statistics, 35, 185; funding mechanisms of, 19, 27; headquarters buildings, *13, 37,* 91; organization of, *chart 36;* seal of, *35;* tools of, *44-55,* 165-166. *See also specific operations, organizations, and persons*
Central Intelligence Group, 10, 13, 17
Chambers, John, 153
Chaos (project), 127-128, *142-*143
Checkpoint Charlie, *94*
Child, Julia, 8
Chile, *144, 145*
China, *map 104;* and Afghanistan, 156, 165, 167; Belgrade embassy bombing, 185; and CIA domestic spying, 142; CIA operations in, 17, *28-30;* and Soviet Union, 122
Church, Frank, 128, *129,* 140
Church Committee, 128-129, 140, 142, 144-145, 146, 147
Churchill, Winston, 11
Chuvakhin, Sergei, *172-*173
CIA. *See* Central Intelligence Agency
CINTELCO (telephone supplier), 37
Civil Air Transport, *29,* 67, 131
Clark, James, *182*
Clarridge, Duane (Dewey), *157-158, 159,* 160-162, 171
Clay, Lucius, 21
Clinton, William, 179, 181, 184, 185
Code pad, *50*
Codes, Air America, *134*
Code training key, *51*
Cohen, William, *158-*159, 160, 161
COI. *See* Coordinator of Information
Colby, William, 6, 103, 120, 121, 127-128, 129, 141, 143, 144, 151; and Chile, 144; and CIA domestic spying, 127-*129,* 141, 143; and CIA "mole" hunt, 121, 127; and
CIA origins, 6, *8;* departure from CIA, 129; and Laos, 108; and Vietnam, 103-*105,* 115, 118-*121, 119,* 127; and Welch, *151*
Communications equipment, *44, 50-51, 52-53,* 165-166
Communists: and CIA role, 11, 61-62; Eisenhower policy on, 57. *See also specific countries*
Congressional hearings, 143, 145, 148, 170. *See also* Church Committee
Continental Air Service, *139*
Coordinator of Information, 8
Corcoran, Thomas (Tommy the Cork), 64
CORDS program, 115, 118-121
Corona satellite, 76, *116*
Counterspy (magazine), 151
Counterterrorist center, 162
Cuba, *map 64, timeline 97, 99, 101;* assassination plots against Castro, 76, 77, *146-*147; Bay of Pigs invasion, 32, *56,* 57, 62, 64, 65, 76, 77-91, *78,* 79, *80,* 84-85, *87,* 88-89, *90,* 147; missile crisis, *91,* 93, *96-101, 96-97, 98;* and Nicaragua, 155, 158, 160
Cubela, Rolando, 147
Currie, Lauchlin, 12
Czechoslovakia, 67, 68, 125

Dalai Lama, *29, 30*
Dar es Salaam embassy bombing, 185
Davis, Robert, 80
Dawson, Bob, 131
DCI. *See* Director of central intelligence
Dead-drop spike, *49*
DeForest, Orrin, 120
Dema, Jusuf, *25*
Deutch, John, 183
Dialer, *44*
Díaz, Carlos, 71
Directorates, roles of, 37
Director of central intelligence position, 37
Dobrynin, Anatoly, *timeline 97,* 101
Dominican Republic, 66, 146
Donovan, William J. (Wild Bill), *6-10, 12,* 13, 104
Dooley, Thomas, 17
Downey, John, 28, *29*
Droller, Gerry, 78, 79
Dulles, Allen, *28, 32,* 42, 61, 83, *timeline 95;* appointed as deputy director for plans, 31; appointed as director of central intelligence, 32; and Bay of Pigs invasion, 77, 78, 79, 83, 84, 91; and Berlin, 40, 42; and CIA origins, *8;* and Guatemala, 66, 67, 68, 69, 76; and Iran, 58, 59, 61; and Olson, 150; and Popov, 33; retirement of, 91; and U-2 spy plane, 72
Dulles, John Foster: death of, 76; and Guatemala, 63, 67; and Iran, 58, 61; law firm of, 31; named secretary of state, 32
Durenberger, David, 160

Egypt, *73,* 156, 165
Eisenhower, Dwight D.: anti-Communist platform of, 57; and Castro, 76-77, 78, 146; and CIA leadership, 32; departure from office, 76, 82; and Guatemala, 62, 63, 64, 67, 71; and Iran, 57, 58, 61; and Laos, 106; and U-2 spy plane, 73-74
Eliot, T. S., 126

El Salvador, 155, 158
Ervin, Sam, *128*
Esterline, Jacob (Jake), 78, 81, 83, 89
ExComm, *98*, 99-100; *timeline* 99
Executive Order 9621, 10

Family jewels" memo, 128, 140
FBI. *See* Federal Bureau of Investigation
Fecteau, Richard, 28, *29*
Federal Bureau of Investigation: and Ames,
    172, 173, 175, 176, 177-179; and CIA "mole"
    hunt, 124; and Watergate scandal, 127
Fiers, Alan, 169, 171
Film containers, *49*
Ford, Gerald: and CIA assassination plots,
    128, 147; and Colby retirement, 129; and
    Olson, *150;* and Rockefeller Commission,
    140, 143; and Welch, 151
Forrestal, James, 18, 21
France, 122
Frei, Eduardo, 144
Fuchs, Klaus, 12

Garbler, Paul, 125
Gardner, Meredith, 12
Gates, Robert, 157
Gaulle, Charles de, 122
Gehlen, Reinhard, *39*
George, Clair, 166, 171, 179
Germany, *timeline* 95; and Ames, 175; Berlin
    as spy capital, 33-34; Berlin crisis of 1961,
    91, 93-97, *94;* Berlin tunnel, *14,* 17, 38-42,
    43; Berlin Wall, 171, *180-181;* BND origins,
    39; and Liebing, *41;* Stasi files, *182*
Ghaffar (Afghan commander), 166-167
Ghorbanifar, Manucher, 168
Giancana, Momo Salvatore (Sam), *146,* 147
Gold (project), *14,* 17, 38-42, *43*
Goldwater, Barry, *147,* 161
Golitsyn, Anatoli Mikhailovich, 122-126, *123*
Golos, Jacob, 12
Gorbachev, Mikhail, *167*
Gordievsky, Oleg, 177
Gottlieb, Sidney, *148-*150
Gouzenko, Igor, *6-7,* 11, 12
Great Swan Island, *map* 64, 79, 86
Gromyko, Andrey, *timeline* 99
GRU (Soviet military intelligence service),
    32-34, 38, 93-95, 174, 175
Guatemala: *map* 64; and Bay of Pigs invasion,
    64, 77, 79, 80, 81; coup of 1954, 32, 62-71,
    66, 68, 69, 70, 72, 76, 77, 78, 82
Guevara, Ernesto (Che), 71

Haney, Albert, 64-66, 69
Hart, Gary, 158-159, *160*
Harvey, William, 39-42, *40*
Hasenfus, Eugene, 169-*170*
Hawkins, Jack, 81, *82,* 83, 89
Hayden, Sterling, 8
Helms, Richard: and Bay of Pigs invasion, 78;
    and Chile, *144;* and CIA domestic spying,
    128-129, 142; and CIA "mole" hunt, 124;
    and OSS, 8; and Southeast Asia, 104, 139;
    and Watergate scandal, 126-127, *128*
Henderson, Loy, 59-60
Herman, Bill, 58
Hersh, Seymour, 127, 140, 141
Hillenkoetter, Roscoe, 13, 19, 21, 22, 31
Hind Mi-24, 163
Hitler, Adolf, 8, 39
Hollis, Roger, 122
Honduras, *map* 64, 66, 67, 68, *152,* 153

Hoover, J. Edgar, 9, 124
Hoxha, Enver, *22,* 23, 24, 25
Hughes, Howard, *117*
Hughes Glomar Explorer, 116-*117*
Huk guerrillas, 15-16
Hunt, E. Howard, 66, 69, *78-79,* 86, 125, 126
Hussein, Saddam, 185

India, 183-184, *185*
Indonesia, 61-62
Intelligence Identities Protection Act, 151
International Telephone and Telegraph Cor-
    poration, 144
Iran: hostage crisis, 61, 153-*155, 154;* Iran-
    Contra affair, 157, 167-171, *169, 170;* Mosad-
    deq ousted, 32, 57-*61, 60,* 169; shah over-
    thrown, 61; and Stinger missiles, 167
Iran, shah of, 57-*61, 60*
Iraq, 184, 185
Israel, 168, 185
Italy, 17, 18-21, *19,* 144
Izvestia (newspaper), 38

James, Daniel, 71
"Jedburgh" team, *9*
Johnson, Kelly, 72
Johnson, Lyndon: and Castro, 146; and CIA
    briefs, 35; and CIA domestic spying, 128,
    141, 142; and Laos, 107, 112; and Vietnam,
    113, 115, 120, 142

Karlow, Peter, 125
Kennan, George, 18, 21, 25
Kennedy, John F., *timeline 95, 99, 101;* assassi-
    nation of, 107, 123-124, 125, 147; and assas-
    sination plots against Castro, *146,* 147; and
    Bay of Pigs invasion, 82-84, *87-91;* and
    Berlin, *92, 93;* and CIA "mole" hunt, 122,
    123-124, 125; and CIA procedures, 76, 91;
    and Cuban missile crisis, 96, 97-*100, 98;*
    funeral of, 151; and Laos, 107
Kennedy, Robert, 87, 99, *146,* 147; *timeline* 97,
    101
KGB (Soviet intelligence service): and
    Afghanistan, 156; and Ames, 172-179,
    175; and Berlin, 41-42; and CIA "mole"
    hunt, 104, 121-126, *127;* and CIA role, 171;
    and Cuban missile crisis, 97, 101; and
    Popov, 38
Khrushchev, Nikita, 75, 95-97, 100, 101;
    timeline 95, 97, 99, 101; and Berlin, *92, 93,*
    95-97; and Castro, 77; and Cuban missile
    crisis, 97, 100-101; and U-2 spy plane,
    74, *75*
King, Joseph Caldwell (J. C.), 65-66, 78
Kingsley, Rolfe, 125
Kisevalter, George, 33, 34
Kohane, Milica, 33, 34
Kolbe, Fritz, 31
Kollek, Teddy, 18
Korea, 28-29
Kovich, Richard, 124-125

Lair, James William, *106-107,* 108, 112, 113
Lansdale, Edward, 15-17, *16,* 27, 28, 78
Laos, *map* 104
Laos secret war, *106-114,* 115; and Air
    America, 107, 108, 109, *110-111, 130-139;*
    cease-fire, 139; CIA analysis in, 120; CIA
    expansion effort in, 103, 106-111; U.S.
    withdrawal from, 114-115; Vang Pao role
    in, *106-107,* 111-115

Lashbrook, Robert, 149-150
Lebanon, 168-170
Lee, Duncan C., 12
LeMay, Curtis, *timeline* 97
Lenin, Vladimir, 31, 116
Letter interception kit, *45*
LeVier, Tony, 72
Liebing, Gertrud, *41*
Life magazine, 93
Lijek, Cora-Amburn, 154-155
Lijek, Mark, 154-155
Lithuania, 26
Locksmith's equipment, *54-55*
LSD experiments, *148-150*
Lucas, George, 154
Lucy, Roger, 155
Lumumba, Patrice, 146
Lynch, Grayston L. (Gray), *82,* 83, 85, 86

McCarthy, Joseph, 57
McCarthy, Roger E., *30*
McCone, John, 91, 97-100, *98,* 104; *timeline*
    95, 99
McCord, James, 126, *127*
McFarlane, Robert, 162, 168, 169, 171
McNamara, Robert, *98, 100*
Mafia, 146, 147
Magsaysay, Ramón, 15-16
Maheu, Robert, 146
Marks, John, 148
Martinez, Eugenio, 126, *127*
Martynov, Valery, 174, *175*
Mathias, Charles, *147*
May, Alan Nunn, 11
Meese, Edwin, 170
Meir, Golda, 126
Mellons, 8
Memorial stars, at CIA, 35
Mendez, Antonio, 153-155
El Mercurio (newspaper), 145
MI-6. *See* Secret Intelligence Service
Miami Herald, 79
MK Ultra program, *148-150*
Mongoose (project), 147
Mosaddeq, Muhammad, 57-61, *59*
Motorin, Sergei, 174, *175*
Mussolini, Benito, 8, 19, 31

Nairobi embassy bombing, 185
National Imagery and Mapping Agency, 37
National Photographic Interpretation Center,
    96, 97-99; *timeline* 97
National Security Act, 13, 141
National Security Council: and CIA mission,
    18, 21-22, 35; creation of, 13; and Cuban
    missile crisis, 99; and Guatemala, 64; and
    Iran-Contra affair, 168; and Nicaragua, 162
New York Herald Tribune, 42
New York Times: and Bay of Pigs invasion, 82;
    and CIA domestic spying, 127, 128, 140,
    141, *142;* and Guatemala, *71*
Ngo Dinh Diem, 17, 103, 105
Nicaragua, *map* 64; and Bay of Pigs invasion,
    81, 83; CIA in, *152,* 157-162, *158, 159, 160-*
    161, 183; election of 1990, 171; and
    Guatemala, 66, 67, 69; and Iran-Contra
    affair, 167, 168-*170;* Ortega in, 155
Nicholson, Harold, 182
NIMA. *See* National Imagery and Mapping
    Agency
Nixon, Richard: and Chile, *144;* and China,
    29; and CIA domestic spying, 141, 142,
    143; and Laos, 107, 114; and Watergate

scandal, 127
North, Oliver, 162, 168-*169*
Nosenko, Yuri, 123-*124*
NPIC. *See* National Photographic Interpretation Center
NSC. *See* National Security Council

Ober, Richard, 142-143
Office of Policy Coordination: and Albania, 22-26; and CIA leadership, 27, 31; creation and mission of, 21-22; and OSO, 31; and Poland, 26-27
Office of Special Operations, 19-20, 31
Office of Strategic Services: and CIA origins, 6-10, 13; and CIA tools, 44; logo of, *9*
Oliva, Erneido, 80
Olson, Alice, *148, 149, 150*
Olson, Eric, *148, 150*
Olson, Frank, *148*-150
OPC. *See* Office of Policy Coordination
Orta Cordova, Juan, 147
Ortega Saavedra, Daniel, 155
OSO. *See* Office of Special Operations
OSS. *See* Office of Strategic Services
Oswald, Lee Harvey, 123, 124, *125*
Oswald, Marina, *125*
Ouane Rattikone, 111

Pakistan, 156, 163, 164-166
Palestine, 185
Palme, Olof, 126
Parker, Evan, Jr., 118
Pastora Gómez, Edén, 158-*159*
PB Success (project), 66
Pelletier, Jean, 154
Penkovsky, Oleg, 93-*95*, 97, 99, 100, 101; *timeline 95*, 97, 99, *101*
Peurifoy, John E., 67
Philby, Harold (Kim), 22-*23*, 24, 25, 39, 122
Philippines, 15-*16*, 27, 28
Phillips, David Atlee: and Bay of Pigs invasion, 78, 79, 82, 89; and Guatemala, 66, 69, 71, 78
Phoenix program, 115, *118-121*, 127
Photographic equipment, *44, 46-49*
Pilatus Porter aircraft, *136-137*
Pinochet Ugarte, Augusto, *145*
Plausible deniability doctrine, described, 22, 77
Poe, Tony. *See* Poshepny, Anthony
Poindexter, John, 169
Poland, 26-27
Polyakov, Dimitri, 174, *175*
Popov, Pyotr Semyonovich, 17, 32-34, 38, 41
Poshepny, Anthony (Tony Poe), *112*
Powers, Francis Gary, *74*
Project Honetol, 124-126

Quarters Eye, and Bay of Pigs invasion, 78, 82, 83, 84, 86, 87, 89, 91

Radio equipment, *50-51*, 165-166
Radio Free Europe, *17*, 27
Radio Liberty, 17, 27
Radio Moscow, 101
Radio Warsaw, 27
Reagan, Ronald: and Afghanistan, 167; and Casey, 156-*157;* and Iran-Contra affair, 168, *169*, 170; and Nicaragua, 162
Revolucion (newspaper), 85
Rio Escondido (ship), 86
Robertson, William (Rip): and Bay of Pigs invasion, 65, 83, 85-86; and Guatemala, 64-

66, *65*, 68, 69, 82
Rockefeller, Nelson, 140
Rockefeller Commission, 140, 143, 148, 150
Roosevelt, Franklin D., 8, 9
Roosevelt, Kermit, 57-61, *58*, 64, 169
Roosevelt, Theodore, 57
Rosenberg, Ethel, 12
Rosenberg, Julius, 12
Rosewood files, 182
Rosselli, John, 146-147
Rusk, Dean, 84
Ruwet, Vincent, 149

Safecracker's equipment, *55*
Salku, Hysen, *25*
San Jose *Mercury News,* 183
San Román, Pepe, 89
Sass, Fred, *130-131*
Satellites, spy: development of, 32, 74, 76, *116;* post-Cold War uses, 165, *183, 184*
Savang Vattana, 112
Schlesinger, James, 127, 140
Schneider, René, 144-145
Schorr, Daniel, 147
Secord, Richard, 162
Secret Intelligence Service, *timeline* 95, 99; and Albania, 22-26; and Berlin, 15, 17, 38-42, 95; and Popov, 33, 34
El Shifa plant, 184-185
Shultz, George, 168, 170
Silver (project), 39, 40
SIS. *See* Secret Intelligence Service
Smith, Frenchy, 134
Smith, Walter Bedell, 31, 58, 61
Somoza Debayle, Anastasio, 66, 155, 158
Soutchay Vongsavanh, 111
Soviet Union, *timeline* 95, 97, 99, 101; and Afghanistan, 153, *156-157, 162-167*, 171; and Albania, 22-26; and Ames, 171-179, *175;* and Berlin, 15, 17, 38-*42, 43, 92*, 93-97; and Castro, 77; and CIA domestic spying, 142, 143; and CIA "mole" hunt, 104, 121-126, 127; and CIA role, 6, 11-13, 104, 181; and CIA tools, *116*, 117; and Cuban missile crisis, 96-101; fall of, 171, 181; and Guatemala, 63, 68, 71; and Iran, 57, 58, 61, 168; and Laos, 106, 107, 108; and Nicaragua, 155; and Poland, 26-27; and Popov, 32-34, 38; and U-2 spy plane, 72-74, *75*, 76; and Vietnam, 103. *See also specific organizations and persons*
Spielberg, Steven, 154
Spry, Charles, *123*
Squillacote, Theresa Marie, *182*
Stalin, Joseph: and CIA origins, 11, 12; CIA proposal to assassinate, 31-32; and Guatemala, 63, 71; and Italy, 20; labor camps of, 21; resistance to, 25-26
Stand, Kurt, *182*
Stasi (East German intelligence service), 182
Stevenson, Adlai, 84
Stinger missiles, 164-165, *166-167*
Stormie Seas (ship), 23-24
Strategic Air Command, *timeline* 101
Sturgis, Frank, 126, *127*
Sukarno, 61-62
Syria, 61

Tairova, Margarita, 34
Taylor, Kenneth, 154, 155
Tenet, George, 185
Thailand, *28*
Tibet, 29, *30*

Time magazine, *32*, 60
Tito, Josip Broz, 22, 27, 122
Tolkachev, Adolf, *175*
Trafficante, Santos, 146
Triangle (project), 112
Trohan, Walter, 9-10
Trujillo Molina, Rafael, 146
Truman, Harry: and CIA leadership, 27, 31; and CIA origins, *10*-11, 12-13; and CIA role, 21; and Communist strategy, 11, 17, 18
Turner, Stansfield, *155*
TWA flight 800, *183*

Ukraine, 25, 26
United Fruit Company, *62-65*, 71
U-2 spy plane, *timeline* 97, 99, 101; and Cuban missile crisis, *96-97*, 99; development of, 32, *72*, 76; and Powers, 73-74, *75*, 76; and satellites, 116

Vanderbilts, 8
Vang Pao, *106-107*, 108, 111-115, *130-131*
Vann, John Paul, 120
Varenik, Gennadi, *175*
Variety, 154
Venona project, *12*
Vienna, 32, 39, 40
Vietnam, *map* 104; coup attempt, 103; Lansdale in, 16-17, 28; and Laos, 106, 108, 111, 112, 113, 114, 131; strategic-hamlets program, 104-*105*
Vietnam War: and Afghanistan, 164, 165; cease-fire, 114; CIA analysis in, 120; and CIA domestic spying, *140-141, 142-143;* escalation of, 105, 113, 120; Phoenix program, 115, *118-121*, 127; propaganda poster, *115;* Saigon evacuation, *102, 139*
Voice of Liberation, 66, 70

Walsh, Lawrence, 170-171
Warren Commission, 124, 125, 147
Washington Post, 42, 184
Watergate scandal, 126-*127, 128*, 140
Webster, William, 179
Weinberger, Caspar, 168, 171
Weir, Benjamin, 168
Welch, Richard, 151
Wheeler, Jack, 164
White, Harry Dexter, 12
Willauer, Whiting, 67
Wilson, Charles (defense secretary), 58
Wilson, Charles (congressman), *164*, 165, 167
WIN forces, 26-27
Wisner, Frank Gardiner, *20*, 23, 24; and Albania, 22-26; appointed as deputy director for plans, 32; and Berlin, 40; and CIA leadership, 27, 31; death of, 76; and Guatemala, 64-66, 69, 72, 78; and OPC creation, 21-22; and Poland, 26-27; Stalin assassination proposed by, 31-32
Woolsey, James, 179, 183
Worthen, Diana, *177*
Wyatt, Mark, 19, 20
Wyden, Peter, 78

Yothers, Charlie, 119
Yousaf, Muhammad, 165
Yugoslavia, 22, 27, 122

Zahedi, Fazlollah, 57, 59, *61*
Zemurray, Samuel (the Banana Man), *63-64*
Zhukov, Georgy, 34
Zuñiga, Manuel, 84

TIME® LIFE BOOKS Time-Life Books is a division of Time Life Inc.

TIME LIFE INC.
CHAIRMAN AND CHIEF EXECUTIVE OFFICER: Jim Nelson
PRESIDENT AND CHIEF OPERATING OFFICER: Steven Janas
SENIOR EXECUTIVE VICE PRESIDENT AND CHIEF OPERATIONS OFFICER: Mary Davis Holt
SENIOR VICE PRESIDENT AND CHIEF FINANCIAL OFFICER: Christopher Hearing

TIME-LIFE BOOKS
PRESIDENT: Joseph A. Kuna
PUBLISHER/MANAGING EDITOR: Neil Kagan
VICE PRESIDENT, NEW PRODUCT DEVELOPMENT: Amy Golden

SECRETS OF THE CENTURY
Inside the CIA

Editor: Esther Ferington
Design Director: Cynthia Richardson
Deputy Editor: Kirk Denkler
Text Editor: Edward P. Moser
Assistant Art Director: Janet Dell Russell Johnson
Associate Editors/Research and Writing:
Nancy C. Blodgett, Annette Scarpitta (principal)
Senior Copyeditor: Mary Beth Oelkers-Keegan
Picture Associates: Amanda Stowe, Diana Bourdrez
Editorial Assistant: Patricia D. Whiteford
Photo Coordinator: David M. Cheatham

Special Contributors: Charlotte Anker, Ronald H. Bailey, George Constable, James M. Lynch, (text); Mary Jo Binker, Kevin Mahoney, Rosanne C. Scott (research/writing); Arlene Borden, Gregory Domber, Michael Evans, Charlotte Fullerton, Christine Hauser, Anthony J. Sheehan, Terrell D. Smith (research); Constance Buchanan, Janet Cave, Lee Hassig, Robert Speziale, Karen Sweet (editing); John Drummond (art); Susan Nedrow (index); Roy Nanovic (overread)

Correspondents: Maria Vincenza Aloisi (Paris), Christine Hinze (London), Christina Lieberman (New York); valuable assistance also provided by Angelika Lemmer (Bonn), Caroline Wood (London)

Separations by the Time-Life Imaging Department

NEW PRODUCT DEVELOPMENT: Director, Paula York-Soderland; Project Manager, Karen Ingebretsen; Director of Marketing, Mary Ann Donaghy; Marketing Manager, Paul Fontaine; Associate Marketing Manager, Erin Gaskins

MARKETING: Director, Peter Tardif; Marketing Manager, Nancy Gallo; Associate Marketing Manager, Terri Miller

Senior Vice President, Law & Business Affairs: Randolph H. Elkins
Vice President, Finance: Claudia Goldberg
Vice President, Book Production: Patricia Pascale
Vice President, Imaging: Marjann Caldwell
Director, Publishing Technology: Betsi McGrath
Director, Editorial Administration: Barbara Levitt
Director, Photography and Research: John Conrad Weiser
Director, Quality Assurance: James King
Manager, Technical Services: Anne Topp
Senior Production Manager: Ken Sabol
Manager, Copyedit/Page Makeup: Debby Tait
Production Manager: Virginia Reardon
Chief Librarian: Louise D. Forstall

ISBN 0-7835-1951-6

10 9 8 7 6 5 4 3 2 1

OTHER PUBLICATIONS

COOKING
Weight Watchers® Smart Choice Recipe Collection
Great Taste~Low Fat
Williams-Sonoma Kitchen Library

DO IT YOURSELF
Custom Woodworking
Golf Digest Total Golf
How to Fix It
The Time-Life Complete Gardener
Home Repair and Improvement
The Art of Woodworking

HISTORY
Our American Century
World War II
What Life Was Like
The American Story
Voices of the Civil War
The American Indians
Lost Civilizations
Mysteries of the Unknown
Time Frame
The Civil War
Cultural Atlas

TIME-LIFE KIDS
Student Library
Library of First Questions and Answers
A Child's First Library of Learning
I Love Math
Nature Company Discoveries
Understanding Science & Nature

SCIENCE/NATURE
Voyage Through the Universe

For information on and a full description of any of the Time-Life Books series listed above, please call 1-800-621-7026 or write:
Reader Information
Time-Life Customer Service
P.O. Box C-32068
Richmond, Virginia 23261-2068